IF

CHRONICLES OF SAN QUENTIN

Also by KENNETH LAMOTT

THE STOCKADE

THE WHITE SAND OF SHIRAHAMA

CHRONICLES
OF SAN QUENTIN

The Biography of a Prison

BY KENNETH LAMOTT

DAVID McKAY COMPANY, INC.

New York

COPYRIGHT © 1961 BY KENNETH LAMOTT

Library of Congress Catalogue Card Number: 61-17447

First edition

MANUFACTURED IN THE UNITED STATES OF AMERICA

VAN REES PRESS   •   NEW YORK

Most of the original research for this book was done by my wife, Dorothy (Nikki) Wyles Lamott, who brought to the job her experience as a researcher and reporter. Whatever merits this book may have as history are largely her work. The shortcomings, of course, are mine alone.

CONTENTS

ILLUSTRATIONS

CHRONICLES OF SAN QUENTIN

Chapter I

WABAU

ON a bright, warm Monday in May, 1960, a stooped and rather heavy-featured thirty-eight-year-old man named Caryl Chessman sat down in chair "B" in the small steel room in San Quentin prison where the state of California executes its condemned criminals. While two guards rapidly strapped down Chessman's arms and legs, other guards kept wary eyes on the sixty reporters and official witnesses, as if they expected a demonstration in favor of the prisoner.

Chessman turned to one of the sea-green windows and spoke to the reporters outside. "Tell Rosalie I said good-by," he said. (Rosalie Asher was one of his lawyers.) Then he added, "It's all right." A woman reporter made a circle of her thumb and forefinger, and Chessman smiled slightly.

At 10:03 the executioner pulled the cherry-red lever that dropped a bag of cyanide pellets into the tank of acid. Chessman breathed deeply for twenty seconds, then he raised his eyes to the ceiling, and his mouth fell open. At 10:05 he coughed. A minute later his face broke out with sweat and saliva dribbled from his mouth. He fell forward, his body straining against the straps; he cried, and his body heaved. At 10:12 he was pronounced dead by a prison medical officer, who had been listening to Chessman's heartbeat through a long stethoscope tube that passed through the wall of the gas chamber. The doctor estimated that Chessman had been conscious for only thirty seconds of the nine minutes it had taken him to die.

Although the warden of San Quentin said afterward that there had been nothing unusual about the execution, and although he was technically correct, Chessman's long-drawn-out march from courtroom to gas chamber had been one of the most extraordinary and curious affairs in the social history of our times. Somehow, the condemned man's shrewd and stubborn fight to stay alive had struck a sensitive nerve and provoked a worldwide reaction that was hard to account for merely on the merits of his case.

The Chessman case is still fresh in our minds, but it is only the most recent of the many occasions on which San Quentin has acted as a mirror to the contradictions and ambiguities that are usually hidden under our conventional attitudes toward crime and punishment. From its haphazard founding in the days of the Gold Rush, the great prison on the shore of San Francisco Bay has faithfully reflected the curious combination of guilt, vengefulness, and prurient fascination that has been the dominant theme in our treatment of our criminals. Both for this reason and for its own gaudy history, which contains full measures of violence, brutality, greed, sex, alcohol, and corruption, San Quentin has fairly earned its position of eminence among the walled prisons of the world.

The history of San Quentin prison properly begins in 1849 with the great migration of adventurers to the banks of the Sacramento, the Feather, the Yuba, the American, the Cosumnes, and the Mokelumne. Although American settlers had arrived in California long before gold was discovered early in 1848, the great invasion of miners did not begin until the steamer *California* dropped anchor in San Francisco Bay on the last day of February, 1849. During the remaining months of 1849, some fifty thousand vigorous and aggressive young men streamed into northern California.

Besides the North Americans there were thousands of Spanish-speaking Central and South Americans, French, and Germans—many of them escaping the aftermath of the political upheavals of 1848—and a sizable contingent of Australians, who in many cases came all but directly from the convict hulks of Botany Bay and Van Diemen's Land.

During the first six months of 1850 the population of San Francisco was increased by two thousand women from New York, New Orleans, and the sinful cities of Europe. They were the vanguard of an invasion of young women few of whom were of notable chastity. Although some are said to have devoted themselves to such useful pursuits as washing clothes, keeping house, and raising children, the vast majority abandoned themselves to every conceivable variety of dissipation and bawdiness, creating a social milieu which has been vigorously described in Herbert Asbury's classic *The Barbary Coast.* The prevailing moral atmosphere of the 1850's has been preserved in the ditty which begins:

> The miners came in forty-nine,
> The whores in fifty-one;
> And when they got together
> They produced the native son.

As the city spread out from Portsmouth Square over the surrounding hills, the districts that remained to the poor, the unfortunate, and the wicked became clearly defined. The pioneer whores, sluttish and unlettered females from Mexico, Chile, Peru, and other countries of Spanish America, congregated in rough shanties in the neighborhood of Clark's Point and up the adjoining slopes of Telegraph Hill, while a Little Chile of other Spanish-American outcasts sprang up north of Washington Street. On upper Broadway and Pacific streets were found the grogshops and sporting houses of the escaped convicts and ticket-of-leave men from Australia and Tasmania. Here in Sydney Town drinks were drugged, throats were cut, and women had sexual congress not only with drunken miners but also, for the instruction of the curious, with such partners as boars and Shetland ponies.

Both in the city and in the mines criminal activity was encouraged by the presence of abundant wealth, very little of which was, so to speak, nailed down. Furthermore, it was almost as hard to hang onto one's life as to hang onto one's property. Although there is no general agreement among the historians on the precise numbers of homicides, somewhere around four thousand persons seem to have been murdered in California in the years from 1849 to 1855. In 1855 the prosecuting attorney in a murder trial declared that in San Francisco alone there had been twelve hundred murders in four years, with only one conviction. This works out to five murders every six days, which seems excessive in a city of forty-five thousand people.

In the mining camps the whip, the noose, and the branding iron were applied to the sound of that glorious cry of American popular justice, "Give him a fair trial and hang him." In the city life was somewhat more relaxed, the politicians being not merely powerless but notoriously unwilling to undertake any vigorous measures against the criminal population. This state of affairs was hardly to be marveled at since the odds were eight to five that an officeholder was, by even the most liberal standards of public morality, a scoundrel. One of the board of supervisors was James P. Casey, an ex-convict from Sing Sing. Judge Ned McGowan, of the court of sessions, had fled from his post as a Philadelphia policeman after having been accused of having had a hand in a bank robbery. Billy Mulligan, the keeper of the county jail, was an infamous New York tough. The police courts were described by a conservative historian as "bulwarks of defense for the scoundrels who ran the elections and the thieves, murderers, and disreputables who voted under their direction."

It is one of the stock truths of social life that men are hardly eager to act on the subtleties of the law in a world in which today's millionaire becomes tomorrow's ragged desperado, and in which today's outcast is tomorrow's hero. California in the 1850's was surely a classic example of the mobile—or open-ended —society, and the institutions of the law were modified to accommodate the people they served.

Both in the camps and in the city the Anglo-Americans distinguished themselves by the ferocity of their treatment of their Spanish-speaking brethren, whether native Californians or immigrants like themselves. The most amateur psychologist can see in the behavior of the Anglo-Americans a massive sense of guilt prompted both by the shameful war that had given California to the United States and the Americans' studied disregard of Mexican property rights. (It is worth noting in this connection that one of the signers of the Treaty of Cahuenga, which, in January, 1847, confirmed the United States' possession of California, was the explorer-soldier-politician John C. Frémont, whose principal warlike acts in the farcical and unnecessary conflict had been to spike a battery of rusty old guns and shoot down three innocent Californian civilians not far from the isolated point of land known as Punta de Quentin.)

The indifference of the police, the impotence of the courts, and the ferocity of the Anglo-Americans toward their Spanish-speaking brethren were all displayed in the first major outbreak of violence in San Francisco in the summer of 1849. On a Sunday afternoon in July a band of fifty or sixty young ruffians who called themselves the Hounds marched on the miserable shanties of Little Chile with the ostensible purpose of collecting a debt owed a shopkeeper. Whether the debt was collected or not is not recorded, but by nightfall the unfortunate Chilenos had been thoroughly burned, beaten, shot at, raped, and plundered.

Decent citizens banded together, collected a relief fund, organized a posse, pursued the Hounds, and arrested their leaders, who were locked up in the brig of the U.S.S. *Warren*. The trial was a straightforward, although extra-legal, proceeding, which found eight of the leaders guilty and dealt out stiff sentences. Two of the Hounds were sentenced to ten years at hard labor in any penitentiary the governor might name.

If the story ended here, it could be counted a victory for Anglo-Saxon justice and the decent instincts of the majority of the citizens. The real point of the story is quite different: A few days after they were found guilty, the convicted ruffians were turned loose. It had been noted that the nearest penitentiary was a couple of thousand miles to the east, and the Hounds' political friends did the rest. The Hound leaders were advised to clear out, and they did, which wasn't a bad bargain considering the harshness of their original sentences. It would still be a long time before a California felon had much reason to fear sure and speedy punishment at the hands of the duly constituted authorities.

In August, 1849, a month after the trial, conviction, and release of the Hounds, the city government of San Francisco took note of the realities of urban life and bought, for use as a city prison, the stranded hulk of the brig *Euphemia,* lying near what is now the corner of Battery and Jackson streets. (The word *brig* requires a word of explanation. A brig, as in the case of the warship on which the Hound leaders were confined, is a shipboard jail. A brig, as in the case of the *Euphemia,* is a two-masted square-rigger. *Brig,* in local usage, was also applied indiscriminately to any hulk used as a prison.)

Although the *Euphemia,* in its reincarnation as a prison, has been described as being about as useful as a chicken coop, its purchase indicated the presence of a decent minimum of responsibility on the part of the town council. Other politicians throughout California made similar gestures; by the end of the year there were county jails in San Francisco, San Jose, Monterey, Santa Barbara, Los Angeles, and San Diego.

Crime continued to flourish and criminals continued to be

caught, and, sometimes, convicted. In the absence of a state prison, or the firm determination to build one, the politicians took recourse to a legal fiction. In April, 1850, all the county jails were solemnly declared to be state prisons, and the county authorities were authorized to use prison labor on public works. Events moved in their usual fashion. It was not until eight months later that the first prisoner was entered on the register of state convicts. The pioneer convict was Charles Currier, a cabinet-maker by trade and a thief by avocation. Born in Massachusetts, he was twenty-two years old, stood five feet eight and one half inches tall, and had light hair, blue eyes, and a fair complexion. He was convicted of grand larceny in Sacramento, sentenced to two years, and entered on the register January 25, 1851.

Although there was no state prison in which to lock up Currier, a prison had not been entirely forgotten. Early in 1851 plans for a state prison were included in an offer made to the state legislature by a former Mexican general named Mariano Guada-lupe Vallejo. Vallejo proposed to give the state the sum of $137,000, in return for which the legislators were to move the state capital from San Jose to a city he proposed to raise for them on the northeastern shore of the northern arm of San Francisco Bay. His chief associate in this ambitious venture was a Demo-cratic politician named James M. Estell.

Vallejo and Estell went further than merely offering twenty acres of land for the state prison They were prepared, they said, to build the prison themselves and then to take over its operation. The terms were generous: Until a prison building went up, Vallejo and Estell promised to buy prison hulks, hire and pay the officers and guards, clothe and feed the convicts, and offer rewards should they escape. As their *quid pro quo,* they asked only to be given a free hand in putting the convicts' labor to any use they wished.

In looking over the offer, the legislators had one thing in mind, and that was money. A senate committee discovered that of twenty "commodious and well-adapted" state prisons in the East, only four yielded a profit. They reported with dismay that the average deficit was more than $100,000 a year. Acutely aware of the chronic exhaustion of the California state treasury, the senators fell over each other in their haste to accept Vallejo's munificent offer. The tone of breathless gratitude was set by the chairman of the house and grounds committee, who said that Vallejo's offer breathed the spirit of an enlarged mind for which he deserved the thanks of his countrymen and the admiration of the world, and that his offer looked more like the legacy of a mighty emperor to his people than the donation of a private rancher. The most impressive thing of all was that it was going to cost the state hardly a penny.

Nothing is more indicative of the forward-looking optimism of Vallejo and Estell than the fact that on April 25, 1851, when they formally leased for a period of ten years the bodies and labor of all of California's state convicts, exactly five prisoners had been entered on the rolls. Although it consisted of only these five prisoners, a contract, no buildings, and two enterprising politician-generals, California at last had a state prison.

Vallejo and Estell form an instructive contrast in the curious processes of history. Both were men who loomed large in California, but Vallejo has been embalmed in the school histories as a lofty-minded and farseeing statesman, while Estell has simply dropped from sight. As it happens, both men were among the notable scoundrels of their time.

Much has been written about Vallejo's statesmanship in supporting the American cause after it became clear that California was destined to join the Union, but little has been said of the revolting cruelty of his treatment of Indian rebels and Mexican enemies who were unfortunate enough to fall into his hands. It was these atrocities that led his nephew, Governor Juan Bautista Alvarado, to remark that the next best thing to sending prisoners to the devil was to send them to Vallejo. California's first convicts were granted few mercies, but one of them was that Vallejo himself never took charge of the prison.

James Madison Estell, Vallejo's partner, was a major general by virtue of his command of the 2nd Division of the California state militia. He was an adventurer and politician by trade, a man of some ability, but his mind was wild and injudicious and his tongue was one of the foulest ever heard in a public hall.

When he signed the prison contract, Estell was forty-one years old. To one admirer he appeared "tall and of grand bearing, brave and able," but his sworn enemy, the San Francisco *Bulletin,* described with relish Estell's "hideous face and Cain-branded countenance" and predicted that his name would be handed down to posterity as the vilest of the vile.

Leasing the bodies of the state convicts to Vallejo and Estell may strike sensitive readers as a cruel solution to the prison problem, reminiscent of chattel slavery and the galleys. In theory, leasing was deplorable and in practice it was a stench in the nostrils of Jehovah, but the prisoners were probably no worse off than they would have been in the hands of the state.

Before diving into the tangled history of the lease, it is a useful corrective to remind ourselves that the present age is not uniquely enlightened, either from the standpoint of morals or of simple humanity, nor were the mid-1800's a dark age. Vallejo and Estell, Governor McDougal, and the California legislators were contemporaries of Emerson and Thoreau, of Lincoln and Walt Whitman, of Hawthorne and Melville. They lived in a time distinguished by works of lively intelligence and moral sensitivity, beside which our own time appears gray and callous.

It was, furthermore, a time in which the articulate public took an earnest interest in both the administration of justice and the plight of the prisoner. In Europe such reformers as Voltaire, John Howard, Jeremy Bentham, and Cesare di Beccaria had awakened men's consciences and set off a revolution in the treatment of crime and criminals. The institution of the penitentiary itself was the most tangible result of this revolution. Today it takes an effort of the will to peel away the modern associations of the word *penitentiary* and remind ourselves that it was intended as a place for penance and reformation rather than punishment.

In this country the Pennsylvania Quakers had pioneered a prison system aimed at the moral rehabilitation of the criminal. Briefly, the Pennsylvania system, as developed by the Philadelphia Society for Alleviating the Miseries of Public Prisons and practiced at the Eastern Penitentiary in Philadelphia, prescribed complete solitary confinement of each convict, his only human contacts to be of the uplifting variety supplied by clergymen, schoolteachers, workmasters, and enlightened prison officers and guards. Throughout the nineteenth century there was a running ideological battle between the missionaries of the Pennsylvania system and those of the competing arrangement which had been worked out in the prisons of New York State. Here, the convicts slept in solitary cells at night, but worked together, though silently, in the prison shops during the day. The advocates of both systems preached reformation rather than punishment.

The California lawmakers, who were not ignorant of these developments, debated the advantages and disadvantages of the two systems, but at first no one seriously urged the adoption of either.

As soon as the lease act took effect on July 1, 1851, a board of prison inspectors began to meet at regular intervals, but, as the secretary noted, the meetings were exceedingly brief, no prisoners having yet been received. It was not until December 3 that Governor McDougal placed in the newspapers a short one-column advertisement directing sheriffs to turn state prisoners over to Estell and Vallejo. Estell added a postscript to the advertisement, advising the sheriffs to deliver the prisoners to Colonel John C. Hays, sheriff of San Francisco.

Hays and his subordinate and bosom friend, Major John Caperton, had acquired custody of the convicts by virtue of a subleasing contract worked out with the two generals. They fitted out the hulk of the old bark *Wabau* as a prison ship and on December 18 hired the steamtug *Firefly* to tow it across the bay where the forty convicts aboard were put to work in a quarry on Angel Island, the largest island in the bay. Hays kept the more docile prisoners in his unfinished and insecure county jail ashore, from which they were driven out in chains to cut and grade the San Francisco streets.

Jack Hays had brought to California a reputation as the bravest and most gallant of the Texas Rangers. At the head of Hays' Rangers he had fought in Mexico under Zachary Taylor and Winfield Scott, and had led his horsemen down the streets of Mexico City itself. He stood only five feet eight, but he impressed people as a heroic figure, the tallest, one of them said, he had ever seen leading cavalry into the teeth of the enemy.

As the keeper of the state convicts, however, Hays was something of a disappointment. One historian has written that of twenty-five prisoners delivered to him, twenty-five escaped. This is a gross exaggeration, and is, furthermore, unfair to the memory of the gallant colonel. The fact is that a month after he took command only seventeen of the forty-odd prisoners on the hulk locked up their three guards, relieved them of their weapons, commandeered a boat, and took off for the eastern shore of the bay. Although Hays himself led the vigorous pursuit, seven of the convicts made good their escape.

Public criticism of this and subsequent escapes was not the only reason Hays had to be unhappy with his bargain. The prisoners weren't earning their keep, and before five months were up he and Caperton had dropped $11,000 of their own money.

Hays went to Estell, but Estell, who had been reading the newspapers, declined to take the convicts back. He was, he said, frightened by the losses, but whether he meant the loss of convicts or the loss of money he didn't say.

Estell was now the sole owner of the original lease because Vallejo, whose affairs had not been prospering, had given up his interest in the contract in the winter of 1852. Estell eventually agreed to release Hays from his sublease if the legislature would pass a law providing for the construction of a prison building ashore. Hays and Caperton were so anxious to get rid of the convicts that they personally lobbied the bill through the assembly and senate. There was at least one vote on which they could count—Estell was now a state senator.

It was thanks to these various machinations that on May 1, 1852, the legislature passed an act directing the prison inspectors and the commissioners of public buildings to select and buy a prison site of not more than twenty acres. Estell put up a bond of $100,000 and Governor John Bigler confirmed his lease of the state convicts.

Later a bored prison clerk practiced his penmanship by writing on a blank page of the daily log the doggerel

> Philadelphia is my native place,
> America is my nation,
> San Francisco is my dwelling place,
> San Quentin my destination.

In hindsight it seems inevitable that the California state prison should come to San Quentin, but at the time Point Quentin was well down the list. There was no question in anybody's mind of the ideal permanent site for the prison. The isolation offered by any of the three major islands in San Francisco Bay—Angel, Alcatraz, and Goat—appeared to be ideal.

The advantages of an island were lyrically described by a legislative committee:

A prison erected on one of these islands could be easily guarded from approach from without, and escape rendered next to impossible, and at the same time, in a place remote from the busy hum of city life, the discipline necessary to the proper training of criminals and their reclamation from vice would be much more effectually enforced. Here there could be spacious enclosures for workshops, for exercise grounds, for bathhouses, and all the other adjuncts of an enlightened system of prison discipline. Here would be uninterrupted opportunity for that mental reflection which is the strongest corrective of vices, encrusted on man's nature, by guilty association. Here the inmates of the prison could look out to the bustling life of San Francisco, and it is not to be doubted that the deprivation they would daily be made to feel, of the pleasure of social intercourse with their fellow men, separated as they would be by an impassable barrier from society, would serve as a severe and most wholesome corrective.

The three commissioners who were appointed to buy land for the prison first looked at Goat Island (now euphemistically called Yerba Buena), and then at Angel Island, but both were turned down because, it was said, their titles of ownership weren't clear. Although one commissioner held out for a site named Bull's Head, near the town of Martinez, the majority voted for Point Quentin. On July 7, 1852, the state paid Benjamin Buckalew, who a little earlier had been active in San Francisco politics, $10,000 for twenty acres at the point of the peninsula. It turned out later that Buckalew's title to the land was questionable, and the choice of Point Quentin blew up a violent political storm, but here, as all the world knows, was where the prison stayed.

At the time of the purchase the convicts had been moved to Goat Island, where they were being worked under the supervision of John McDougal, who only seven months earlier had been governor of California. Universally known as "I, John" from his fondness for gassy proclamations beginning with the words "I, John McDougal," he was one of those colorful eccentrics who from the beginning have been drawn to California. An unsuccessful miner turned politician, a buffoon, and a drunkard, McDougal affected a costume consisting of ruffled shirt, buff vest and pantaloons, and a blue coat with brass buttons. Although the ex-governor's connection with Estell aroused accusations of skulduggery, McDougal was actually one of the few men in California who knew anything about running a prison, having once been superintendent of the Indiana state prison.

It is probably not far from the historical truth to imagine this curious character, resplendent in his ruffled shirt and brass buttons and only partly sober, directing operations from the poop as the bedraggled old hulk was towed across the bay from Goat Island and moored in the shelter of Point Quentin. According to a tradition which need not be disbelieved just because it is suspiciously pat, the historic settlement took place on Bastille Day—July 14—1852.

Chapter II

NO PARADISE FOR SCOUNDRELS

NORTH of the Golden Gate San Francisco Bay is bounded on its western shore by the peninsulas and sheltered coves of Marin County. The smallest of the Marin peninsulas was called Punta de Quentin by the Californians. At first the Americans called it Point Quentin; later it became Point San Quentin. Point San Quentin is a hook of land about a mile and a half long and about three-quarters of a mile wide. Its steeply rising hills, green in the winter and spring and brown in the summer and fall, are the dividing ridge between San Rafael Cove to the north and Corte Madera Cove to the south. The only native trees are live oaks. In 1852 there were a few acres of not very good clay land along the southern shore where the state had bought its twenty acres. The hills contain blue granite of a quality fair enough to justify the commercial quarrying that goes on to this day.

The commissioners who selected the point cited not only the deposits of clay and rock but also the healthy climate, the good water, the abundance of wood, and the accessibility of the point to the steamboats that were the principal means of transportation around the bay. They neglected to add that the water could be only obtained by drilling wells, that the wood was mostly scrubby oaks, and that, except at the point itself, the bay shore to the north was little more than salt marshes, and to the south, mud flats.

In retrospect it would appear that, whether their motives were pure or not, the commissioners could have done much worse. Point San Quentin is isolated and yet easily accessible from San Francisco, about twelve miles to the south, and from the Contra Costa shore four miles to the east. The point lies three miles south of San Rafael, the county seat, which was founded in 1817 by the Franciscans as the second northernmost of their chain of missions. In 1852 San Rafael was a small town that served as the commercial and social center for the county's people, who, for the most part, lived on scattered farms.

Inland from Point San Quentin rolling hills rise to the 2,600-foot peak called Tamalpais, or, more commonly, Mount Tam. The slopes of Tamalpais are covered with live oak, manzanita, chinquapin, toyon, fir, and redwood forests as well as with the dense underbrush called chaparral. On the western slope of Tamalpais bold and broken headlands descend steeply to the Pacific.

The climate of Marin County varies considerably, from the cool fogs of the ocean shore through the warm valleys to the moderate climate of the bay, which is shared by Point San Quentin. The temperature rarely rises above 90° F. or falls to freezing. Almost all the rain falls during the months from October to April. Fogs are not uncommon, but they are neither so frequent nor so dense as the folklore has it. On the whole, the climate is as pleasant and healthful as human beings can reasonably expect.

St. Quentin himself was a third-century Roman who was beheaded by pagan Gauls after having had iron spits run through his body from head to foot. When Quentin's head was mercifully struck off, it is said that a white dove issued from his severed throat and flew to heaven. Quentin would have made a splendid patron saint for the California convicts, except that he had nothing at all to do with the naming of Point San Quentin. The point was named after an Indian warrior, a sub chief of the great Chief Marin, who led the Licatuit Indians in their last stand against Mexican troops.

In 1824 Lieutenant Ignacio Martinez pursued a band of Indians under Quentin to the isolated point of land south of the mission at San Rafael, defeated them there, and took Quentin prisoner. Quentin was taken to San Francisco, where the Franciscan fathers at the Mission Dolores put him to work as skipper of a lighter on the bay. Later he went to work in the same capacity for General Vallejo.

The sainting of Quentin was a peculiarly Anglo-Saxon ceremony. General Vallejo's explanation can hardly be improved upon:

> The spot in which the struggle occurred, with such a happy termination for the whites, between Lieutenant Martinez' troops and Quentin's Indians, was, after the capture of the red chief, known as "Punta de Quentin" (Quentin's Point); but it was reserved for the North Americans to change the name of that place, and to call it "Punta de San Quentin." I believe that the change may be attributed to the fact that a large number of them arrived in California under the belief that the inhabitants of this country were very zealous Catholics, and desiring to gain their good will added *San* (Saint) before the towns or villages that they visited. I remember having heard on various occasions "Santa Sonoma," "San Branciforte," and "San Monterey," and pursuant to this custom, they added San to Quentin.

The actual canonization of Chief Quentin appears to have been performed by the prison commissioners in their report of 1853.

During the height of the gold excitement more than five hundred ships were beached or left riding at anchor in San Francisco Bay, deserted when their crews and even their officers abandoned them for the mines. Some of these ships rotted at their moorings and sank. Others were beached and became warehouses and hotels. The *Euphemia,* as we have seen, became the first San Francisco city prison, while the *Wabau* became the first state prison.

Although hulks had served as prisons in England and Australia for years before the Gold Rush, they were going out of use at just about the time of which we are writing. The prison brig had no positive advocates in California; it was only a makeshift until a permanent prison could be put up ashore. Yet, until a building was erected, there was no escape from it, though the life of the prisoners aboard was one of such dismal cruelty that it became apparent even to the politicians.

On Bastille Day, 1852, there had been forty or fifty prisoners aboard the brig; by the end of the year the number had tripled. On fair days the able-bodied men worked ashore preparing the site for the first building; at night they were locked below, four or five men to each eight-foot-square compartment. During the warm summer days they stewed in their own juices, while in the rainy winter they stayed below day after dreary day. In the mornings the effluvia of fesces and sweat and general decay was so strong that the guards refused to go below until the lower decks had been aired out. As a committee of senators and assemblymen observed with restraint, "These unfortunate people ... present a pale, careworn appearance." The committeemen were distressed, but not too distressed to find a silver lining.

> As regards food [they reported], it is plain and substantial; the bread is of a superior quality, and as good as any to be found on any table in this country. The quantity appeared amply sufficient, if one might judge from what was left on the table after the prisoners had finished their dinner of bread, soup, and meats.

A word or two of explanation may be useful toward the understanding of this report and of the other similar documents. It is an article of faith among official prison visitors that, so long as it contains no recognizable insect carcasses, rocks, or mouse droppings, prison bread is equal to the finest in the country. Joseph, no doubt, heard the same from the Pharaoh's baker. Similarly, friendly committees never fail to interpret the leaving of food on the table as a tribute to its abundance rather than a criticism of the cook or the quality of the raw materials.

Besides one or two reports of this nature nothing survives in the way of a reliable account of life on the brig. No ex-convict, no officer, or guard wrote his memoirs of life on the brig at Point Quentin. The San Francisco newspapers had not yet discovered the copy that could be made of the state prison, a topic that in later years was to sustain them through dry seasons as the barrel cactus sustains the thirsty traveler in the desert. It is a situation to make a historian weep, for the committeemen were of such delicacy that nowhere do they comment upon the life of the women who were confined aboard the brig.

Firmly established in the folklore of San Quentin is the story that among the prisoners on the brig were three San Francisco whores named Dolores Martinez, Scotch Mary, and Russian Kate. As with most folklore, there is some truth here and some imagination.

The first woman to be sentenced to a term in the state prison was a thirty-three-year-old Scotswoman named Agnes Read, who was committed for a term of one year for helping a prisoner to escape. She was entered on the convict register on July 8, 1852, exactly a week before the brig was towed to Point Quentin. There is, however, no record of whether she was actually aboard the hulk or whether she had remained in Jack Hays's jail. Similarly we have only the register to vouch for the existence of the Mexican washerwoman Perquita Saledano or the Chilean Carmine

Nuñez, both of whom were convicted of theft in the summer of 1852. Even more tantalizing is the person of Lilly C. Smith, a blonde, hazel-eyed circus rider from New York who was convicted of grand larceny in San Francisco in November, 1852, and duly entered on the register. But even Lilly Smith seemed to slip from the memories of the guards who, three years later, were to testify about the behavior of the women at San Quentin. It might be argued that these females received little attention because, according to the ungallant testimony of the prison register, Carmine was cross-eyed, Perquita had only one eye, and Lilly C. Smith was ruptured, but the guards were not noticeably finical about their women. Although it was at about this time that John Gray, the lieutenant of the guard, began to slip into the pleasant habit of visiting the women's cabin for relaxation, we do not know if it was Agnes Read or Perquita Saledano or Carmine Nuñez or Lilly C. Smith or Dolores Martinez who first seduced him from the stern path of his duty.

It was with this Dolores Martinez, who was committed to prison on the same day as Lilly Smith, that we find ourselves at last on firm ground. The life of the women at San Quentin becomes vastly clearer not long after Dolores and one other but unidentified woman were moved ashore in May, 1853, to a wooden shack known as the Middle House or the Overseer's House. In June they were joined by a Scottish girl named Mary Anne Wilson, who, with Dolores, was to figure prominently in the first of the many scandals that have brightened the annals of San Quentin.

Dolores was only nineteen and Scotch Mary was twenty-nine years old. They had both been convicted in San Francisco and sent across the bay for one year, Mary for robbery and Dolores for manslaughter. Mary listed her occupation as servant while Dolores called herself a washerwoman. They were small girls, Dolores standing a little under five feet and Scotch Mary a bare half inch over. Dolores was dark, while Scotch Mary was fair and blue-eyed, but it is unhappily necessary for us to rid ourselves of the pleasant but vulgar picture of a flashing-eyed señorita and a bonnie Scotch lassie. Dolores was squat and pockmarked, while Scotch Mary's face was scarred. They were drabs, and there is no reason to suppose that they looked anything but what they were, particularly after several months at Point Quentin.

The life they led in the Middle House had little resemblance to the legislators' pious dream of a prison "remote from the busy hum of city life" where the convicts would be reformed by the wholesome corrective of being deprived of "the pleasure of social intercourse with their fellow men." Although the windows of the Middle House were slatted over and the doors were stout, Dolores and Scotch Mary were practically overwhelmed with the attentions of their fellow men.

To begin with, John Gray, the semiliterate lieutenant of the guard who was known for his harshness to the male convicts, simply moved into the women's room. Although he usually slept with Dolores, Scotch Mary was also seen in his bed. Mary, however, was generally known as Judge Thompson's woman. (The title borne by J. N. Thompson, the captain of the guard, had, one guesses, survived from a previous appointment in another state.) Thompson, like Gray, was a drinking man, and both drunk and sober, both day and night, he was seen by his guards visiting the females in their rooms, pulling Mary into his lap and tumbling her into bed. With more delicacy than Lieutenant Gray, Thompson continued to maintain his official sleeping quarters in the deckhouse of the brig, but this was no obstacle to his easy relations with the women.

Thompson and Gray were not the only men with whom Dolores and Mary had, as one witness noted with antiseptic disapproval, "free sexual intercourse." Two male convicts were assigned to help them with the officers' and guards' laundry, and, as the same witness described their relationship with the girls, "those convicts were inside of the house a part of the time with the females and out of sight of any guard, and had sufficient opportunity for intimacy if they had felt disposed." From what we know of the deplorable moral characters of these young women it is hard to believe that they did not sometimes feel so disposed. Nor was this all. Two other convicts who described themselves as the girls' husbands were allowed to visit them in their quarters all day Sunday although the men were herded back onto the brig at night.

The girls were free to come and go as they pleased. Estell and his employees had done their best to make life at the prison as comfortable for themselves as they could, and the girls shared in the amenities. A cookhouse had been built and a boarding-house for the guards and free workmen. Estell himself owned the first bar, which was tended in the cookhouse by a guard named George Woods. Another bar was run by a man named Parker on Benjamin Buckalew's property about five hundred yards from the prison grounds. Still another bar was established on the prison brig itself by Asa Estes when he succeeded Judge Thompson as captain of the guard in 1853. Estes himself tended this bar. The women drank wherever they pleased, going as far from their quarters as Parker's tavern, where they spent the money they had made washing and sewing or touched the guards for drinks. Scotch Mary in particular had the name of being partial to her whisky.

These domestic arrangements lasted for only about a year. By the middle of 1854 Dolores, Scotch Mary, and the other women had been discharged, and for a time San Quentin was without any female convicts. Judge Thompson had already left Estell's service and Lieutenant Gray had been transferred to one of the Marin islands, where about eighty prisoners had been put to work in a quarry. The scandalous goings on at San Quentin were reduced markedly in their variety, though not, as it became clear, in their over-all color.

The twenty or thirty men who served on the guard line when they were not assigned to more congenial duties such as tending

bar had been recruited from various walks of life. The majority
were described as being former rangers, and the nice ambiguity
of this term is probably the best guarantee of its truthfulness.
A ranger, particularly in southern California, was a member of
one of the mounted posses that acted as an auxiliary police,
but in San Francisco a ranger was one of the criminal types who
frequented the Barbary Coast. Guards were hired wherever they
could be found, and we have the testimony of the first prison
doctor, Alfred W. Taliaferro, that they were on the whole "brave
and desperate men, but somewhat addicted to dissipation." (Dr.
Taliaferro, who was in and out of San Quentin for twenty years,
came of the Virginia family that pronounces its name as if it
were written *Tolliver*.)

Even as it is now, the profession of prison guard was woefully
ill paid. For the sum of $50.00 a month—once it rose briefly
to $75.00 but dropped again to $50.00 and then to $40.00—the
guard was expected to work eighteen hours a day the week
through. All the day guards were on duty from four in the
morning until sunset, and then four men were assigned to the
night watch. Each was armed with a percussion rifle or musket
and a Colt's dragoon revolver drawn from the stores of the state
quartermaster general, but their numbers were wholly inadequate
to keeping the convicts safely inside a prison without a wall.
Besides this, the physical arrangements at San Quentin were mad-
deningly inconvenient. Three times a day the entire body of
working convicts had to be marched from the site of the building
to the cookhouse and back again.

Furthermore, escapes were frequent and often bloody. Estell
himself told the legislature that "I have the mortification daily
of seeing the graves of my guards, murdered by the hands of
infamy, and meeting others, maimed for life, whilst in the discharge of their unenviable duty." The guards protested with
understandable emotion: "Every hour of the day we literally carry

our lives in our hands, and that at any moment is liable to be wrested from us."

In spite of these brave protestations it is hard to avoid the conclusion that the guard line at Point San Quentin was a refuge for unreformed alcoholics. The various estimates made of the precise incidence of intemperance can be reduced to the consensus that well over half the guards were habitual drunkards. There was only a little disagreement over the extent of Lieutenant Gray's drunkenness. Some of his colleagues remembered him as being drunk two-thirds of the time. Others claimed they had never seen him sober.

The crude democracy of drinking men blurred even the line between guard and convict. Male convicts were almost as welcome as Dolores and Scotch Mary in the bars, and it was not uncommon to see Judge Thompson or Gray buying a round of drinks for seven or eight thirsty trusties. On New Year's Day, 1853, or 1854, convicts joined the guards in seeing the old year out. The high point of the evening was a fight in which one convict bit off another's nose. On other occasions roistering convicts provoked barroom brawls with the masons who had been imported to work on the prison building.

The first attempt at reform came in June, 1854, when Samuel W. Haight, the uncle of a subsequent governor of California, bought a one-fifth share of the prison contract and took over the active management whenever Estell was away, which was often. Haight fired ten guards for drunkenness and did his best to close down the bars, but he continued to supply liquor to the captain of the guard in order, he explained, "to keep the guards from the groceries that were kept near the grounds"—which seems to mean that he hoped that if he gave them some liquor they would keep their hands off his private supplies.

There were few compensations besides whisky to serving as a guard. Several men exercised squatters' rights in the sur-rounding hills, clearing the land and building their cabins with convict labor, but most of them seem to have lived from day to day, going to their posts as often as not half-seas over with the liquor that was their only escape from Point San Quentin. One can be justified in wondering if the guards or the prisoners were the more desperate.

The building of the penitentiary authorized by the legislature in May, 1852, began, inauspiciously but typically, with the closing of a contract with the San Francisco Manufacturing Company, the firm which Estell and several friends had established to exploit the convicts' labor. Estell and his cronies proposed to build a prison which would be an architectural marvel, a nonpareil, a second-to-none. The plans envisaged a 20-foot wall running in a rectangle 500 feet by 450 feet, with a Roman tower with battlements at each corner. Rising tastefully from other locations, according to one description, were to be Doric columns, arches, and minarets. Besides the cell block, the buildings were to include guards' quarters, an armory, a mess hall, cells for the female convicts, the best privies devisable, a laundry, and a bell tower, all to be constructed of the finest materials by the most cunning workmen.

This marvel was never to arise. The newspapers, disappointed contractors, and speculators raised a mighty howl that Estell's contract would bankrupt the state; the attorney general threatened to get out an injunction; and the *Alta California* denounced "the most stupendous fraud that was ever attempted by the officials upon the people of any state in the Union." Whenever assemblymen and senators showed up at Point San Quentin, Estell's men laid on the whisky, but all the extra supplies they shipped in to entertain committeemen were not enough to ward off a legislative finding that somebody had been guilty of fraud.

The contract was accordingly canceled in May, 1853, and new commissioners were appointed to take over the prison. The commissioners had the law on their side, but Estell had the prison and refused to give it up. Eventually, after he had dropped the Doric columns, the Roman towers, the minarets, the bell towers, and the wonderful privies, Estell was permitted to proceed with the construction of the first cell block.

Within four years of its completion in January, 1854, this cell block was called the Old Prison; it was also known as the Stone Building (or simply the Stones) and, more picturesquely, as the Old Spanish Prison. The last name has led many present-day San Franciscans to conclude that it was built by the Spanish or Mexican governments of California. This of course, is sheer mythology. The point of the name was that it was built in the Spanish-colonial style, with cell doors opening onto galleries on the outside of the building. Unlike most American prison buildings, there was no massive cell house surrounding the block like the shell around a walnut kernel.

The Stones consisted of two stories, 180 feet long by 24 feet wide. The upper floor was divided into 48 cells, arranged in two rows of 24 each, back to back. The cells were 10½ feet long by 6 feet wide, and were originally intended to hold two prisoners each. The first floor was divided into two rooms. One, called the Long Room, 160 feet long, was a dormitory. The other, the turnkey's office, occupied the easternmost end of the building. By the time all the bills were in, the Stones had cost the state $135,000, but it was a good and substantial building, and its construction was probably the only case in which Estell gave the state of California fair value for its money. The Stones stood until the winter of 1959, and its stout stone walls resisted the wrecking machines to the end.

From the very beginning until the present day the wardens of San Quentin have sweetened their evenings with the pleasant illusion that after the next cell house has been completed every convict will have a room of his own, gross immorality will cease, and the voice of the turtle will be heard in the land. Like the millennium, this glorious day has never arrived.

In the winter of 1853, as we have already noted, the prison brig, which had been fitted out for fifty convicts was holding more than three times that number. By the time the Stones was ready in January, 1854, the convict population had climbed to about two hundred and fifty, and by the end of that year more than three hundred prisoners were on hand.

Barely a year after the Stones was built each of the forty-eight cells held four prisoners. The only air came from the Judas hole in the solid iron door; the only amenities were four wooden bunks and a night bucket. Less desperate convicts were quartered dormitory fashion in the Long Room on the first floor.

Besides discharges, escapes, and deaths there was only one road of relief. That was the removal to the larger of the two Marin islands of about eighty convicts. The Marin islands lie less than a mile from the shore of San Rafael cove. The larger is a bare 300 yards long by 100 yards wide. The only marks of civilization were a few Indian shell mounds and rows of buckeye trees the Indians had planted as a food crop. Here, under the cold and bloodshot eye of Lieutenant Gray, the convicts broke rock in Estell's quarry by day and by night were driven into an old brig. There is no record left to tell us if this was the *Wabau*, towed off the San Quentin mud flats and a mile up the bay. In any case, there is no further mention of the brig at Point San Quentin.

Visitors to San Quentin in 1854 complained that they couldn't tell the convicts from the guards. Convicts and guards alike wore shabby civilian clothes, the convicts because that was all they had, the guards because that was all they could afford. Nobody was very well washed or barbered, even by Gold Rush standards. Some of the men who carried guns were convicts. Some of the men who didn't carry guns were guards. Not even by the degree of drunkenness could one tell the prisoner from his keeper.

There was one further similarity: Just as the guards came from the lower orders, so did the prisoners. San Quentin, like all other prisons then and now, held few successful criminals. (A successful criminal is, by definition, one who is not caught.) Convicts are, in the words of the criminologist Hans von Hentig, the proletariat of the criminal world. They are, at best, poor and without influential friends. More commonly they are simply too incompetent at their various illegal trades to stay out of trouble. Although this is a general truth, it was even more true in San Francisco of the 1850's. The Board of Prison Inspectors was merely reporting the facts when it stated in 1855 that few of the men at San Quentin were daring and intelligent criminals, but that most of them were stupid, ignorant, and submissive.

The prison inspectors undoubtedly found it easier to arrive at this judgment because such a disproportionate number of the convicts were foreigners. There were two good reasons for the foreign population of the prison. The native-born patriots of the Know-Nothing party, who were girding their loins to capture the governorship in 1855, were, for once, quite right when they protested that California was overpopulated with gallows birds from foreign parts. Second, the native-born white scoundrel was (as he still is) accorded a distinct advantage by the various arms of the law involved in his apprehension and conviction. Consider for a moment the plight of a San Francisco cook entered on the register under the name of Ai Yai, who was arrested on suspicion of grand larceny, found guilty, and sentenced to San Quentin in the fall of 1853. Who would go Ai Yai's bail? Who would bribe the police or speak to a friendly politician on Ai Yai's behalf? Who would pack the jury with Ai Yai's friends? Who would undertake to present Ai Yai's case privately to the judge?

Ai Yai and his compatriots represented not only the most exotic national group, they were also the least understood. Bret Harte's grossly libelous "The Heathen Chinee" appears full of brotherly feeling when compared with the corrosive hatred and absurd anthropology of the anti-Chinese agitators. (According to a notorious state supreme court decision of 1855, Chinese were solemnly declared to be American Indians and hence incompetent to testify against white men.) The Chinese, both their names and their queues casually mutilated by the long-nosed barbarians into whose hands their misdeeds had very properly delivered them, shuffle across the pages of the convict register in a woebegone procession: A Hing, A Mor, Ah Hoy, Ah Lum, Wang You Fou, Ah Wah, Ah You, Me Sing, and inevitably, Ah Fuck.

About one in every eight convicts was a Mexican or native Californian, although to count these men among the aliens is to involve oneself in the prejudice of the times. The Irish, Scots, and English together accounted for the largest national delegation from overseas, with the Irish well in the lead. (Among these Britishers were the Sydney Coves, who, though Australian by involuntary naturalization, were British by birth.) France and Chile also sent respectable delegations, though neither country could match the sovereign states of Massachusetts or New York. In all, thirty-one foreign countries accounted for something more than half the convicts.

Their crimes were, of course, various, but three-quarters of them were thieves of various denominations. The remainder had been convicted of every crime in the dreary catalogue of the penal code: murder and manslaughter, rape, sodomy, perjury, forgery, assault in its various degrees, mayhem, assisting prisoners to escape, arson, receiving stolen goods, and so on.

Their sentences were severe but not Draconian. Of forty-four convicts who share a page of the register in 1852, twenty-one were serving sentences of only one or two years. Only seven men had drawn sentences of more than five years. Two years later only fifteen of the original forty-four were still in prison. Nineteen had been discharged, five had escaped, three had been killed, and two had been pardoned.

In age, the large majority were in the prime of vigorous young manhood. The number of convicts over forty was insignificant, but one in ten was under the age of twenty. Laborers and sailors appear to have been the most prone to crime—or at least the most unlucky in the matter of arrest and conviction—but other trades were well represented. We can find on the prison rolls four confectioners, a vine dresser, four musicians, a soldier (one soldier to sixty-two sailors!), two lawyers, a circus rider, a *carbonero* or charcoal maker, several *vaqueros* or ranch hands, one physician, a pianoforte maker, a trainer of horses, and two gamblers. The occupation of one prisoner, received from Mariposa County on April 15, 1854, is not given, but one can hope that it will someday be subjected to scholarly investigation. The convict's name is listed simply as Jesus.

While there was ample work around the prison for carpenters, blacksmiths, and other skilled workmen, the great unwashed mob of prisoners could, by the terms of the lease, be put to profitable labor by the San Francisco Manufacturing Company. The company was engaged principally in supplying stone and brick to the San Francisco market. The stone came from the quarry on Marin Island; the brick was made from the native clay in a sixteen-acre steam brickyard adjoining the prison. Here a multitude of prisoners labored from sunrise to sunset seven days a week. (Estell, his business partners, and his guards clung to the fiction that Sunday work was required only in emergencies, but the condition of emergency was chronic.) Other men, more fortunate than the brickyard workers, were sent into the hills with axes to chop firewood for the brick kilns. These earned the hatred of nearby landowners by going about their duties with a fine disregard for property rights. Other men manned the schooner *Mariposa* and the sloops *Pike County* and *Marin,* which carried the brick and rock across the bay. San Quentin brick went into the San Francisco custom house, the Navy Yard at Mare Island, the first prison on Alcatraz Island, and the harbor fort which still stands on Fort Point, under the southern abutment of the Golden Gate Bridge.

The sailors ranked high in the aristocracy of San Quentin, but there were others who ranked higher; these were the trusties who kept the prison records, who were issued guns and assigned to guard posts, and who were seen drinking in the saloons of San Rafael and even strolling along the streets of San Francisco.

Estell's contribution to the quasi-science of penology was a trusty system the like of which has never been seen before or since. It was a system which was administered with absolute capriciousness, prejudice, and partiality, and which survived Estell by twenty years. A convict who made himself agreeable and useful could expect to live a life not much more rigorous than he had lived outside of prison; if, in addition, he came of a respectable family, Estell positively overflowed with good fellowship.

On July 1, 1854, Thomas McFarland Foley, a young Scottish-born San Francisco printer, was received at San Quentin to begin a three-year sentence for killing John H. Dunn, the editor of the *Pacific Police Gazette*. Estell met Foley as he stepped ashore at the steamboat wharf and escorted him to the superintendent's office. Foley himself described the meeting in a letter which he wrote a week later to Judge Solomon Heydenfeldt:

> [Estell] accepted my pledge of honor, and placed no restrictions on my liberty, and gave orders that I should live at his hotel, outside the guards, and receive the same fare, after the officers, in the dining room. He also placed upon me the injunction that his liberality toward me should be avoided in my communication with friends, lest such indulgence should subject him to the censure of the community. What blessings are conferred upon the unfortunates whose luckless fate consigns them to the discipline of a state prison—to be placed under the benevolent guardiancy of such a humane gentleman as General Estell. He is always alive to every feeling of sympathy and consideration toward those who are placed under the charge; and it is only to be regretted that there are so many whose depraved natures are ever ready to take advantage of any indulgence which

he offers, and thereby involve him in difficulty. The superintendent, Mr. Tice, seems to be a perfect gentleman, and
Mr. Gray, Captain Brouder, and Lieutenant Hays are declared to be without parallel; in fact, they seem to be everything that is desirable in officers.

The elevated tone of this communication was hardly flawed
by its conclusion: "And now, all that is necessary to 'cap the
climax' of my comfort, is a few plugs of common tobacco."

This was not all that Estell did to make Foley's stay at San
Quentin comfortable. He told his superintendent, A. Jackson
Tice, that Foley was a well-educated gentleman who had come
with a letter of introduction from a mutual friend (who was
probably Judge Heydenfeldt). The young printer, Estell said,
should never have been convicted, and he expected him to be
pardoned before long. In the meantime, he ordered Tice to give
Foley full liberty and to let him pass in and out at his convenience.
He was to sleep in the guards' boardinghouse (the "hotel" of
Foley's letter) and to eat with a Judge Gates, who, like Foley,
was a man of education who had fallen on bad times. Gates was
steward at the boardinghouse.

Barely two weeks after he had stepped off the San Francisco
steamer Foley was made a guard, assigned to the night watch, and
given a gun. So far as we know, he performed his duties as well
as any of the free guards until the day came when he simply
walked away from the brickyard, where he had been chasing the
prison hogs away from the soft bricks. He left behind a note for
Estell, promising to send back as soon as he could the $500 he had
taken from the prison safe.

It is hard to say how many trusties there were at any particular time, since Estell and his guards naturally tended to
underestimate the numbers for publication. A report of three
years later names fifty-three trusties with their jobs, which range
from assistant physician to servant in Estell's San Francisco house.
At this time there were probably thirty or forty. One of them,

a man named Dewing, lived with his wife in a cottage off the grounds. The others were less fortunate in their sleeping arrangements, occupying the Long Room or having rooms of their own in the various wooden houses around the grounds, but they suffered few restrictions.

The chief trusty in point of responsibility was Thomas Brown, alias E. J. Briscoe, an English-born forger, who was clerk in the prison office and carried the keys to the prison safe. In the fall of 1854, with only two years of his five-year sentence gone, Brown became restless and asked Estell if he might go to San Francisco to circulate a petition for his pardon. Estell not only told Brown to go ahead, but also lent him one of his own horses and suggested he stay for two or three days. Brown led the horse aboard the next steamer that stopped at the wharf, and, debarking at San Francisco, proceeded to visit old friends from the prison.

Among these was the same A. Jackson Tice who had been superintendent when Foley was committed. Tice had left the superintendency in July, 1854, as the result of a conversation with Estell. Estell had asked him if he wanted to stay and then had said, "If you will take $10,000 of the stock [of the San Francisco Manufacturing Company], you can stay here as superintendent as long as you please—and if not, there is another man, a Mr. Turner, who will take it, but you shall have the preference." Tice had turned down the offer and gone into business on Leidesdorff Street. He willingly signed Brown's petition.

Brown then proceeded down Montgomery Street, where he was seen by Thomas Young, a former engineer at the prison, and Henry Baker, who had been secretary of the San Francisco Manufacturing Company. Baker didn't recognize Brown, but Young pointed out the convict on General Estell's horse. Brown stopped, and there was a general conversation, during which he solicited the two gentlemen's signatures.

Unfortunately for his chances of pardon, Brown fell victim to the occupational disease of forgers and check writers—an inability to resist the juxtaposition of paper and pen—and forged a check on the firm of Macondray & Co., importers and commission merchants. His forgery was promptly detected, and his excursion to San Francicso ended with a new sentence of ten years added to his original five-year term.

Brown was not the only convict to be let loose on the streets of the city. Thomas Young recognized other trusties on Montgomery Street, among them a young English boy, Joe Francis, who had been convicted of carrying a master key to the county jail. Most familiar to San Franciscans were the convict crews of the prison boats who laid over along the Embarcadero after crossing the bay with cargoes of rock or brick. Although the convicts were supposed to be locked in the holds while the boats were in port, they weren't. The cook of the *Pike County,* a trusty known to the guards as Mr. Harris, was in the habit of spending the night ashore with his wife. It shouldn't have surprised anyone when he simply failed to return from one such connubial visit.

Chapter III

THE FIRST SCANDAL

THE first of the many scandals that have revolved around San Quentin broke in the winter of 1855 when Estell's unconventional ideas of prison discipline could no longer be ignored even by his supporters in Sacramento. In October, 1854, Governor John Bigler, a close friend of Estell, wrote the prison inspectors, asking that in view of the "peculiar state of things" at the prison they render him a report as soon as possible.

The inspectors did not get around to submitting their report before the end of January, but the substance of what they had to say moved the legislature to appoint a committee to investigate further. When the committee convened at the prison in March, they discovered that the rumors of queer goings on were substantially true. They were principally distressed by the frequency of escapes, by the endemic drunkenness, by Thompson and Gray's housekeeping arrangements, and by Estell's casual ways with money.

In the matter of escapes, the committee found the prison bookkeeping so wildly inaccurate that it was hard to tell exactly how many prisoners were on hand, and that much less possible to count the dead and missing. Surviving prison records, however, show that in the fifteen months from March, 1854, to June, 1855, one hundred and fourteen convicts escaped from Estell, an average of nearly eight a month. The largest single escape of this period had been made by twenty-two men from one of the Marin islands who had got away in one of the prison boats. Of the other escapes, some were bloody outbreaks from the Stones, but the vast majority were made by trusties, who had many opportunities simply to walk away. The occasional fogs not only hindered the detection and pursuit of escaping convicts but also dampened the powder and caps of the guards' rifles, a fact which was as well known to the convicts as to the guards. Once a convict was well away from San Quentin he could take refuge in the heavily wooded slopes of Mount Tamalpais, where a floating population of escaped convicts lurked in the firs and redwoods, living off game and terrorizing local residents, who complained repeatedly that their virtuous wives and daughters were exposed to the horrors of rape. (In view of the repetition of this theme, it is interesting to note that the one instance of rape of which we have certain knowledge, an attempt upon the person of a rancher's wife, was made not by a convict but by a guard.)

For convicts with money or influence a safer and more gentlemanly way of departing from San Quentin was to secure a pardon. Although Estell was never actually convicted in court of selling pardons, his conduct in this matter was at best flagrantly indiscreet. Pardons were known to have been written out not only by Estell himself but also by the convict clerks in the prison office. There was, furthermore, a well-founded belief among the Mexican women of northern California that Estell's price for a pardon was about $200.

The most circumstantial testimony came from a stout Mexican woman named Juana Carillo, who testified that she had handed Estell himself $195.50 in cash for the pardon of her son and had been given a receipt, which she produced for the committee's inspection. Two or three months after the money had changed hands Mrs. Carillo's son was discharged from San Quentin and was last seen heading toward the gold mines. Mrs. Carillo's only complaint was the length of time it had taken to free her boy. She had, as a matter of fact, returned to the prison to thank all hands for their help in the matter. Asa Estes, who had succeeded Judge Thompson as captain of the guard, returned her visit, staying overnight at her house in San Francisco, where he shared the bed of a Mexican girl who boarded there. "They appeared," Estes testified ungratefully, "to be lewd women."

The committee professed itself generally distressed by the social life of the officers and guards. The general drunkenness and the sale of liquor to convicts were solemnly found to be not in the best interests of discipline. Although it was noted that there were currently no female convicts on hand, the committee listened to abundant testimony concerning the relations of Judge Thompson and Lieutenant Gray with the women. (The tone of this testimony may be gathered from this sample: "Capt. Thompson ... was very familiar with a female convict named Mary Ann Wilson. I have seen him pull her down toward his lap and handle her familiarly.")

In the course of its hearing the committee also recorded testimony on half-a-dozen other subjects of more or less scandalous nature. Although the prisoners were supposed to have Sundays free from work, they appeared to have been sent to the brick-yard regularly on the Sabbath. This was, in a sense, balanced by the fact that the guards themselves worked sunrise to sunset with no relief except for meals. Benjamin Buckalew, the former owner of the twenty acres on the point, testified to the bad blood between himself and Estell brought on by Estell's encroachments on his property. The prison books were said to have shown purchases of twice as much food as would have been required by standard army rations for the same number of men. Estell, it turned out, had not paid the guards since some time the previous spring.

The outcome of the hearings was a recommendation that the

state buy out the contract. The negotiations that followed were complicated by Estell's friendship with Governor Bigler. Bigler first vetoed an act that would have bought the contract outright, and then turned around and approved another bill providing for the state to take over the prison if Estell would voluntarily give it up. This put Estell in a cruel position, for he neither wanted to give up the prison now that he saw some future profit in it, nor did he want to keep it unless the state would agree to build a secure wall. An exchange of stiff notes followed, the negotiations being terminated when Estell appeared on the streets of Sacramento armed with a double-barreled shotgun with which he said he was going to blow a hole through Bigler wherever he found him.

Bigler stayed out of Estell's range, and two weeks later, on June 1, 1855, Estell quietly turned over San Quentin to three men who had been appointed to run the prison in the name of the state. It was not until somewhat later that Estell was to have a revenge that was even sweeter than the violent physical dissolution of John Bigler.

Philosophers of the moral grandeur of free enterprise may find a congenial text in the events of 1855 and 1856, when public graft replaced private profit as the mainspring of the management of San Quentin. The danger had been seen clearly by the joint committee which, in recommending that the state take over, had warned: "If an old, well-trained, cunning politician is placed in charge, the scheme will surely and speedily fail." (A cynic might add that there was nobody better qualified to warn against graft than the old, well-trained, cunning senators and assemblymen of the committee.)

With his usual flair, Major Horace Bell wrote of the change of management that "There was such a gathering of the clans as was never known on that side of the bay. Offices were multiplied. The guards were doubled and sinecures created. Still not one in five could be provided for, but they were all invited to hang up their hats, eat, drink, and be merry, until something could be done for them, which caused some of the committee facetiously to designate our state prison as the 'Loafers' Asylum.' "

While many of Major Bell's reminiscences belong more to mythology than to history, his rendering of the moral climate of the new administration is, if anything, muted. As the state found out before the end of the year, the new directors, Major John Love, Richard N. Snowden, and William H. Palmer, spent the public funds as if there was no end to them. In the seven months between their assumption of control and the end of the year they managed to run through precisely $382,226.84. As a measure for comparison, the state's estimated expenses for the entire fiscal year 1855–56 were only a little more than $700,000, with a mere $60,000 earmarked for the prison.

Where the money had gone was a question which occupied a good deal of legislative time the next year, but without any really satisfactory explanation coming out of the investigation. Although it was shown that the contractors had made excessive profits, it was never proved that any of this money found its way into the directors' own pockets. Nevertheless, it took a good citizen of childlike faith to believe that it hadn't.

The physical condition of the prison and the prisoners, the demoralization of the guards, the strained political situation, and the legacy of maladministration inherited from Estell all called for the abilities of men of practical and moral intelligence above the average. Judging from their actions, the new directors appear to have been merely rather stupid and rather venal.

In the day-to-day management of the prison as well as in the awarding of contracts, directors Snowden and Palmer turned over their authority to John Love. The principal contract that Love had at his disposal, and the one that created the greatest scandal, was for the prison wall. In August, 1855, Love awarded the wall contract to a builder named James Smiley, who recruited gangs of stonemasons and bricklayers and joyfully went to work. The wall that grew up under his direction was a prodigy of jerry building. Grossly out of square to begin with, it ran raggedly from nine feet high up to the twenty feet called for in the contract. It was only two feet thick in places. The mortar was green and damp and had been mixed with salt sand from the beach. The stonework was laid in lime and sand, with only a camouflage of good mortar on the outside.

If Love or Smiley had exercised reasonable discretion they would probably have escaped the unwelcome interest of another investigating committee. But Love's term of office was up at the end of 1855, and when the new directors, who had been elected in November, took over the prison on New Year's Day, the smell of graft was too strong for even a seasoned politician to ignore. As the subsequent investigation revealed, Love had spent the fourth of December making out warrants to Smiley to the total value of $125,157 in partial payment for the misshapen, moist, and doughy wall that other contractors estimated at $50,000. In February the investigating committee applied a tape measure to the already famous wall and reported that they had found *prima-facie* evidence of fraud. Major Love, who a month earlier had demanded an investigation to clear his reputation, didn't pursue the matter any further. Neither did the state.

After hearing alarming estimates of the cost of running San Quentin, the committeemen took a deep breath and recommended that the state lose no time in getting out of the prison business and returning the prison to a private contractor. How a contractor could profitably work an institution that threatened to bankrupt the state was a matter which nobody explained satisfactorily.

Before returning the San Quentin convicts to General Estell we shall pause for a moment to admire a picture of Alexander Bell, the chairman of the board of prison directors, which has come to us from the pen of the high-spirited Major Horace Bell. A good friend of the prison director, but no relative, Horace Bell wrote that "Aleck was about the handsomest man on the coast, near six feet high, as lithe as a Delaware and as graceful as a statue." He was an adventurer by vocation, and had distinguished himself as a member of William Walker's filibustering expedition to Nicaragua. But let Major Bell tell the story:

> Aleck Bell was the luckiest man of the day, and this is the way his good luck cropped out.
>
> There were two Alexander Bells in Los Angeles, both captains, one having served under Taylor in Mexico and the other having served under Stockton and Kearney in California. The latter was a wealthy, most popular, and estimable citizen of Los Angeles, and the former was a first-class adventurer and noted rustler. Colonel Butts, of bear-fighting fame, was the Know-Nothing delegate from Los Angeles to the state convention and suggested Alexander the rich as a nominee on the state ticket for state prison director, an office with a $3,500 annual salary thereto attached and with perquisites of many more thousands thereto belonging. When the state ticket was announced, Alexander the rustler swore he was the man, interviewed Butts, promised him the prison beef contract if he'd keep mum, was the first to take the stand at the ratification meeting, accept the nomination, and pledge *his* influence to the ticket. He next went to his rich namesake, begged his acquiescence, and, notwithstanding several indignation meetings, Alexander the rustler brazened the thing through, claimed his election, got his certificate, took his seat as president of the board, swamped the whole directory in less than three months by incurring immense debts for reckless prison expenditures which brought down the wrath of the legislature, and the board was abolished.
>
> Aleck was the most openhanded, whole-souled, generous, and liberal of men, and his heart opened and yearned

toward these former friends [whom he found at San Quentin] now in prison rags and half starved, and he hied him to San Francisco, and bought the best of blankets, underwear, boots, hats, black doeskin pants, red shirts, and warm coats for his family of five hundred convicts [and] two suits each; had the prison renovated from floor to roof, the convicts shaved, shorn, scrubbed, and made comfortable, and had the prison larder stocked, and the table supplied in such style as would have bankrupted a second-rate hotel; cigars and tobacco were furnished, and forlorn indeed was the poor convict whose throat got cobwebbed for the lack of whisky. Alas for the poor devils at San Quentin, Aleck so ran the thing in the ground that in less than a month a committee of the legislature investigated the prison management, and on their report, during the third month, as before stated, the directory was wound up.

Although this cannot be given very high marks as history, in rendering the political atmosphere of the 1850's Major Bell comes off better than many of his more sober colleagues. Major Bell had thoroughly confused the board headed by John Love and the board headed by Alexander Bell, as well as adding some glorious flourishes of his own, but the picture he draws of the handsome, reckless, and kindhearted Aleck Bell is a pleasant contrast to the moneygrubbing scoundrels who preceded and followed him at San Quentin.

Estell did not have to wait long for a thoroughly satisfying revenge against Bigler for his betrayal in the matter of the prison contract. Between 1852 and 1855 California was invaded by the American, or Know-Nothing party, which had sprung out of the native-born Protestant's suspicion of foreigners and Catholics. Know-Nothingism became a rallying point for dissatisfied California Democrats, among whom was Estell. Estell established himself as a leader of the first Know-Nothing convention in

Sacramento in August, 1855, and managed the nomination of a
hitherto-undistinguished young man named J. Neely Johnson
who, with Estell's help, soundly beat Bigler for the governorship.

Not long after his inauguration the grateful Johnson wrote
to the assembly, reminding it of the expensive experiment that
had taken place at San Quentin and approving a bill authorizing
the prison commissioners to undertake arrangements for returning
the prison to private hands, provided the contract wouldn't cost
the state more than $15,000 a month. Estell, who had managed to
get himself elected again to the legislature, this time as assemblyman, promptly stepped forward and offered his services for a
modest $10,000 a month. Five days later the commissioners, hav-
ing neglected to advertise for any other bids, were able to report
that they had negotiated a new contract with Estell. At the time
nobody was heard to object to the scandalously profitable terms
of the contract.

In its internal affairs, Estell s second occupation of San
Quentin was a bleak repetition of his earlier tenure. Where the
food had been bad enough before it now became even worse:
spoiled beef, maggoty hams, wormy flour, rusty mackerel, and
coarse brown bread. The prison had been crowded before; now,
besides the 192 men crowded into the 48 cells, an additional 226
were crammed into the Long Room below. When Estell tried to
put up a new building, it collapsed with a tremendous crash.
Where, before, it had been hard to tell the convicts from the
guards, now the difference was plain to see. The convicts were
unbelievably filthy, they were visibly starved, and many of them
were barefoot.

Although the law required the prison commissioners to draw up
a set of rules for the government of the prison and to see that
these rules were followed, the commissioners simply endorsed
the existing rules and didn't bother to see that they were put into
effect. Under these circumstances it shouldn't have been much of
a surprise to anybody when the irresponsible and greedy Estell

managed once again to run the affairs of the state prison into a dreary mess.

The moralist may deplore the brutality they reveal, but the historian can only rejoice at the existence of the original prison logs which, beginning in 1856, give us our first clear account of the day-to-day events at the prison. Kept by hand in bound ledgers, the delicately shaded script records the weather, the number of prisoners, and such usual or unusual events as escapes, rebellions, congressional visitations, deaths, and punishments.

It is from these logs that we can see for the first time the extent to which San Quentin was governed by the whip. This was something for which Estell cannot be personally blamed; as the logs make clear, the appalling brutality of the floggings was a matter which was—often literally—in the hands of the captain or the deputy warden. There is in any case little to choose in this matter between Estell's regime and that of the 1856 prison directors, who were by contrast reasonably humane and enlightened individuals.

After his cruise aboard the frigate he called the *Neversink*, Herman Melville wrote with disgust and loathing and passion of shipboard scourgings of a dozen, eighteen, or twenty lashes. At San Quentin, ten years later, floggings of one hundred and fifty lashes were not uncommon. It is true that in the Navy the victims were, technically at least, free men, while at San Quentin they were convicts, but there is no reason to suppose that the convicts' nervous systems were any less sensitive.

Flogging offenses ranged from the obviously serious to the comparatively trivial. One day James Hudson took fifty lashes for stealing and "general inattention to his duties as cook"; the next day Leonard Tufts took one hundred and fifty for planning a general rebellion. Convicts were given thirty lashes for weakening their chains, ten for lying, eighteen for fighting, thirty for insubordination, sixty for escaping, twelve for stealing, and thirty for "indulging in the most disgusting propensities." The month of February, 1856, saw eleven floggings, none particularly serious but involving a total of two hundred and twenty-two strokes of the whip.

When the deputy warden or the captain of the guard took a personal dislike to an erring convict, there was nothing that set a limit to the ferocity of the punishment. Henry Wilson was one of those flogged with thirty lashes for weakening his chains; ten days later Wilson was given fifty more for being involved in Tuft's abortive rebellion; a day later he took twelve strokes more. Bearing in mind the physical consequences of an expert flogging —the torn skin, the infected flesh, the swellings, the scabs—it is hard to feel anything but wonder that he survived at all. Yet he did, and his punishment seemed moderate by comparison to that dealt out a few months later to William Scott, recaptured after a bloody escape from Marin Island. On the day he was brought back, Captain George Wells gave Scott one hundred and twenty lashes; two weeks later Wells administered another fifty-five, for a total of one hundred and seventy-five. Scott too survived, but the log says nothing of his physical condition after the floggings.

The prison officers showed some individual preferences in the matter of the instruments used. Wells generally used a rawhide whip, while John Gordon, who served as superintendent under both Estell and the state directors, appears to have preferred a rod or a leather strap fastened to a handle which could be held in both hands. Although it could be made to cause as much pain as the rawhide, the strap didn't break the skin and, apparently with official visitors in mind, Gordon flogged the convicts across the buttocks, where the marks wouldn't show.

For lesser offenders and as a supplement to flogging there were chains of various weights and lengths. The working parties who graded and excavated the prison roads were chained together, while for the chaining of individuals there were long chains, short chains, heavy chains, light chains, single irons, double irons, and cross irons. A convict under punishment might be chained to the wall of his cell or he might be sent to work with the ball and chain dragging from his ankle. There was also solitary confinement on bread and water, with or without chains.

It was not until later, when San Quentin passed under the benevolent administration of the state, that torture became a recognized instrument of prison policy and the convicts became familiar with the dungeon, the ladder, the water cure, and the jacket.

As it turned out, it was not Estell's notorious mismanagement of the prison that loosened his grip on San Quentin so much as his involvement in the murder of James King of William, which to this day remains the most celebrated murder in the history of California.

James King of William was an unsuccessful Montgomery Street banker turned crusading newspaper editor. (The "William" was a patronymic which he had adopted to distinguish himself from other James Kings, and also, one suspects, for the sake of the romantic ring it gave his workaday name.) On the afternoon of May 14, 1856, King's paper, the *Bulletin*, appeared on the streets with an editorial charging that a politician named James P. Casey had served time in Sing Sing and had achieved public office by stuffing ballot boxes. Casey immediately called on King in his office and protested that his past was nobody's business but his own. King ordered him out, but at five o'clock, when King left the *Bulletin* for the day, Casey was waiting outside. He fired once with a Navy revolver, wounding King in the chest. Casey ran into a police station and gave himself up; King was carried into an office building where he was thought to be on the mend, until, six days later, he died.

This murder becomes part of the story of San Quentin because Estell, who was a friend of Casey's, had boldly stationed himself

on Montgomery Street during the assassination. He appeared
as a witness at the inquest on King, and, although his account
of the shooting differed in some significant details from the stories
of more disinterested eyewitnesses, he was never proved to have
been criminally implicated with Casey. But the Vigilance Committee, which had sprung into new life to do justice in this case,
hanged Casey and showed an uncomfortable interest in Estell's
affairs, while the *Bulletin* published documented accounts both
of Estell's personal corruptness and of his outrageous management of the prison. If he was not arrested, the only reason was
that his crimes had been committed in Marin County, while the
Vigilance Committee had limited its activities to San Francisco.

The crimes with which Estell was charged were many and
various. First, he was said to have murdered a man in Missouri
and to have escaped punishment only through the intervention of
a man he was now employing at San Quentin. Second, Estell had
opened a fraudulent post office on the plains, promising emigrants
to deliver letters back home for a fee of a dollar per letter; then
he had burned the letters to save himself the trouble of making
delivery. Third, he was accused of having instigated at least one
murder in Marin County. Fourth, he had tolerated the licentious
behavior of his officers with the abandoned wenches committed
to their care. Fifth, he had let prisoners buy their way out of
prison, with the result that the state was being pillaged by gangs
of escaped convicts. Sixth, he had had two Negroes taken from
San Quentin to New Orleans to be sold as slaves. Seventh,
he had perjured himself in telling his story of the shooting
of James King. There was more, but mostly in the form of varia-
tions on these major themes.

Estell answered with one of the most scurrilous speeches ever
delivered in a public hall. His fellow assemblymen were at first
astonished and then delighted when he accused King and his
wife and brother of whoring, pimping, and thieving.

The violence of Estell's speech was due in part to the visit, a week earlier, of an unfriendly investigating committee to the prison. The committee's first move had been to have every convict called into the yard, where they were herded into a circle. Then the prison roll was called. As each man heard his name, he walked out of the circle. There were almost four hundred convicts at San Quentin, and the committeemen had ample time to observe the filth, the rags, and the absence of shoes and stockings. They also were given an opportunity to observe the disciplinary regime. When convict Donnelly 1008 failed to answer to his name, the guards tracked him down to his hiding place in a bush behind the prison. He was dragged back and flogged with fifty-three lashes for the encouragement of the others and the instruction of the committee.

The committee sailed to Marin Island and took muster there also, as well as counting the trusties working on the ranches and assigned to the prison boats (one of which had modestly been named the *Estell*). When they were through, there were still six names on the muster roll for which no corresponding bodies could be found. The committee set out to track down one of these, a robber named Francisco Esparza. At Point San Quentin they had been assured Esparza was on the island. At the island they were told that Esparza was on a boat. When they checked the boat crews, no Esparza was found. They returned to the prison and asked Estell about Esparza. Estell said he'd never heard of the man. The committee was disturbed, particularly when they found that Esparza had last been seen working as a servant in Estell's house in San Francisco.

By the time the committee left San Quentin they had concluded not only that Estell was incompetent and a liar but that he was, as the Vigilance Committee had charged, criminally guilty of helping prisoners to escape. They rebuked the Marin County grand jury for having failed to indict the prison officers involved and reminded everybody concerned that the law provided that anyone conniving at an escape should serve the same term as the escaped prisoner.

Of the positive recommendations they made, the most important called for the state to station a resident agent at the prison to ride herd on the lessee, for a reformatory rather than a disciplinary regime, for the adoption of a prison uniform, and for a law forbidding the sale of liquor within two miles of the prison. These were all splendid ideas; none of them was adopted until years later.

So far as Estell's contract went, they declared it void. Estell threw up his hands and cried to heaven that he had once again bankrupted himself by his devotion to his duty. He demanded that the state bail him out, for not only the convicts but also the officers and guards were, he said, suffering grievously. The state, he went on, was responsible because it had paid him his monthly $10,000 in twenty-year bonds rather than in cash. Moreover, his credit had been ruined by the attorney general, who had delivered an opinion that the lease was unconstitutional.

What with one thing and another the legislature had at last had enough of Estell. They advertised for a new lessee, but nobody came forward, and, as it turned out, it was Estell himself who engineered his own removal from the prison. His lease remained in effect, but in May, 1857, Estell assigned the remaining four years of the contract to a businessman named John F. McCauley, whose tenure at Point San Quentin remains one of the liveliest chapters in the history of the state prison.

Chapter IV

THE ART OF POLITICKING

JOHN F. McCAULEY was one of the tens of thousands of young men who came to California by way of the Mexican War and the Gold Rush. Born in Virginia, he had, like Estell, lived in Missouri. In his middle thirties he tired of Missouri and enlisted in the Army to serve in the Mexican War. Mustered out, he kept on the move, arriving in California in 1850.

McCauley got his first toehold in San Quentin when, in 1855, he was awarded the prison beef contract during the directorship of Major John Love, the famous wall builder. (Later some unpleasant things were said about the honesty of McCauley's bills; the refusal of the legislature to pay him in full stiffened his resolution to extort every penny he could from the state.) His arrangement with Estell called for a fifty/fifty split of the monthly $10,000 due under the contract, with McCauley to keep any profit he made from working the convicts. He was, according to one writer, a "forceful, determined man, not much of a humanitarian or philanthropist, who cut his cloth in the management of the prison according to the money there was in it."

Money was, in fact, the single and entire key to McCauley. He ran the prison like the forced-labor camp which it was. By the end of 1857 the life of the San Quentin convict had fallen several steps from even the low condition it had occupied under

Estell. McCauley ignored the physical needs of the convicts, ignored the orders sent down from Sacramento, ignored the suggestions of his own prison officers, ignored everything but his profit, and left the prison a wealthy man.

This took some doing. McCauley worked the convicts in the brickyard from daybreak to breakfast at nine o'clock. The convicts then worked until four in the afternoon, when they were fed dinner. Sixteen hungry hours followed until breakfast the next morning. In spite of the urgent recommendations of the last investigating committee, McCauley bought no shoes or socks, and the prisoners went to work with their feet wrapped in rags. Nor did McCauley provide any uniforms; the convicts wore their civilian clothes until the rags dropped from their backs. Conditions in the four-man cells were worse than ever, and in the Long Room three hundred men and youths, including a fifteen-year-old boy, slept in three-decker bunks stacked so closely together that the only way for a convict to enjoy his lousy straw mattress and single ragged blanket was to crawl in from the end. Dr. Taliaferro was still on call from his home in San Rafael, but he wasn't encouraged to visit the prison. McCauley refused to throw good money after bad chasing escaped prisoners, and although as many men escaped from him as from Estell, he cut the guard force in half. He paid his eighteen guards only $40.00 a month.

The only items recorded in McCauley's favor come from the folklore. He is said to have opened a keg of whisky in the prison yard every Saturday afternoon and to have declared that Sundays were ladies' day, with the convicts' spouses and sweethearts having the freedom of their cells. He is also reputed to have distributed a coarse tobacco called "nigger heel" to all men who attended diligently to their work.

In the summer of 1857 the prison commissioners hired an architect named M. F. Butler to design a building which was actually built later on as a combined hospital, female prison, male lockup, and dungeon. Before work began they decided to erect another cell block instead. On August 20 Butler delivered the plans to Estell, who promised that work would begin directly. During the remaining months of the year Butler returned to San Quentin five times, but, as he reported glumly to the commissioners, not a brick had been laid.

The state officials were not pleased with McCauley, but as they found out in 1858 he knew his rights and was prepared to fight tooth and nail for every penny he thought he had coming to him under the contract. The issue in which McCauley had his first chance to show his toughness was precipitated by Neely Johnson, who in his farewell message to the legislature in January spoke out against the inhumanity of farming out the convicts and recommended that the prison be abolished. He pointed out that San Quentin, even under the lease, gobbled up a quarter of the state's budget. Rather than spending another penny on San Quentin, the prisoners, Johnson said, should be returned to the county jails. Although it was the incoming governor, John B. Weller, who was to carry the battle to McCauley, Johnson struck the first blow by cutting off the $10,000 due McCauley and Estell for running the prison during the month of December.

As a politician, John Weller had been something of an infant prodigy. Before he was twenty-one he had been elected district attorney of his native Butler County, Ohio, so greatly were his neighbors impressed by his rare oratorical talents and his political zeal. His career as a passionate Democrat was noted largely for his platform eloquence. California historians have generally treated Weller as a glib blowhard, but he entered the state prison imbroglio as the most capable man who had yet had anything to do with San Quentin.

In his inaugural address Weller reminded the legislature of the exorbitant cost of maintaining the prison, and pointed out that its annual budget of $160,000 was larger than the entire Indiana state budget and more than four times the amount New York spent on three prisons holding two thousand convicts. He

SAN QUENTIN, 1859

THE FIRST GREAT FIRE, 1876

STRIPES, 1871

THE PRISON, 1893

Roy D. Graves

SAN QUENTIN VILLAGE

SUNDAY VISITORS, 1915

Dr. L. L. Stanley

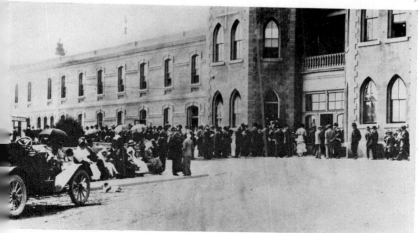

Roy D. Graves

THE PORCH, AROUND 1900

WOMEN'S QUARTERS, AROUND 1905

Roy D. Graves

California State Library

TB WARD, 1921

THE CANTEEN

San Quentin Prison

260

San Quentin Prison   *Marin County Historical Society*

W. H. T. DURANT   DR. A. W. TALIAFERRO

WARDEN   JOHN E. HOYLE

Roy D. Graves

San Quentin Prison

RALPH H. NEW, GEORGE MANTLO, CLINTON DUFFY, JULIAN ALCO

DR. LEO L. STANLEY   WARDEN FRED R. DICKSON

San Quentin Prison   *San Quentin Prison*

San Quentin Prison

LOOM ROW

SACK ALLEY

San Quentin Prison

ROAD CAMP, ABOUT 1916

THE WAR EFFORT

THE BALL CLUB

FIELD DAY, 1921

Roy D. Graves   *California State Library*

SARAH BERNHARDT   PROFESSOR GALLUR
VISITING SAN QUENTIN   AND HIS BAND, 1921

THE BIG SHOW, NEW YEAR'S DAY
San Quentin Prison

San Quentin Prison

A DOOR IN THE STONES

San Quentin Prison

A MODERN CELL

SIBERIA

San Quentin Prison

CONDEMNED ROW, OLD AND NEW, ABOUT 1940

THE GALLOWS   THE GAS CHAMBER

California Department of Corrections

THE BIG YARD AND THE UNEMPLOYED, 1958

THE GARDEN BEAUTIFUL, ABOUT 1930

San Quentin Prison

San Quentin Prison

MESS HALL, OLD STYLE

MESS HALL, NEW STYLE

San Quentin Prison

San Quentin Prison

EAST BLOCK

left the solution of the problems up to the legislature, who, in what must by now have been reflex action, sent another committee to San Quentin.

Estell must have failed to warn McCauley that the committee was on its way. In any event, when the committee arrived unannounced, they found one hundred and twenty-five prisoners entirely barefoot, and a good many more wearing strips of old gunny sacks or blankets on their feet. The committee protested, and the next day quite a few of the previously barefoot convicts appeared in brand-new shoes. McCauley explained with a straight face that the convicts had hidden away their shoes so as to look as pitiful as possible when the committee arrived. The committee noted with massive irony that they had "failed to discover the secret place where were concealed the missing shoes of the shoeless prisoners, although the committee do not undertake to state, positively, that such secret place *may not* be in existence, and hereafter discovered by the closer scrutiny of more interested parties."

The lack of shoes was not all that was wrong. The convicts' clothing in general was so scanty and so threadbare that they suggested to the author of the committee report that "the commonest street beggars, sleeping by the wayside and begging their daily bread, would, by comparison, have the appearance of newly Parisian-clad gentlemen." The committee reviewed the other ways in which McCauley had abused the convicts, and wound up with a list of ten points in which McCauley had failed to live up to the terms of his contract.

The daily press was divided in its reaction. The *Alta* published an article generally favorable to Estell, but the *Bulletin,* sneering that this had been written by Estell himself, trundled out its editorial howitzer to destroy the "Big Jailer," as they had christened him. (In the *Bulletin's* eyes, Estell was still the archfiend and McCauley was his creature.) For several days the air around the *Bulletin's* office on Montgomery Street was full of smoke and fire, canister and grape. "The only compromise that should be made with Estell would be accepting his self-banishment from the state, instead of imprisonment in the walls of San Quentin, where he would only further corrupt the base wretches now confined within its limits."

A few days later the *Bulletin* published the committee report in full and fired off another mighty blast.

Read this document carefully and judge if the warfare made by the *Bulletin* upon the infamous Estell for the last two years has not been a justifiable one—one that the welfare of the state imperatively demanded should be made and prosecuted until this thieving vampire was forced to lose his hold upon the veins of the public, which he had gorged himself by sucking dry for years already. When we first opened our batteries upon this overgrown and swollen murderer and public plunderer we were prepared for a desperate battle. . . .

And again, after characterizing Estell as an "embodiment of vice and filth," the *Bulletin* cried,

The horrid exposé of the brutality, vice, corruption, filth, and mismanagement of the prison fully confirmed all previous reports, and was enough to make the heart sick to think that so much villainy and cruelty could be suffered so long to exist in the midst of a civilized community.

Even allowing for the overblown journalistic style of the times, these were strong words. Estell fought back by encouraging the legislature in a red-herring investigation of the activities of the Vigilance Committee of 1856 and circulated a pamphlet answering the committee's charges. But this time his tactics were unavailing.

On February 1, while the committee was writing its report, the Board of Examiners again refused to approve Estell's and McCauley's monthly claim for $10,000. The attorney general didn't bother to disguise his pleasure in rendering the opinion that not only was the payment unconstitutional, but that the entire leasing arrangement was illegal. When the committee formally presented its report on February 26 it itemized the various abuses of which McCauley had plainly been guilty. On the same day the assembly rushed through a bill which declared the lease null and void and directed Governor Weller to proceed to San Quentin to take physical possession of the prison.

McCauley's first reaction to being dispossessed was deceptively mild and reminiscent of Estell's delaying tactics. In Sacramento on Saturday, February 27, 1858, McCauley wrote to Weller, agreeing to evacuate San Quentin if the state would only make good his financial loss. Weller, however, was determined to take over the prison on his own terms, and, emboldened by McCauley's humble reply, he departed Sacramento on Sunday, accompanied by his youngest son, Charles, Lieutenant Governor Joseph Walkup, Secretary of State Ferris Forman, Major W. R. I. McKay, and several other gentlemen. McCauley left Sacramento the same day, agreeing to meet the governor's party in San Francisco the next morning.

The next morning the governor and his friends patiently waited for the boat to San Quentin which McCauley had promised to have ready for them. McCauley showed up and apologized for the delay; he would, he said, be ready in just a couple more hours. Weller was prepared to wait, but directly McCauley had left the room a friend of the governor's dropped in with the alarming news that the business that was delaying McCauley was an application for an injunction to keep Weller out of the prison. Weller and his companions hustled to the water front and lost no time in hiring a Whitehall boat, an open-air water taxi propelled by oarsmen. The oarsmen set a course for San Quentin, across about twelve miles of water. The governor's boat was clearing the point of Angel Island when they observed another

Whitehall boat in full chase. The passenger of the second boat was McCauley, and in his hand was a piece of paper.

Weller and his party debarked at the San Quentin wharf and hurried to the prison office, which they found in charge of John Simms, a follower of McCauley who sometimes acted as superintendent. Simms was a foxy-looking character with something of the air of a riverboat gambler. The governor demanded the keys to the prison. Simms said he didn't have the least idea where they were. A veteran guard who was in the office volunteered the information that the keys were kept in the strong room. Weller ordered the door battered down, the keys were taken, and the guard was put in temporary charge. Next, Weller demanded the prison seal. Simms said it was in his pocket, but he'd be damned if he'd give it up. Weller's party tackled Simms and captured the seal in his pants pocket. The entire proceeding had taken about twenty minutes.

At this point McCauley ran panting into the office, the injunction clutched in his hand. He was immediately joined by the local sheriff, the county clerk, and a county judge, all of them stout McCauleyites and all prepared to use their official powers to keep the governor out of San Quentin. Why they didn't remains something of a puzzle. The best account of the affair says simply, "The governor had acted with such promptness that they were all struck with amazement and they quietly surrendered at discretion."

Weller let McCauley stay at San Quentin and told him he could use convict labor to load the brick that had been burned during his occupation. McCauley took advantage of this permission to demonstrate again that he was such a habitual rascal that he couldn't bear to pass up the chance to turn even the smallest illegal profit. Between nine and ten o'clock on the night after Weller's victory the captain of the *Pike County* was surprised when his vessel was boarded by a working party of prisoners carrying three crates of prison hogs and two of chickens. The hogs and chickens were followed by two of McCauley's guards, men with the melodious names of McCoy and McClannahan, who explained that the livestock was to be delivered to a friend of McCauley's in San Francisco. The skipper took the animals, McCoy, and McClannahan across the bay and returned the next day to San Quentin, where McCauley was congratulating himself for having outwitted the state once more.

Even though the entire business had its comic aspects, Weller came out of it well, managing the expulsion of McCauley with dignity and firmness. Back in Sacramento he reported dryly to the legislature, "I was compelled to use a little force." To all appearances the battle of San Quentin was over, but the truth was that Weller had survived only his first and easiest skirmish.

As he wrote ruefully at the end of the year, Governor Weller spent most of his time during 1858 on prison affairs. He remained in personal charge at San Quentin until May 1, when he became one of a trio of prison directors, the other two being Lieutenant Governor Joseph Walkup and Secretary of State Ferris Forman.

Three days after he took over control Weller wrote to the assembly a letter which he devoted largely to his philosophy of penology.

You will allow me to suggest [he wrote] that the practice of the courts in sending men to prison for long periods will defeat any attempts, no matter how well directed, at what is regarded as one of the great objects of all human punishments—reformation. There are a number of convicts who have, for the first offense (grand larceny), been sentenced to imprisonment for ten years, and some fifteen. If a reformation cannot be effected within the first two years of confinement, there is scarcely any hope of it. He begins to look upon the officers as his enemies, selected by an unfeeling people to torture and oppress him. His heart becomes callous, and all the warm and generous impulses of his soul are annihilated;

he broods upon the wrongs which he thinks society has inflicted upon him, until at length, after years of suffering, he is thrown back upon the world a hardened wretch. Under our system, at the expiration of his term he is driven from the doors of the prison in rags and without a cent to purchase a meal of victuals. He has been in the state prison, and men are unwilling to employ him.

More than one out of ten prisoners were under twenty-one years old, and Weller, who had seen boys of fifteen and sixteen jammed into the Long Room with the rest, spoke out strongly for the establishment of reform schools, or, failing that, suggested that youthful offenders be kept in the county jails. In addition, Weller told the legislature that he intended to use his pardoning power whenever a sentence seemed to him to be too severe, and promised to restore the rights of citizenship to all former convicts with clean records. "I will guard as faithfully as I can the public weal," he wrote, "but if I must err, I prefer erring on the side of mercy."

But as is the unhappy case with most reforms, the gap between the ideal and its realization remained a wide one. There were some slight changes in organization, but these consisted mainly in filling the jobs vacated by McCauley's men with friends and supporters of Weller. Weller himself pointed out that he had been acting as warden for two months and that it was clearly absurd to expect the governor of the state to continue as full-time warden, leaving the legislature to go its own willful way. The directors were consequently inspired to create a new position, which they called chief warden, and to nominate Lieutenant Governor Walkup to fill the post. The directors hoped—soundly as it turned out—that a grateful legislature would pay Walkup for his time. As so often happens in public affairs, a temporary accommodation became a permanent institution. For years afterward the lieutenant governor was ex officio warden, an arrangement which solved the perennial problem of what to do with the lieutenant governor but did nothing to guarantee the prison a competent and honest warden.

From the viewpoint of the convicts the most welcome change was the construction of a new building to relieve some of the pressure on the Stones. McCauley had built a mess hall and a kitchen, but he had failed to construct a single new cell. Within three days of taking over Weller had somewhat improved matters in the Stones by partitioning the Long Room into six smaller rooms, permitting some segregation of the more hardened inmates. More important was the construction of a building containing more living quarters. This building, finished in 1859 and still standing, contained dormitory rooms, rooms for female prisoners, a twelve-bed hospital, and, in its basement, fourteen dungeon cells. Because some Marin County prisoners were kept in this building for a while it was called the County Jail, but it is now known as the Old Hospital.

The fourteen cells which were built of rock and brick in the foundations of the new building had been ordered as a reform measure intended to provide a means of punishment less revolting than the rawhide. Here in the solitude of an 11½-by-6 foot cell, chained to an iron eye embedded in stone, the erring convict could meditate on his sins until, chastened both by his removal from society and a diet of bread and water, he came to see the necessity of mending his ways. This, at any rate, was the theory.

Weller had ordered work to begin on the dungeon as soon as he took command in March, 1858. By the end of the month, when eight of the cells were ready, a convenient opportunity had arisen to test their effectiveness. Sixteen prisoners who had tried to capture the sloop *Black Cloud* had been seized. Instead of sending them to the whipping post, Weller ordered them to the dungeon in two shifts, each shift staying underground for a week on a diet of bread and water. When they emerged, their heads were half-shaved, and they were kept in this grotesque condition for a matter of months. But they were not whipped.

The rawhide and the leather strap were not completely abandoned, but for some time the prison logs show almost daily commitments to the dungeon. When the board of directors began to meet, Walkup and Secretary of State Ferris Forman endorsed Weller's enthusiasm for the practical and humane advantages of the dungeon after considering the comparative merits of flogging and such punishments as the water torture. So far as practical grounds went, the directors thought a spell in the dungeon would touch the sensibilities of even the "Mongolians and Africans" among San Quentin's polyglot population. As for the humanitarian grounds, the directors agreed that flogging was an abomination which should be reserved for only the hardest cases. But they took the sensible precaution of having the whipping post erected just before the entrance to the dungeon cells.

Like the humane men they were, the directors took steps to see that the dungeoned convicts would not become the victims of sadistic guards.

The officers of the prison have been instructed [the directors wrote] to treat these men as human beings entitled to commiseration, and who may yet become useful citizens. In their intercourse with them they are to receive all the kindnesses compatible with their security. The convict is sent to the prison to be deprived of his liberty and compelled to labor as an expiation of his crime, and any other punishment besides that which is absolutely necessary to accomplish this and enforce the discipline of the prison is not only unlawful but inhuman.

So it was that high-minded men with the best of intentions put into use the dungeon which was to remain the shame of San Quentin for eighty years.

In July, 1858, McCauley fired off the first shot in what was to become a battle of such complexity that we shall leave its details to scholars of the law. The battle in the courts ended with the state supreme court sustaining a judgment against Weller of more than $12,000 for forcible entry and detainer, the damage having been the smashing of the strong-room door. McCauley also started another action against Weller as an individual, a suit for $100,000 for trespass, but this was apparently intended merely as a harassing action on a vulnerable flank, for it was at length quietly dropped. McCauley's most imaginative tactic, however, was not in the courts. In the winter of 1859 he embarked on a campaign to impeach the character of Lieutenant Governor Walkup, who since the previous May had been acting as warden.

Walkup was the perfect lieutenant governor, loyal but undistinguished. His obituarist described him as a man of plain, unassuming manners but of great sincerity of character, who was decided and honest in his political views. It was the greatest of ironies that Walkup should have been caught in behavior that his enemies could represent as indecent and immoral.

Joseph Walkup's weakness was an amiable one: He enjoyed a friendly drink and a little social dancing after a hard day's work at the prison. San Quentin was far from being a social desert. Parker's tavern, which had been the locale of many a drunken brawl during the early days, still flourished inside the prison boundaries, while within sight of the prison in the other direction an express agent named Robinson ran a hotel and bar he called the Point House. Here Robinson and his wife and their three children entertained the cream of San Quentin society: Chief Warden Walkup, Dr. Taliaferro, Charles Robinson, who had succeeded Gordon as superintendent, and Lieutenant John C. Morton. Here, too, came ladies and gentlemen from surrounding hamlets and travelers from San Francisco. Among the guests were also the wife and daughter of a trusty named Gilman; while Gilman drank in the bar, his ladies danced with the male guests. There were those who claimed to have seen two female convicts among the dancers as well as the wife and daughter of an outlaw named Jack Phillips, but neither of these charges was ever proved. The music for these affairs was provided by a fiddler whose name was Stephen Jackway, but who was generally known by the more euphonious name of Jackaway.

Jackaway was a trusty with the reputation of being the most faithful prisoner at San Quentin. McCauley had made him gatekeeper. Jackaway had performed his duties in this post so conscientiously that when McCauley needed three convicts to go into the woods to cut spars for a schooner he was building, he chose Jackaway. One of the other convicts escaped, but the faithful Jackaway returned with the spars. McCauley rewarded him by sending him to work on the ranch of William Hicks, who lived twenty miles from the prison. Here he stayed until Weller brought him back with the other farmhand trusties and put him to work handling livestock in the stable outside the walls.

Until his discharge in January, 1859, Jackaway slept outside the walls and came and went as he pleased. Sometimes, when Robinson was entertaining, Lieutenant Morton would take Jackaway and his fiddle to the Point House as an accommodation to the innkeeper. Among those who danced to Jackaway's fiddle was the gregarious chief warden.

Between dances Jackaway was rewarded with a drink. Sometimes, as the evening wore on, he was seen to be a little tight. One night, when Walkup was there, Jackaway got more than a little tight, and in the early morning put away his fiddle, saying, "I'm tired and I'm damned if I'll play." There was a small row over this, and the party broke up as a result.

Now all this was innocent enough, or at least so it seemed to Walkup and the other prison officers. It is doubtful if anyone would have been seriously distressed by Walkup's sociability if McCauley had not set his friend John Simms to spy on the new administration. Simms, who, it will be recalled, was the officer in whose pants pocket the prison seal had been captured, frequently traveled from his home in San Rafael to San Francisco by way of the Point San Quentin steamboat landing. Whenever he fell into company with a prison officer—encounters which may not have been entirely accidental—he turned the conversation toward the latest prison gossip. In this way he heard about the dances at the Point House and about the simultaneous presence there of the convict Jackaway and the chief warden. Simms gratefully promised to say a good word for his informant if the prison could be returned to McCauley.

Friendly legislators spread the word in Sacramento that Walkup had been living the life of a degenerate Roman emperor, beating innocent prisoners half to death for his amusement, engaging in indecent and immoral practices (this turned out to be the dancing), and embezzling the taxpayers' money. Ignoring the report of a senate committee which endorsed Weller's improvements, McCauley and Estell's friends in the assembly packed an investigating committee with their own men and sent if off to nail the warden's ears to a door. Their real target was Weller, who would be a candidate for renomination later in the year.

As expected, the assembly committee listened to McCauley's testimony and found Walkup and his subordinates guilty on all counts. Even while they were meeting, however, another packed committee arrived at the prison, this one being a committee of senators friendly to Weller and Walkup. After expressing polite surprise at finding their colleagues from the assembly already in session, the senators found that Walkup had managed the prison so splendidly that there was no cause for complaint at all.

Faced with two flatly contradictory reports, the legislature did nothing. This was precisely the outcome hoped for by Weller's enemies, who were afraid that if he was admitted to have run the prison successfully, he would be an invincible candidate for renomination. Neither they nor anybody else expected their maneuvers to end with McCauley again in possession of the prison.

McCauley himself was among those who recognized the purely formal political nature of the proceedings. Although his legal claim had been affirmed in March, when the supreme court directed that the prison be returned to him, McCauley let it be known that he was open to any reasonable settlement. A joint committee heard McCauley and Estell's terms, which were that they would give up all future claims to the prison in return for $120,000 (ten months' payment under the contract) plus an additional sum of almost $100,000 that McCauley claimed was due him personally for his property on the prison grounds. Because the legislature was scheduled to adjourn within a week, McCauley hoped to push through his demands without giving the state any chance to negotiate. Instead of taking the bait, the committee reported his offer without recommendation. The legislature appropriated the money to pay a judgment of almost $8,000 against Weller, and adjourned, leaving McCauley in possession of San Quentin.

Chapter V

McCAULEY'S REVENGE

THE prison log for May 13, 1859, contains only the sober entry, "The Warden, on behalf of the State, delivered up the Prison and prisoners to John F. McCauley, Esqre." Behind the bare bones of this sentence lies a puzzle of considerable magnitude.

There are two splendidly circumstantial and splendidly contradictory accounts of McCauley's return to San Quentin. Since there is no possible way in which the two can be reconciled, the only fair course is to present the reader with both. For the livelier, and probably apocryphal, account we are indebted to James H. Wilkins, who served as a prison director a number of years after the events he describes.

He came over from San Francisco on a chartered ferryboat with a full official list, a number of invited guests, and a brass band [Wilkins wrote of McCauley's return]. The procession formed on the wharf at San Quentin Point, the band playing the melody: "We'll all get drunk when Johnny comes marching home."

Many voices joined in the refrain. Next came McCauley with the eminent Marin jurist, County Judge Frink, on his right, whose decision the Supreme Court had just affirmed, and Chief Counsel A. P. Crittenden on his left. [Eleven years

later, as he sat with his wife on the deck of another ferryboat, Crittenden was shot through the heart by the notorious
Laura D. Fair.] Distinguished invited guests followed, and
what might be called a lifesaving corps, with demijohns,
case goods, and solid refreshments, brought up the rear.

Warden Walkup and his officers were drawn up at the
front gate of the prison, ready to turn over the works officially when the rather odd procession approached. The lieutenant governor, as warden, stepped forward, and presented
the keys, which McCauley accepted rather ungraciously. Then
the restored potentate had a word to say "for the good of
the order." McCauley did not have the intellectual powers
of his great English namesake, but possessed a rough gift of
speech and a wicked tongue. Addressing the rival assemblages,
he recounted in detail the long story of the wrongs that had
been done him—how he had been set upon and despoiled by
a combination of pirates, porch climbers, and horse thieves,
but through the courage and high acumen of the judiciary—
here the speaker glanced significantly at Judge Frink—their
plans had been frustrated and he had come back trium-
phantly to his own. Then, turning to the late officials, he
remarked, "You get, and don't let me see your ugly mugs
around my prison again!"

Everyone, except the dismissed officials, gave three cheers
for Johnny McCauley. The convicts, who had thronged to
the main gate, with the enthusiasm of their kind for any old
change, turned loose a mighty shout and the band played
"Annie Laurie." McCauley, touched by this enthusiasm of
the inmates, went inside the yard and delivered an address
to the convicts, conjuring them to believe that Johnny
McCauley was their sincere well-wisher and friend. The prisoners' hilarity was further heightened by an order for free
distribution of grog and the promise of a bang-up Sunday
dinner.

It was a red-letter day for San Quentin prison. Refreshments, both solid and liquid, had been prepared on such a
liberal scale that a considerable contingent from San Rafael,

scenting wassail from afar, were gladly welcomed to the feast. Everyone acquired something nice, all the way from a souse to a fist fight.

The San Franciscans returned home late in the afternoon. Over the calm waters of the bay, as the specially chartered ferryboat rounded Angel Island, floated the voluptuous strains of dance music by the band, indicating that the returning guests were still having a fairly good time of it.

Wilkins claimed to have had this story direct from old residents of San Rafael who had taken part in the jamboree and confesses only to have added a daub of color here and there. But even allowing for generous daubs of color, his story is hard to reconcile with the newspaper reports. Wilkins' account appeared in the *Bulletin* sixty years after McCauley's return. But on the afternoon that McCauley repossessed San Quentin the same newspaper had printed an account so different that it is hard to believe it describes the same event.

According to the *Bulletin's* correspondent, McCauley went about the recovery of his property in an entirely businesslike manner. He went to San Rafael and put into the hands of his friend Sheriff Doub the writ of restitution, commanding the sheriff to put Governor Weller out and to put McCauley in. McCauley, some friends, and some of his old officers accompanied the sheriff to the prison at about seven in the morning. Acting Warden John C. Gordon was called out, and the sheriff read the writ to him in a loud voice. Gordon replied that he was ready to obey, and surrendered the prison.

The sheriff, ex-Warden Gordon, and the captain of the guard proceeded inside the walls, where the convicts were at breakfast. They were called out of the mess hall and lined up in a double column along two sides of the wall. The captain then called muster; as each convict's name was called, he marched to another side of the yard. The muster showed that all convicts were present, 605 men and two women, one white and one Negro. "The general description of these people may be summed up as wretched, squalid, dirty, debased, and lost," the *Bulletin*'s correspondent wrote. "They are not dressed in uniform, except indeed that they were uniformly ragged and filthy."

The report makes clear that in spite of Weller's good intentions the state administration of San Quentin had gone the way that many other reform administrations have gone. For three months the six hundred prisoners had been without regular employment after the last clay on the prison grounds had been made into brick. During the night the convicts were packed into their still-lousy beds; in the day they were turned loose in the yard to amuse themselves as best they could. Gordon had been using the strap freely to keep this restless mob in hand.

This is not to say that no permanent improvements had been made. Most apparent were the physical changes that had been made during McCauley's absence. The county jail had been finished, complete with the dungeon in its basement. The prison office, a two-story building inside the walls, which later became famous in California criminal circles as the Porch, had also been finished. Quarrying had been started on prison property. Two more wharves had been constructed, and two roads, North Cannon Road and South Cannon Road, had been built around the walls. The main yard had been partly paved with bricks, and a smaller yard had been excavated and filled. New guardhouses had replaced the frame-and-canvas shacks McCauley's guards had used.

Dr. Taliaferro found the health of the prisoners and the general sanitary condition of the prison improved. There was less stomach and bowel distress, but the incidence of respiratory disease was going up as the prison became more crowded. (Flu was the most common complaint. "The men when locked up are literally piled one upon another," Dr. Taliaferro warned. "This fills the rooms with animal heat and impure air.")

In the matter of escapes, the state showed a considerably better record than either of the private contractors. Where McCauley had lost seventy-two prisoners in 1857, the state had permitted only nineteen escapes during the ten months of 1858 during which it had control. Furthermore, state officers had recaptured 26 of the convicts who had escaped from McCauley. Ironically, the state's record was marred by its failure to pay the advertised rewards, an oversight for which McCauley had been criticized.

As soon as his repossession had been confirmed, McCauley proceeded to discharge most of the employees appointed by Weller, even firing Dr. Taliaferro, who had served as prison surgeon since Estell's day. McCauley announced a program of hard work. Brickmaking, presumably on new clay lands, and stonecutting were to be resumed, and convicts were to be put to work sewing and making shoes. Road gangs would be sent out to various parts of the county. The guard force was to be cut to 15, but these men, armed with rifles and revolvers, would be stationed atop the wall, from which eminence the men in the prison enclosure would be at their mercy. Nobody expected McCauley to be humane, but he gave every audible indication of being a stern and efficient master.

It may have been pure bad luck, but it surely must have given some comfort to the former chief warden and his dispossessed employees when, a bare week after McCauley's return, fourteen of the most desperate convicts escaped from the dungeon under circumstances that suggested either, the connivance or colossal carelessness of McCauley's guards. If there was any doubt left that, so far as escapes went, McCauley was but Estell writ large, it was resolved by the events that followed immediately. Three days after the recaptured fugitives had been locked up, a guard discovered that someone had driven a nail into the touchhole of the six-pounder cannon at the Point, hiding the nail under the usual priming powder. The cannon was reprimed and fired off, and the guard put on the *qui vive*.

The escape came as expected, only two days after the discovery of the sabotaged cannon. Forewarned, the guard might have been expected to be ready, but the escape turned into a major rebellion, and one which in several ways was a blueprint for the greater prison breaks of the next five years.

At one o'clock on the afternoon of June 27 the lower gate was opened to let the brickyard crew—mostly Mexicans and Indians—return to their work. Outside the gate stood John Spell, the gatekeeper, and George Lee, a guard who acted as superintendent of labor. They had counted about a hundred and fifty convicts into the brickyard when a group of fifty men suddenly turned on them, slammed the gate, locked it, and seized Lee and Spell prisoner. Pushing the two guards ahead of them at the points of their daggers, they rushed across the brickyard and took the road that leads toward Corte Madera and Mount Tamalpais.

The alarm was given, but the ringleaders had planned their moves efficiently. The guards inside the yard couldn't get out, while those on the wall didn't dare fire for fear of hitting the hostages. Instead, they turned their weapons on the hundred prisoners who had been left behind in the brickyard. Some of those who had refused to escape made their way safely to the east gate, where they were admitted, but the rest saw the rifles and cannon of the guard aimed at them. They fell on their knees and crossed themselves and cried out that they didn't want to escape, but the cannon was fired anyway at the miserable wretches, killing one man and wounding several others.

Meanwhile, under the leadership of a desperate fellow named Francisco Lulio, alias Acapulco, the fugitives were making progress toward the mountain. They dropped Spell because he couldn't keep up, but they drove Lee ahead of them with his hands tied. They had managed to get three miles from the prison when horse guards caught up with them and opened fire. Lulio raised his dagger to stab Lee, but a charge of buckshot caught the convict full in the face, and he fell to the ground so severely wounded he was thought to be dead. Lee escaped, and the surviving convicts scattered.

After this it was mainly a matter of hunting them down in the hills and gulches and shooting them. Sporting citizens turned out with their shotguns and deer rifles to join the guards. The captures that were made were incidental; the guards shot to kill.

Lulio's body was carried back to the prison, but before he could be buried he began to show signs of life. Instead of going to the graveyard, he went to the hospital. Lulio lost an eye but survived to take a prominent part in other bloody and desperate ventures.

McCauley ordered the entire convict population locked in their cells, where they remained for five days while the guards shook the prison down for knives. Governor Weller and Ferris Forman and other gentlemen from Sacramento showed up, unwelcome but within their legal rights, and personally verified that there were still 567 prisoners in the institution. McCauley's guards not only found the knives they were looking for but also discovered that a prisoner named Frederick Billings had been smuggling out "scurrilous and untrue" stories for the San Francisco newspapers. Billings went into the dungeon.

Even though their San Quentin correspondent was chained by one leg to the dungeon wall, the newspapers had no trouble keeping up with affairs across the bay, which tended to be all too public for McCauley's peace of mind. Besides more escapes, there was evidence that neither Estell nor McCauley's manners with money had improved during their exile. McCauley was known to have pocketed at least $200 from incoming convicts and to have relieved a Spanish woman, whom he later committed to the state insane asylum, of her gold rings. Estell continued to appropriate prison property for his own use. Owing the firm of Jones & Smith for the whisky that had lubricated his campaign for the state assembly, Estell paid them off with a yoke of the prison's best oxen, still clearly bearing the prison's brand, SP, on their left flanks. The oxen were later recovered, but this was no thanks to Estell. Three other yoke of oxen were shipped away on the *Pike County* to satisfy other creditors. The *Pike County*, rerigged as a schooner, disappeared for a time as the result of private negotiations by Estell.

As the year went on it became increasingly clear to more and more people that, regardless how much money it might save the taxpayers, a private contract was no way to run the state prison. The *Bulletin* was not alone when it demanded that, whatever it cost, a final end had to be put to the system of farming out the management of the state convicts.

Getting rid of McCauley the second time was even harder than it had been in 1858. With the Supreme Court decision in his pocket, McCauley sat tight and didn't encourage visits by representatives of the state. On the state's side failure had brought recriminations, with the ousted directors and the attorney general snapping at each other for neglect of duty. Attorney General Thomas H. Williams suggested that the directors do whatever they thought best, but pointedly refrained from offering to start the proceedings. Forman took this in bad part.

Since the last legal skirmish the characters involved had undergone one important change. In January, 1859, Estell had withdrawn completely from San Quentin affairs, selling his interest in the contract to a prominent businessman named Lloyd Tevis. Under this agreement McCauley and Tevis were to hold joint possession of the contract, with McCauley receiving three-quarters and Tevis one-quarter of whatever could be squeezed out of the state treasury. Three months after selling out to Tevis, Estell died.

Estell's old enemy, the *Bulletin,* which two years earlier had filled its columns with thunderous denunciations of his various iniquities and demanded his banishment from the state, noted Estell's death with two lines in the "Deaths" section of the vital statistics: "In this city, April 26, General James M. Estell, formerly of Madison County, Kentucky, aged forty-nine years." It was a strangely quiet ending for a man who for eight years had not only been at the center of the highly public affairs of San Quentin but who also had wielded considerable power in California politics. It was not until 1890 that Estell's better qualities were described by an anonymous writer in the San Francisco *Call*, who remembered his impressive bearing, his personal bravery, and his talents as a politician.

In the fall of 1859 McCauley had some legal successes, and the year 1860 opened with a political omen favorable to his continued prosperity. In January John Weller was defeated for United States senator by the governor-elect, Milton S. Latham. McCauley was so exhilarated by the good news that he ordered the prison artillery to fire a monster salute of thirty-one guns in commemoration of the political death of his enemy. (Weller moved to Louisiana after the Civil War, and died in New Orleans, in 1875, of smallpox.)

McCauley had the state over a barrel, and he knew it. In view of the legal situation, the state had only the alternatives of negotiating at a disadvantage or of letting the contract run its course, which would leave McCauley in possession until March, 1861, at $10,000 a month. There was strong pressure to get McCauley out of San Quentin, and after a false start earlier in the year the legislature in April authorized a board of commissioners to settle all of McCauley's various claims, to buy out his contract, and to take physical possession of the prison. There was, however, still a long way to go between passing the bill and getting McCauley's name on the dotted line; as the prison clerk noted in the log for May 17, everyone concerned was "waiting for to know who is going to keep the prison this summer."

The negotiations had their amusing features. McCauley and Tevis declined to attend the first meeting called by the board of commissioners; the commissioners later retaliated by shutting their office door in the contractors' faces. McCauley protested that he wasn't trying to get the last penny due him, but only a quarter of a million dollars to keep him from further loss. Although the legislature knew precisely McCauley's price for selling out—and knew, moreover, that in the light of the court ruling he had every chance of getting it—they obstinately put off appropriating quite enough money to satisfy him. The negotiations dragged on from April to August. Finally, in August, McCauley and Tevis formally accepted the state's offer of a grand total of $275,000, of which $30,000 was to settle McCauley's claims against Weller, $240,000 was to settle the state's contractual obligations to McCauley, and $5,000 was to ensure the physical surrender of the prison and the contract. McCauley was given two more months, at $10,000 a month, to wind up his business at San Quentin. He was also paid a little more than $15,000 extra for physical equipment at the prison.

On August 11 McCauley turned over the keys to Lieutenant Governor Isaac N. Quinn, who took charge of the prison while McCauley continued to work the brickyard. Quinn stopped all Sunday work, but otherwise things remained much the same. Two weeks after Quinn became warden the indestructible one-eyed Francisco Lulio led a break of fifteen chain-gang men who were filling and grading near a wharf. They managed to disarm three or four guards and to seize the boat *Nip Cat*, but the alarm bell was rung before they could get under way, and the boat was retaken. After the evening lockup the next day, the escapers were hauled into the yard and flogged with from forty-five to one hundred and sixteen lashes.

McCauley left San Quentin on October 11 with a characteristic flourish. According to the local correspondent of the French-language *Echo du Pacifique,* McCauley addressed a political meeting of Marin County citizens in the following words, which surely have lost nothing in translation and retranslation:

My children, I am delighted to see you so happy at my departure. Believe me, if I give up the prison, it is to minister to your pleasure. It is now your turn to do something for me. Send my friend John Simms to the Assembly. This can make no difference to you, and to me it would be a great favor. It is true Simms is a little stupid and that he can't write his name; but a member of the Assembly never has occasion for sense and need not know how to write.

The *Echo*'s correspondent wound up his dispatch with the prophecy, "Be this as it may, Monsieur John Simms will not be elected from this county." He wasn't.

McCauley left San Quentin a rich man. Although whenever it had served his purpose to cry bankruptcy he had done so, he retired to his farm near Galt, in Sacramento County, with a total from the state of about $125,000 in cash and another $100,000 due him in six months. In company with Tevis he lent out money to Sacramento County farmers, took hard cases to the courts, closed out mortgages, and saw his capital multiply. When in 1896 he died on his farm in his seventy-seventh year, the *Bulletin* wrote of him:

It is now a good many years since he retired thither, closing the books of a long and active life in our midst. On rare occasions since then was his prim figure, once so familiar, seen on our streets. He was almost unknown to the present generation of politicians and businessmen, and passed the sunset of his long life quietly on his farm, in affluence and among his immediate kin.

In California the Civil War was little more than the thunder of distant guns. While the rest of the country marched into its age of heroes, California engaged in patriotic demonstrations. At San Quentin the war years brought more than the usual amount of bloodshed and gunfire, but this, of course, was sheer coincidence.

During its first eight years at Point San Quentin the state

prison had been managed in the spirit of improvisation which dominated the social and economic life of the Gold Rush era. After the final ejection of McCauley, however, the prison fell into the hands of men who were primarily professional politicians rather than pirates. The distinction is a nice one, and the change was more a matter of style than of substance. The prison remained a rich piece of political spoils, but the looting was now carried on more in line with the ancient traditions of American state politics.

The act that the legislature had passed in 1858 after John Weller had expelled McCauley remained the law governing the prison until 1880. During these twenty years the prison was in the hands of a board of directors comprised of the governor, the lieutenant governor, and the secretary of state. Although the prison was usually managed from day to day by a deputy warden, the lieutenant governor was the ex officio chief warden. He drew $10.00 for every day he spent at the prison in addition to his $75.00 a month salary as a prison director. Although by comparison with Estell's $10,000-a-month contract this looks like very small potatoes indeed, the lieutenant governor was, in fact, handsomely paid. Simply by certifying to his presence at the prison he could draw $3,650 a year, plus $800 for service as a director, which gave him a grand total of $4,450 with house, food, and horses thrown in free. This was at a time when the highest-paid prison warden in the rest of the country, at the Massachusetts State Prison at Charlestown, was paid $2,500. Another advantage which the warden of San Quentin had over his colleagues elsewhere was that nobody expected him to know much about running a prison.

The power of distributing patronage, however, was not in the hands of Lieutenant Governor Quinn but in those of the governor, John G. Downey. Downey was a good fellow, a Democrat, an Irishman, and a citizen of Los Angeles. It was clear to Downey that the office of state prison guard could be filled only by good fellows, Democrats, Irishmen, and citizens of Los Angeles. In the process of finding jobs for the faithful, Downey got rid of most of the experienced officers, replacing them with men who have been precisely described as "cheap skates and bar-room bummers."

Up to this time the state had not done too discreditable a job in the brief periods during which its agents had operated San Quentin. The building of Major Love's wall had been balanced, as it were, by John Weller's good intentions, but Weller's decency had in turn been canceled out by Joseph Walkup's indiscreet behavior. On the whole, the state's record was fair to good. The convicts had probably been a little better treated during the periods of state control. Discipline had been firmer. In the matter of escapes, the state's record was far and away better than either Estell's or McCauley's. Where the lessees had allowed an average of six or eight prisoners to escape every month, the state had held this to between one and two, an improvement which was brought about largely by reforming Estell's wonderful trusty system.

Physically, the prison had grown by fits and starts, but the building had been done largely either in periods of state control or reluctantly and under great pressure by the lessees. Major Love's crooked wall still surrounded the prison, but even by 1860 his inferior bricks and salt-water mortar were decaying at an alarming rate. In the five acres within the walls the principal structures were the Stones, the two-story brick office building known as the Porch, and, all in one line and adjoining one another, the County Jail, with dark cells and dungeon, the tailor shop, and the mess hall and kitchen. Backed against these buildings were the blacksmith, cooper, and carpenter shops. There was also a brick laundry inside the walls. Later a long, four-story brick factory was built, only to burn to the ground in the great fire of 1876.

The offices and sleeping quarters of the officers and guards were located in a brick building McCauley had put up outside the walls. The guards' bedrooms were described as "cold, damp, fireless apartments, which are almost entirely destitute of every comfort and convenience of life." Here, too, was the warden's office and his bedroom, which, as an inventory noted carefully, contained, among the usual bedroom furniture, a cracked mirror. There was also a barn, a small slaughterhouse, a woodshed, and a two-story building over the main gate. The guard stood duty in five small brick posts, three of which were equipped with artillery pieces: a brass six-pounder, a mountain howitzer, and, in one of the posts commanding the brickyard, a nine-pounder gun.

A little more than five hundred prisoners were turned over by McCauley. Of these, the majority were still foreign-born. At the end of 1860 the prison held 554 convicts, of whom 330 were of foreign birth and 224 native Americans. A third of the Americans came from New York or Pennsylvania; of the foreigners, 87 were Mexican, 41 were Irish, 32 Chinese, and 30 English. About half the prisoners could neither read nor write. By far the greatest number described their civil occupations as "laborer," although, as one jaundiced official noted, few of them showed any signs of having ever put in a day of honest labor. Cooks had replaced sailors as the second most criminally inclined occupational group.

Nobody knows what the convicts thought of the change of administration. Outside the prison walls there was general rejoicing among editorialists and Democratic politicians that McCauley's feudal fief had been delivered up to the representatives of the people. There was also general approval of the new contract system that was negotiated in the latter part of 1861. The advantage over the old and discredited system was that now, with the exception of the brickyard, the prisoners could be worked only inside the walls. Prominent among the contractors was I. N. Quinn, the former chief warden, now turned out by the hazards of politics into the business world. Quinn and his partner bought the brickyard equipment and agreed to employ a maximum of 60 men at a daily fee of forty cents per man. Other contracts provided for the construction and operations of an agricultural tools factory, a cabinet shop, a clothing factory, a cooper's shop, and a cigar factory. The directors were to receive from thirty to seventy-five cents a day for each convict employed.

Although a sophisticated observer would have been safe in predicting that San Quentin was going to see its share of graft and inefficiency, it would have taken a prophet of extraordinary powers to have seen that the prison had entered its bloodiest and most violent years.

Chapter VI

THE BATTLE OF ROSS LANDING

IT IS one of the pleasant staples of political life that a new administration invariably finds things to have been dreadfully mismanaged by predecessors of a different political party. California's first Republican administration, which took office in January, 1862, under the leadership of Governor Leland Stanford, found predictably that previous to their elevation to office San Quentin had been managed by rogues and knaves. Only the stanchest of Democrats could deny it.

When the new prison directors—Stanford, Lieutenant Governor John F. Chellis, and Secretary of State William H. Weeks— took over the prison on January 18, 1862, they were dismayed to find San Quentin in its normal state at a change of administration. Bills were a year behind, and the prison's credit was so shaky that merchants habitually added a stiff carrying charge to their bills against the certainty of long-delayed payment. The buildings and workshops were run down, leaky, and barely habitable. Taking a stand which comes naturally to Republican politicians, Stanford and his colleagues announced that they were going to run San Quentin on sound business principles and make the prison self-supporting.

They were about as successful as most Republicans have been

in their attempts to balance the budget. To begin with, the new directors were faced with problems brought on by the worst winter on record. In January more than twenty-four inches of rain fell, flooding most of the Sacramento and San Joaquin valleys, putting the streets of Sacramento under water, and driving the legislature into San Francisco for the rest of the session which had barely begun. At San Quentin no work could be done, and the unemployed convicts were locked in their cells during the long, rainy days. As spring approached, rumors of trouble in San Quentin began to be heard in San Francisco.

In March the captain of the guard, an officer with the splendidly appropriate name of Blood, was fired for incompetence by Deputy Warden W. E. Robinson. Three months after he fired Captain Blood, Warden Robinson himself was suspended from duty by the resident director, John Chellis. On July 8, before a meeting of the full board of directors, Chellis charged Robinson with four counts of misconduct, two of which involved his handling of prison money and two simple insubordination. Stanford and Weeks found the charges unproven, but, judging from the promptness with which Robinson turned in a letter of resignation, they were acting out their part of a gentlemen's agreement to smooth the matter over for the best interests of everyone concerned. The day after the hearing Robinson resigned, owing "to the want of good feeling on the part of the resident director." The board courteously answered with a letter of thanks for his services.

Thus it was that the day-to-day control of San Quentin passed disastrously into the hands of John Chellis, a politician and sawmill operator by trade, whose only qualification for the office was his election as lieutenant governor of the state, and whose only experience had been the six months he had served as resident director.

After the noon meal on Tuesday, July 22, 1862, San Quentin was preparing to go back to work. In the mess hall the prisoners had finished their scanty portions of beef, beans, and bread, and the waiters were clearing away the tin eating pans and mopping up the sour juices that had spilled over onto the narrow tables. Outside, the sweepers leaned on their brooms, waiting until the working convicts had cleared the yard. Below the mess hall, in the lower yard, the brickyard crew waited for the gatekeeper to open the gate through which they would file back to their jobs. It was a warm, sunny day, as almost all July days are at San Quentin, and the men moved slowly, sluggish in the sunshine.

Lieutenant Governor Chellis sat in the most comfortable chair in the warden's office and digested his lunch. Chellis was a stout, well-nourished man; he must have felt tempted to go into his bedroom next door and lie down for a few minutes. But he stayed in his office, full-bellied, contented, as drowsy as the bluebottles that buzzed against the windows through which he could see the northeastern angle of the walls, and, to the left of the angle, the main gate. Murphy, the keeper of the main gate, was the only man in sight. Beyond the southern end of the wall Chellis could see the quiet waters of Corte Madera Cove, and beyond the water the hills of the Tiburon peninsula. Superintendent Robinson, with whom Chellis had been feuding, had left the prison two weeks earlier, and Chellis had no reason to be worried by the way things had gone since then. We would probably be not far from the truth if we picture him leaning back in his chair, his feet on a lower drawer of the mahogany desk, his hands resting gratefully on his well-filled vest, with no reason in the world not to feel pleased with himself.

At twelve-thirty the keeper of the rear gate swung the gate wide to let the brickyard crew go back to work. There were 131 of them in all, and as they filed out the foreman of the brickworks, a trusty named Miller, kept tally alongside the gatekeeper. Everything was going as it had thousands of times before when ten men who had just been counted through the gate broke out of line and, hugging the cover of the walls, sprinted for the main gate and the warden's office.

The alarm was raised by the guards manning the two gun positions that covered the brickyard, but the little group of convicts scuttling around the walls offered too small and fast-moving a target for their cannon. The gunners brought their pieces to bear on the west gate, but the convict foreman had bullied the rest of his gang back inside the walls. The guards on top of the wall heard the alarm, but by the time they had located the escaping convicts, the fugitives were out of sight.

Chellis had seen the convicts coming. The only question was whether they intended to murder him on the spot or to carry him off as a hostage. Chellis didn't keep even a pistol in his office. He did the only thing he could, which was to take his feet off the drawer, hoist himself out of his chair, and lock himself in his bedroom. It took five or six convicts a minute or two to smash the bedroom door and drag him out.

The rest of the rebels in the meantime had seized Murphy at the front gate and demanded his keys. Tough and stubborn, Murphy refused to give them up, even when they shook him and cuffed him about and threatened him with little inch-long home-made knives. Murphy continued to refuse even after Chellis was hauled to the gate and forced to give him a direct order. Exasperated, the convicts threw the gatekeeper to the ground, kicked him, and stamped on him. After they had thoroughly worked him over, they took the key to the wicket, or outer gate, in his pocket. They smashed the inner gate with an iron bar, and through the main yard of San Quentin was heard the intoxicating cry of "Liberty!"

The cry was answered by virtually every man who was free to run. From the workshops, howling and shouting, came men armed with the tools of their trades: blacksmiths with hammers, coopers and carpenters with knives and hatchets, mechanics with files, tailors with shears, cooks with cleavers. The yard sweepers dropped their brooms and ran for the gate with the rest, and the cell tenders scrambled down from the galleries of the Stones and joined the mob. Above the whooping and screaming and bellowing came the flat reports of the rifles aimed by the gun guards on the walls, but the escaping convicts continued to stream past the wounded toward the gate and freedom. They came until virtually every man in and around the main yard had made a run for it. Left behind were about 115 men of the brickyard crew in the lower yard, the men who were locked in their cells, the bed patients in the hospital, and the incorrigibles who were chained to the walls of the dungeon.

The leaders of the rebellion thought they would find Edward Vanderlip, captain of the guard, in the armory. They broke in, but Vanderlip was not there. Although the armory was stocked with rifles and pistols, they found only a single loaded revolver. The convicts missed a case of sabers that stood in full view and took off with their captured but largely useless firearms. Some of them paused long enough to look unsuccessfully for the commissary officer, whom they blamed for their semi-starvation.

The advance party of the rebels, with Chellis in the van, had already started westward around the walls, heading for Post 5, on the hill north of the brickyard. The gunner at Post 5, Thomas Watson, brought his nine-pounder cannon, loaded with grapeshot, to bear on the advancing column of prisoners. Chellis looked into the muzzle of the cannon and cried, "For God's sake, *don't shoot!*" Watson recognized the lieutenant governor in the nick of time, turned the cannon toward the water, and discharged it harmlessly. He had managed to spike it when the furious convicts seized him, almost as angry as if he had fired into them. They had hoped to turn the nine-pounder against the cannon at Post 10, across the brickyard; infuriated, they threw Watson down the steep slope of the hill and tumbled the heavy gun and its carriage down on top of him. Although the gun carriage was smashed and Watson was badly battered, he survived.

So far, Watson and Murphy had been the only guards to stand to their posts. The rest dropped their arms and ran for their lives; one of them even left his shoes at his post, so swift was his flight. Armed with the rifles and pistols dropped by the guards, the main body of the convicts marched across the brickyard, protected from attack by their hostage. A round of grapeshot whistled over their heads, and then the guards at Post 10 took to their heels.

Under cover of the uproar in the brickyard about a dozen convicts made for the brickyard wharf and tried to get away in the prison sloop. They took the *Pike County* successfully, cut the lines and pushed off, but after that everything went wrong. The tide was low, they missed the channel, and consequently found themselves stuck on a mud bank. Here they perched until guards opened fire at leisure, picking off three men whose bodies fell into the shallow water. The rest surrendered.

The prisoners ashore had better luck. Although Captain Vanderlip had by now organized a pursuit of foot and horse guards, and had managed to round up fifty stragglers, the main body of fugitives, with Chellis prominently displayed, took the traditional escape route, the westward road that runs along the shore of Corte Madera Cove and Corte Madera Creek in the general direction of Mount Tamalpais. Once they reached the mountain, they knew they had a fighting chance of getting away completely.

Nobody knows how many convicts actually took part in the break. The most liberal estimate was that three hundred men, or half the convict population, had broken out; the most conservative was that about two hundred men had been free at one stage or another of the rebellion, with only about a hundred marching away in the ragged procession toward the slopes of Mount Tam.

By the time the first news of the break was carried to San Rafael by a guard on horseback, the number had grown astonishingly. The alarmed citizens heard that four hundred convicts had seized the cannon and small arms and were at that very moment marching toward their town. The men armed themselves and prepared to repel the invasion. While most remained in town to protect their wives, children, and property, a small citizens' posse led by Sheriff Doub rode across the hills toward Corte Madera.

Those who remained in town were treated to an eyewitness report from the convict foreman, Miller, who turned up later in the afternoon to deliver his version of the break to the respectful townspeople. The excitement and the free drinks were too much for Miller; when the prison roll was called later in the evening Miller was counted among the missing.

The news shrank not a bit as it was carried across the bay to San Francisco. The prison surgeon, Dr. J. D. B. Stillman, was in his office at 124 Montgomery Street when, early in the evening, a messenger brought a report that the entire convict population of six hundred had broken out and were bent on murdering Chellis. Dr. Stillman telegraphed Governor Stanford at Sacramento and sent word to Chief Burke of the San Francisco police. Then the surgeon, accompanied by a professional colleague, started for the prison in a small boat.

Chief Burke also wired Governor Stanford. He asked for authority to take a body of armed and mounted men across the bay to scour the woods of Marin County for the fugitive. About nine o'clock the answering wire came from the capital. Burke called on General George Wright, in command at the Presidio, for troops. Wright himself was kept from taking the field by an attack of asthma, but he ordered the Sacramento Rangers to report to Burke for orders. Captain DeMerritt of the Rangers got the order at about ten-thirty and within half an hour had ridden out of the Presidio barracks with forty-five of his troopers. Meanwhile, the governor's brother had organized a posse of mounted San Franciscans, and the energetic chief of police had chartered the steam-

boat *Clinton* for $250. At five minutes past one on the morning
of January 23 the *Clinton* cast off. The whole expedition, particularly the troopers, was in splendid spirits. They were looking
forward to an invigorating morning's work hunting convicts,
and it was exceedingly annoying when a heavy fog and strong tides
and winds slowed the *Clinton* down to a little more than three
knots.

In the meantime, well before sundown, Vanderlip and his little
band of guards were trailing the convicts along the Corte Madera
road. Whenever the guards drew too near, the convicts flourished
their pistols and threatened to blow off Chellis' head. When the
convicts came to the house of the gunner Watson they paused long
enough to turn the place upside down in revenge. Then, three
miles inland from the prison, they came to another house where
a couple named Brevier had seen them coming. Mrs. Brevier had
run into the hills to hide from the expected fate worse than death,
but her husband, whose business had often taken him to the
prison, stayed behind with the hope that the convicts would remember the little kindnesses he had done them. They did, and
they offered him no harm, but they took everything movable that
struck their fancy. The loot included Brevier's best suit, twelve or
thirteen dollars in cash, and a meerschaum pipe that belonged to
Brevier's hired man. In the stable they found a three-year-old
stallion that had never been ridden. They dragged the wild horse
out and urged Chellis to mount.

"What, get on that horse without saddle or anything else?"
cried the already-exhausted lieutenant governor.

The convicts insisted; the lieutenant governor pleaded. At
length the practical joke lost its appeal, and Chellis was permitted
to proceed on foot. Heavy on his feet and unaccustomed to walking, Chellis was having a hard time of it. He was in mortal danger,
but the spectacle of a fat politician dragging himself along
under the July sun was too much of a temptation for the newspaper reporters who described his ordeal. One wrote archly that

whenever Chellis begged to be let go, the convicts prodded him with their little knives "in a place where no bones can be broken," and added, "thus spurred up, the governor *had* to get along pretty briskly for his size."

About this time one of the convicts tried to pick Chellis' vest pocket of his gold watch, but another man interfered. The pickpocket, abashed, returned the watch. It was now about four o'clock.

About four miles from the prison, at a place called Ross Landing, they came to a slough which had to be crossed. Chellis, who was both afraid of the water, and, sweating as he was, afraid of pneumonia, begged to be let go, but the convicts forced him through. The tide had been rising, and the water came up to his chin.

As it turned out, it was Chellis' fatigue that saved him and undid the convicts. Beyond the slough was a high fence. Dripping, chilled, dog-tired, Chellis balked. His bodyguard tried to force him over. Convict hands hoisted the immense lieutenant-gubernatorial stern, but Chellis was too heavy, too clumsy, and too tired. They let him fall back to the ground, and, because there was nothing else they could do, they left him there to his great joy.

When the convicts gave up Chellis they gave up their security. As soon as Chellis was safe, the guards and the sheriff's posse opened fire. The convicts scattered into the marshlands and the brush, and those who were armed returned the fire, as they worked their way toward the foothills of Mount Tam. Sheriff Doub cautiously sent back to San Rafael for reinforcements, and soon every able-bodied man and boy for miles around—160 or 170 by count—had seized a weapon and hurried to join the fight.

The convicts were outnumbered and outgunned; furthermore, they were on foot while most of their pursuers were mounted. When they ran toward the safety of the mountain, the men on horseback went after them. Some were picked off by the riflemen, and some got away, but most were captured or gave themselves up. By eight o'clock a line of 47 recaptured prisoners was walking through the twilight over the road toward San Quentin. When the muster roll was called in the prison yard only 33 were found missing.

The fogbound *Clinton,* with Captain DeMerritt and his Rangers, and Mr. Stanford and his citizens, didn't make the San Quentin wharf until daybreak. The battle had ended hours before, and there was nothing for the San Franciscans to do but to listen to the tales of the prodigies of valor performed by the guards and citizens who had taken part.

The hunt for the fugitives went on. Some were reported from as far away as Los Angeles, but by the end of a month almost all of the escaped convicts were back inside the walls.

In the prison hospital Dr. Stillman and the hospital steward, Russell, counted up the casualties. Thirty-two convicts survived their wounds; four had been killed outright and three more died later.

Brewer was shot through the thighs with a Minié ball which fractured the head of the right femur on its passage out and proved fatal on the ninth week [Dr. Stillman wrote in his admirably concise report]. Bieta, a California Indian, received a shot nearly in the same region. . . . He recovered from his wounds, but died in November of tubercular disease consequent on his injuries. Rodriguez was shot through the lungs with a pistol ball, but is entirely recovered. Blonnel, wounded through the shoulder, had also a buckshot enter the mastoid process of the temporal bone and pass out at the mouth, carrying away portions of the two upper middle incisors. Farrow was shot through the neck from behind, the ball passing out between the trachea and the sterno-mastoid muscle. Both these cases recovered, contrary to my expectations. Twelve were wounded in the lower extremities. One of these, Keller, had his thigh fractured at its middle part by a ball passing entirely through. The chances for saving the man's life were small in any attempt to save his limb, but after mature deliberation upon all the circumstances, he concluded to share the fate of his leg. I respected his determination, and saved his leg, though much shortened.

When the excitement was over, and the participants had run out of an audience for their accounts of daring and marksmanship, when the troops from San Francisco had returned after their outing, and Mr. Brevier's hired hand had bought a new meerschaum pipe, when John Chellis had recovered from the knife wounds in his buttocks and the blisters on his feet, there was one thing that remained clear to everyone who had taken part in the battle. With the exception of Murphy and Watson and one or two others, the San Quentin guards had distinguished themselves largely by the speed with which they had thrown down their rifles and run.

Neither the convicts nor the newspapers allowed Chellis and his guards to forget their shame. Whenever a free man stepped inside the walls, he was greeted with jeers from the convicts, who threatened openly to make another break, and to make sure the next one would be successful. Two weeks after the break eleven guards had resigned, leaving only twelve men on duty to guard six hundred prisoners. Governor Stanford and Secretary of State Weeks were reported to have urged Chellis to stay out of the prison and to have issued strict orders to the guard to fire in the event of another escape, hostages or not. "They go on the principle that the keeper who cannot keep himself out of their hands is no great shakes, and ought not to be spared," the Sacramento *Bee* said acidly. "Perhaps the Secretary of State will take the Lieutenant Governor's place for a while, as he could not be so easily carried away."

Whether or not the comical figure he had cut during the great prison break had anything to do with it or not, Chellis was replaced by T. N. Machin as Republican candidate for lieutenant governor in 1853. He thereupon retired from California politics and went to Nevada, where he made and lost a fortune. Poor Chellis died at the age of seventy, after having dragged himself, sick and destitute, to the house of a friend in a small town in Oregon.

The punishment books for the period following the great break of 1862 have disappeared, and we can only surmise that the dungeon was filled to its capacity of four men to a cell, and that a larger than usual number of candidates for the rawhide and the fire hose were lashed to the whipping post that stood before the dungeon.

Someone in the late 1850's had called the whipping post the Ladder, and this was the name by which it was known at San Quentin afterward. It was not in shape a ladder at all, but a cross inclined at an angle of seventy-five degree to the ground, with thongs top and bottom to secure the hands and feet of the man under punishment. An eyewitness to a flogging has left us a firsthand account of the procedure.

After a prisoner who had been found with whisky had been tied naked to the Ladder, the following conversation took place:

CAPTAIN A. C. MCALISTER: I want you to tell me where you got that whisky.

PRISONER: I can't do it, Captain.

MCALISTER: You can't, eh? Well, I'll have you flogged until you do tell.

PRISONER: Well, Captain, be as merciful as you can, for if you flog me to death, I shall not tell.

MCALISTER (angrily): You won't, won't you? I'll bet you twenty dollars you do tell before I get done with you.

PRISONER: All right, I'll take that bet! I've got twenty dollars that says I'll not tell you anything about it, no matter what happens.

A nod from the captain, and the guard steps forward, and

swinging the heavy cowhide high in the air, brings it down with a sharp, resonant sound upon the bare and quivering back of the prisoner.

"One!"

A scarlet streak follows in the wake of the scarring and cruel blow.

"Two!"

With painful deliberation the vindictive lash again descends with all the force which the trained muscles of the stalwart guard can give it.

"Three!"

The mute, protesting flesh rises in rigid welts and marks the course of each torturing blow.

"Four! Five! Six!" and the sickening scene goes on until a score is told. But the victim's lips are yet silent and his tongue still dumb. His back is scarred and blistered, the blood trickles through twenty bruised and broken channels, and yet no sign escapes him. Not a word is uttered as the exhausted guard stands waiting, and the cruel whip slowly drips crimson drops, foiled in its purpose and baffled in its quest.

There was a refinement of the technique of flogging at San Quentin which made it an even more savage punishment than floggings elsewhere. When an American seaman was to be flogged, he stripped off only his shirt. The British soldier or sailor was made to wear a broad leather band which protected the sensitive regions of his loins from the whip. The San Quentin convict was flogged stark naked, and only the questionable good will of the flogger stood between him and painful and permanent damage to his vital regions.

The other punishment administered at the Ladder was described for publication under the mild and deceptive names of the "cold shower" or the "shower bath." It was more accurately known at the water torture. The convict being prepared for the shower was lashed naked to the Ladder in the reversed position from that assumed for whippings. His face, chest, abdomen, and private parts were exposed to a guard who held a 1½-inch hose equipped with a ¾-inch nozzle. A stream of water under a head of about a hundred feet was directed against the convict's body. If the convict gasped, the stream was forced into his mouth. According to a contemporary account, the physiological effect of the shower was alternately to quicken and retard the heartbeat until "blood bursts from the eyes and ears, and syncope intervenes."

There is really no objective measure of the comparative amounts of pain inflicted by the various common forms of punishment and torture. One man will take twenty lashes more cheerfully than a single day in solitary confinement; another would choose a steady diet of bread and water to ten minutes on the Ladder. John Weller and his colleagues had instituted the dungeon as a merciful and humane substitute for the whip; it need not surprise us that a few years later Dr. Taliaferro made an urgent recommendation to precisely the opposite effect.

Dr. Taliaferro wrote:

> I cannot too strongly reprobate the system of punishment that is sometimes adopted here, by confinement in a place called the dungeon, and dungeon it is in every sense of the word, and in the fullest import. Down there the prisoner is subjected to the very counterparts of what is necessary to health. To have health we must have light, pure air, exercise, warmth, dryness, and good food. Down there, in that horrible hole, the prisoner gets darkness, foul air, dampness, cold, bread and water simply, and no exercise. Without advocating the lash, if no other system of punishment can be adopted, a thousand times more preferable is it than punishing in this abominable hole.
>
> For every reason, human and divine, I hope the doors of this dungeon have been closed forever.

The last flogging officially administered occurred in 1880. The shower was in use for two years longer, but the doors of the dungeon were not closed until our own time, after even more ingenious varieties of cruelty had been practiced on the unfortunate convicts.

The last attempt at a mass escape that San Quentin has seen happened on a Saturday afternoon in April, 1864. Again the brickyard crew was involved, and again there was bloodshed, but otherwise the uprising had little in common with the great revolt in which John Chellis had figured in such an undignified manner. Four convicts were killed on the spot, and six more were badly wounded. Not a single man escaped.

This abortive break brought to an end the ten-year period of mass escapes which had begun in 1854. During these ten years a total of 654 convicts had escaped from San Quentin. At the end of 1864 Lieutenant Governor T. N. Machin was able to report that not a single convict had escaped during the year. In the entire ten years from 1864 to 1874 only 17 prisoners escaped. San Quentin was clearly undergoing a thorough transformation.

Chapter VII

CIRCLE OF THE DAYS

STRIPED monkey suits were introduced in San Quentin after a contract was made in 1864 with the Mission Woolen Mills of San Francisco to supply the prison with cloth striped in gray and black. By the first of November, 1865, almost all the convicts wore the ugly striped suits run up in the prison tailor shop. The jackets were cut with the stripes on the body running vertically and the stripes on the sleeves horizontally; the trousers were made of material with broader stripes. The convicts declined to wear the caps provided for them, and, instead, were permitted to keep on wearing felt civilian hats, which they got by bartering, as they did vests, underwear, and topcoats. In spite of these nonregulation additions for the first time in the prison's history the convicts *looked* like prisoners.

Prison stripes are an American institution, related to but distinct from the broad arrow worn by the English convict. As with so many other ingenious inventions, stripes were devised by a Massachusetts Yankee. Until 1812 Massachusetts convicts had worn a pied costume, half red and half blue. Then, as a means of quickly identifying the various classes of convicts, second-termers were put into red, yellow, and blue stripes, while third-termers wore yellow, red, blue, and black. By comparison, San Quentin stripes were dignified and restrained.

Although the convicts could not be expected to approve of the esthetic or social effect of the stripes, there were some considerable advantages to the adoption of a uniform. Under Estell and McCauley the prisoners had worn their own clothes until they were worn through; then, if they were lucky or rich, they could beg or buy a pair of jeans and one of the red or blue woolen shirts affected by the miners or a hickory shirt. Shoes were harder to come by, and, as we have seen, prisoners often had to go barefoot.

The convicts were a little better clothed after the establishment of the tailor shop in the early 1860's. The practice then was to issue civilian-type pants, shirts, and shoes, but to leave the convicts to their own devices—which meant bartering—so far as warmer clothing went. Although the striped clothing was intended as a security measure, the adoption of a uniform also had the effect of setting some minimum standards of decent dress.

Stripes were only one facet of the general bureaucratization of prison life. The daily routine was also falling into a pattern which it was to follow for many years. The day began with the getup bell, which rang at about six-thirty. The prisoners dressed, triced up their bunks, and stood at the door with their night buckets. Trusties ran up and down the galleries, sliding back the bolts that secured the cells after the padlocks had been opened. The prisoners marched out of their cells with their buckets, emptied them in the cistern known as the Rose Bowl, washed their faces and hands in cold water, and marched to breakfast.

After the factory buildings were built and before a fire destroyed the main workshops in 1876, the men who worked for the contractors ate in messes attached to the shops, just as sailors did aboard men of war. Except for this interlude the convicts ate in a great common mess hall, where there were five hundred numbered seats at the long, foot-wide tables. Waiters passed between the tables, ladling out beans and stew cooked in the five huge copper boilers in the kitchen, poured coffee into tin cups, and dropped a chunk of bread in front of each convict. After the turnkey had mounted a pulpit at the end of the room and brought down a mallet against a board, the men fell to. While they ate, the captain of the yard paced the aisle, alert to any real or imagined signs of trouble. When the mallet sounded again, the convicts stood up and marched out.

The number who went to work and the work which they did varied according to the state of the prison contracts. The major contractors during the 1870's were the California Furniture Manufacturing Company (200 men), Stone & Hayden, tanners and harness makers (125 men), and Porter & Baldwin, shoes (100 men). Besides these enterprises there were at various times a wagon-maker, a knitting mill, a bindery, and a blacksmith shop. The cash income to the prison in a good year was about $20,000.

Housekeeping duties in the prison, tending the flower gardens, grading the grounds, and breaking rock kept still others busy. As the prison grew, it pressed against the hills, making the task of grading and leveling and surfacing a constant one. Of all the jobs, the least sought after was the traditional prison employment of making little ones out of big ones. In the rock pile eighty to a hundred prisoners broke boulders into large rocks, broke the large rocks into medium-sized rocks, and then, with a large rock as a table, broke the medium-sized rocks into little rocks with a steel hammer.

But even with all this activity there was not enough work to keep all the convicts busy. There were always several hundred who were completely unemployed, the total number depending on the size of the prison population and the number of con-tractors in business. During working hours the unemployed were herded into the yard, where, outside the paved areas, the grass grew knee-high. If the prison officers were jittery, all the un-employed men were locked in their cells, where they spent twenty-two hours a day. If they were lucky enough to be let into the yard, they lounged in the sun and bored each other with the classic convicts' tales of the high-priced whisky they had drunk and the high-priced women who had shared their beds when they had lived like merchant princes on the outside. Some played cards, some amused themselves by watching the antics of the insane men in Crazy Alley, some tried to plan an original escape, some plotted homosexual intrigues, some worked at handicrafts—a sailor with a model ship, a Spaniard with a hair cinch, a Chinese with a lace doily—and three or four read books.

At eleven-twenty the dinner bell rang, the mess-hall lines formed again, and the men marched in for their main meal of the day, soup, potatoes, beans, and bread. Fifteen minutes later the turn-key's mallet sounded the end of dinner, and the convicts marched back to their jobs or to the yard. At three-thirty a bell called an end to the working day. The prisoners marched into the mess hall for the third time for a supper of bread and black coffee, then they were marched to their cells, locked up, and counted.

The count, or head count as it is more precisely described, is both a ceremony celebrating the spiritual essence of a prison and a practical necessity, the purpose of which is to assure the officers that they have in their physical control the precise number of bodies that have been committed to their care. Each prisoner must be physically tallied, and an accidental short count or long count is the penological equivalent of a surgeon's leaving a sponge in his patient's abdominal cavity. During the time with which we are concerned the prisoners in the dormitories and multiple cells were counted as they entered their quarters; in the double cells, the men stood inside the barred door; in the single cells, they speeded up the routine by putting a hand through the bars. (There was at least one unsuccessful attempt to cover up an escape by leaving a wooden hand propped in the barred window.)

After lockup the most cheerful place in San Quentin was the Red Room, a dormitory on the first floor of the Old Prison in which trusties slept. From the Red Room could be heard the sound of guitars, banjos, and violins, and sometimes the shuffling of feet when the warden had granted permission for the trusties to invite guests to a dance. At nine o'clock the lights-out bugle sounded, even the Red Room became quiet, and the prison was secured for the night. After this the only activities in the cells were masturbation, fellatio, and pederasty.

The Sunday schedule called for no work in the shops and for church services, but the prisoners were locked up for the day by eleven in the morning. Their chief diversion was watching the holiday makers from San Francisco. The prison log for April 7, 1871, a typical Sunday, notes "Pic Nic & Excursion of the Lone Star Social Club, first of Season." The custom of throwing the prison open to visitors, as if it were an insane asylum or zoo, began in 1860 when the excursion steamer *Clinton* interrupted its trip to the Navy Yard at Mare Island to drop off a hundred curious citizens, male and female, at the Point San Quentin landing. For years a visit to the prison was a prominent feature of middle-class San Francisco social life, with such organizations at the British Benevolent Society, the Montgomery Guards, and the children and parents of St. Ignatius College traveling to the prison en masse. After they had picnicked, the vistors strolled through the yard, where the girls could shudder at the Ladder and thrill to the glimpse of white faces peering through the wickets in the cell doors. There were also occasional dignitaries among the visitors, men such as King Kalakaua of the Hawaiian Islands, who arrived in February, 1881, accompanied by a retinue of distinguished San Franciscans.

These tours of the prison were a logical extension of the institution of the Prison Trotter, an individual who first flourished during McCauley's occupation. The Trotter's duty was to escort visitors through the prison, show them an immaculate model cell, solicit contributions from them at the gate, and induce them to leave behind written testimonials to the splendid condition of the prison and the robust spiritual and physical health enjoyed by the convicts. (Civic organizations and church groups are still encouraged to visit San Quentin, although it would be unfair to call their guides Trotters. They are now engaged in public relations.)

Holidays resembled Sundays, with the addition of festive meals. Not only were Thanksgiving, Christmas, and Election Day observed with holiday schedules, but there were also observances of the anniversaries of the Battle of New Orleans, the Mexican Day of Independence, and the Emancipation Proclamation. On the last occasion, it was noted by the clerk, "the darkies had permission to remain up all night, dancing and singing and a good supper." The greatest holiday of all was the Fourth of July, which, in 1860, was celebrated with a curious menu of "2 Barrells of Peaches made up in Duff and a Chowder." The Fourth seems also to have been a dangerous time in those days, for, not once but twice, unfortunate guards blew off their arms while firing the traditional salute.

There were also a few unplanned diversions. In July, 1874, the log reported that "Yesterday—Sunday 12th—a Yachting party, with a Brass Band came over from the City, and after meandering etc. around the Point marched up the road to the Prison. Capt. [James] Towle invited them inside after Lockup, and they wandered around for about an hour through the Yard, the Band playing several pieces of music greatly for the pleasure, edification, etc., of the prisoners."

On October 8, 1874, San Quentin's population for the first time reached one thousand. The construction of two new cell buildings parallel to the Stones, and the addition of a brick third story to the Stones itself, had been intended hopefully to relieve the housing pressure and allow prisoners to be classified according to the seriousness of their offenses and their apparent chances for redemption. But the population grew faster than the cells, a phenomenon which was first noted at San Quentin in 1852 and which has continued to the present day.

In the Stones, four men still slept in each of the 10-by-6-foot cells, but the 196 cells in the Middle Prison and the South Prison had been built only 9 by 4 feet and could hold no more than two men each. The only sanitary facilities were the night buckets that stank in the corner of every cell. In a Stones cell the only ventilation was through a narrow slit in the ⅜-inch boiler-plate door. (Not even in the open air could a convict escape the smell of excrement; at flood tide the sewage gas was forced back up the gratings in the yard.) The air was also fouled by the fumes of the kerosene lamps which the men were permitted to buy or make. In an attempt to make their cells more livable, some prisoners painted frescoes on the walls or put up shelves to hold their possessions, but not even the most ingenious artist could disguise the fact that life in a San Quentin cell was about the minimum possible anywhere.

One of the essential ideas of prison reformers throughout the nineteenth century was the necessity of classifying prisoners according to the treatment they were to receive. San Quentin was not necessarily more backward than other American prisons in this matter, but the physical layout of the prison offered little chance for separating convicts from one another. The only classification that existed involved the boys of eighteen and under and a rough sort of segregation based on race. The Stones and the new prisons held Anglo-Americans, Europeans, Spanish Californians, and Mexicans. The small number of Negro and Indian convicts were thrown together in one of the rooms in the first floor of the Stones. In 1874 the Chinese were moved from the Stones into the former wagon shop in the basement of the factory building. Here in a room 58 feet by 39 feet were packed 168 Chinese convicts in spite of the prison doctor's protest that it was a "very unhealthy sleeping apartment." Nobody else showed any concern for the welfare of the "China Boys," who, as the result of two decades of anti-Chinese agitation, were regarded by most Californians as a species of anthropoid having neither a completely human form, human emotions, nor a human capacity for pain. The alleged personal filthiness of the Chinese was responsible for the institution of China Wash Day, on which the Orientals were urged to make use of the outdoor plunge. A visitor to San Quentin in 1877 expressed the general opinion of his countrymen when he wrote, "Let him who doubts Darwin compare the contented Chinaman at San Quentin with a well-fed cart horse, and he will need no missing link."

The Chinese convicts were thought, with good reason, to be universally addicted to opium, and much of their activity in the prison was devoted to assuring themselves of a steady supply of the drug, which had to be smuggled in by way of the county road that ran through the prison grounds, or on the persons of bribed guards or visitors. Although Captain McAlister crusaded against opium and drove the price up to $60.00 a pound, it could still be had, and when the pressure was taken off the price dropped to $15.00 a pound. (These prices seem preposterously low in these enlightened days when the law has made narcotics more valuable than gold. The reader must remember that we are writing of a less sophisticated age when a tired mother could legally soothe her teething baby with laudanum while she quieted her own nerves with any of the popular syrups whose active principle was tincture of opium.) Every night the crowded quarters of the Chinese reeked with the fumes of the drug, which was smoked in homemade pipes. The pipes were made of small bottles wrapped in brown paper to prevent cracking. A hole was drilled in the side of the bottle to hold the conical wad of opium and a stem was fitted to the bottle's neck. The pipe was passed around, and for a few hours the happy smokers drifted off into a world far removed from Point San Quentin.

There were those of the English- and Spanish-speaking convicts who also smoked opium, but at this time by and large they preferred alcohol as a soporific and gambling for excitement. Beer was brewed of cereals and garbage stolen from the kitchen, alcohol was stolen from the hospital and the paint shop, and whisky could be bought from corrupt guards or smuggled in by visitors and trusties who had access to the Hill Road. Gambling was, is, and always will be a principal amusement of convicts, but it is doubtful that the pastime flourished at any other American prison as it did at San Quentin in the 1800's. Although there are records of men being flogged for possessing playing cards as early as the 1850's, a visitor in 1868 saw five monte and faro banks in operation at one time. This is the sort of enterprise that could have gone on only with the connivance of the guards, from the captain of the yard on down. The third traditional form of masculine dissipation—women—was denied most of the convicts, except for whatever vicarious thrills could be squeezed from exchanging messages with the six or eight women convicts who lived above the captain's office. In the matter of sex, as has been noted elsewhere, the male convicts had to make do with what they had.

In 1867 it cost the state of California exactly $63.80 to keep a convict alive for the entire year. Of this sum, $53.10 went for food; the remainder was spent on clothing ($7.48), shoes and their repair ($2.36), and bedding (86 cents). There were frequent charges that the convicts were actually being starved (charges which were possibly made by citizens who wondered how you fed a man three meals a day, 365 days a year, for $53.10 or about 14½ cents a day). Dr. Stillman, who was not afraid to make public criticisms of his own, attempted to quiet these charges when, in 1862, he reported that each convict was served a daily average of 12 ounces of fresh beef (gross weight, including fat, gristle, and bone), 7 ounces of potatoes, 2 ounces of bacon, 4½ ounces of vegetables, 7 ounces of fish, 4 ounces of beans, and 25 ounces of bread. This seems more than adequate, so far as volume goes (25 ounces of bread!), but, without casting a shadow on Dr. Stillman's integrity, one suspects that average figures of this sort can most readily be compiled by dividing the purchases appearing on the commissary books by the total number of prisoners. There is notoriously little connection between this figure and the amount of edible food that actually appears on the mess-hall tables of a public institution such as San Quentin.

Nor was there any necessary connection between the number of ounces served of each commodity and its palatability and wholesomeness. By general consent the food appears to have been highly unpalatable but not actually poisonous. Besides the outbreaks of dysentery and diarrhea which might have occurred in even the best-managed institution there seems to have been little distress, in a strictly medical sense, that could be traced to the food. This is aside from the facts that it was monotonous, of inferior quality, badly prepared, offensive to the nostrils, and often mixed with foreign substances.

There were two recourses for the prisoner who found his daily ration insufficient or insipid. He could go to work for a contractor who was obliged to furnish coffee, sugar, and other little luxuries to his men, or he could buy extra supplies from a sutler. Sutlers were favored convicts who traded in food supplied them by the prison commissary, an officer who derived a large profit from encouraging this trade. The food handled by the sutlers was largely the sort that wasn't usually seen on the mess-hall tables—real coffee, fresh vegetables, and so on. Prisoners without ready cash or something to barter had to make out as best they could on the mess hall's beef, bread, and beans.

It was a life which, in the words of one observer, was wretched, squalid, dirty, debased, and lost. Yet the convicts seem, by and large, to have survived it in fairly good shape. Except for occasional epidemics of intestinal infections or flu, and allowing for seasonal fluctuations between the dry summer and the wet winter, the number of sick convicts was usually not more than 5 per cent of the total. Furthermore, few convicts took the prisoner's final and irrevocable protest against the intolerableness of his life—self-mutilation or suicide.

Yet there were those who, driven by the various motives which impel a man to suicide, killed themselves. The most spectacular suicide of the prison's entire history was that of William Smith, who did away with himself in August, 1871. According to the prison log, Smith "threw himself into a boiling cauldron"—presumably of soup or beans—"and was literally cooked, although alive, before being extricated, which was done immediately." Poor Smith lingered for three hours, the manner of his dying and the excruciating tortures of his last hours creating a sensation among the convicts.

Nowhere is the perennial gap between prison theory and prison practice more evident than in the matter of discipline. In 1877 Lieutenant Governor James A. Johnson (who must not be confused with the later warden of similar name) set forth a wholly admirable philosophy of prison discipline. "The cruel and inhuman iron-will rule usual at prisons is not in vogue here," Johnson wrote. "Instead, we treat all who will bear it—and most prisoners do—with kindness, and even courtesy. The plan of individualizing each one, and recognizing each from all others, and requiring something of each as an individual, is the secret method of obtaining good government at an institution like this."

In the same year in which he revealed his secret method of government, Johnson also, for the first time in the prison's history, appointed a guard to act as flogger at an increase of pay of $25.00 a month to compensate him for the extra work.

Although San Quentin continued to be governed by the dungeon, the fire hose, and the whip, it would be unfair to Johnson and the other wardens of this time to neglect to record the two reforms that were virtually the only improvements in the life of the convict from 1860 to 1880. In April, 1864, Governor Frederick F. Low signed the "Goodwin bill," which provided "good-time" or "copper" credit for convicts who stayed out of trouble. The Goodwin bill required the prison directors to subtract from each prisoner's sentence five days for every month of good behavior, and also required the governor to grant a full pardon whenever a convict was discharged. (The point of the pardon is that it restores the prisoner's civil rights, including the right to vote.) Later, an investigating committee claimed that the Goodwin bill had been drafted at San Quentin by a convict who also masterminded the strategy for its passage in the legislature.

When a convict was discharged, he left in a suit of prison-made clothes with three dollars in cash, granted to him by a magnanimous state. Since the money was little more than the steamboat fare to San Francisco, he was obliged to look for a job with empty pockets and the marks of the prison still on him. In 1869 the directors, distressed by this situation, attempted to augment the absurd three dollars of gate money by authorizing the clerk to pay one-half of an employed convict's overtime pay into an account which would be paid him on discharge. But this did the unemployed convict little good, and in any case there was never much money involved.

There was little in a positive way that the directors might be proud of, but at least after the last big break in 1864 they managed the prison without flagrant dishonesty, without more cruelty than was practiced at other prisons, and without starving the prisoners to death. This was something for which a San Quentin convict might be grateful.

There were a few convicts who had cause to feel much greater gratitude. In spite of the general subjection to routine, the ghost of Estell's trusty system lingered on well into the 1880's.

The last of the noted trusties under the lease was a young man named Rodman M. Backus, who was virtually the only prisoner who enjoyed a tolerable life in the last years of Mc-Cauley's regime. He was also the only prisoner of whom it can be said with certainty that he came to San Quentin voluntarily. Backus came of a respectable family and was employed in a respectable job by Wells Fargo until the night when he killed a man he met coming out of the quarters of Jenny French, a woman who lived in an alley off Washington Street in San Francisco. Backus was awaiting his appeal from a conviction of manslaughter when the Vigilantes, after removing James P. Casey and a murderer, Charles Cora, paused long enough for a critical look at the other inmates of the Broadway jail. Backus was alarmed, as was his lawyer, who lost no time in withdrawing the application for a new trial and hustling his client off to San Quentin a jump ahead of the Vigilance Committee. Backus was later seen wandering about freely at San Quentin, shooting birds, and growing fat, brown, and healthy at a time when most of the other inmates were starving. He no doubt owed his pleasant life to the enmity of the Vigilantes he shared with Estell.

One of the most human pictures we have of the life of the favored trusties comes, literally, from the pen of K. H. Keeny, a writing master convicted of murder, who kept the official prison diary from 1873 until his pardon in 1875. Besides setting down the daily events in several colors of ink in a hand that was both legible and gorgeously ornamental, Keeny added marginal glosses and personal notes of his own that are sometimes wryly humorous ("Execution of K. H. Keeny today. Mrs. Keeny arrived in the 11 A.M. boat.") and sometimes pathetic ("My little boy, Lincoln, died today" and later, "My little son, Frank, died in San Francisco of measles today").

We also learn from Keeny that the clerks in the turnkey's department had their own kitchen and ate separately from the general run of convicts. They wore white shirts or complete civilian outfits and were treated as trusted employees rather than as prisoners. Keeny shared with Captain Matthews a concern for the frustrated motherhood of the office canary ("the Canary sat 21 days today when Capt. Matthews broke the eggs and found them rotten") and sympathized with Captain McAlister's efforts to establish a quail house as an adjunct to the officers' kitchen. Keeny occasionally ate with one of the captains, and, except for the awful visits of his spouse, appears to have found San Quentin not too bad.

Later in the 1870's observant visitors remarked on the presence of several gentlemen who wore well-cut civilian clothes and occupied positions of trust, and yet who were not members of the guard force. The ambiguity of their position at the prison was puzzling except to those visitors who recognized in the most elegant of these functionaries a San Francisco forger of poll-tax receipts named Newt Morgan, who for several years in the 1870's was the acknowledged Duke of San Quentin.

Newt Morgan, a young man in his early thirties, fair in person and dandified in dress, was chief clerk in the prison office, where he flourished under the fond gaze of Captain McAlister. He was not merely pre-eminent among the seventy-five trusties, he was the Chosen One of the entire population of thirteen hundred convicts. Besides acting as Captain McAlister's guide, philosopher, and friend, he controlled the trade in prison-made goods and installed his chief accomplice, one Hayes, in a tobacco and newspaper stand just inside the front gate. Like his patron, Hayes was permitted to wear civilian clothes. According to the San Quentin custom, the generality of trusties ate at the guards' table and slept in the houses of the prison officers or elsewhere outside the walls. Morgan lived more elegantly in a private apartment in the hospital, where he was said to be served by his own convict cook.

Morgan found his job pleasant and congenial. Not the least congenial of his duties was the task of locking up the female prisoners in their rooms on the second floor of the captain's office. Although he might accept whatever favors were offered him by the ragged women upstairs, Morgan did not have to depend on them for companionship, for he was free to pass through the walls as he pleased, and on Sundays to receive his own guests. When the morning excursion boat from San Francisco docked at the wharf at ten-thirty, there was often a party of

Morgan's friends aboard, made up of fashionable young men and fair young things who, as the curious old saying goes, were no better than they should be. Captain McAlister turned his office over to Morgan, champagne corks popped, and the young people were reported to have had a merry time. On these occasions Morgan was accustomed to inviting a girl into an office in the rear of the building, from which they emerged refreshed and with Morgan feeling little pain at the rigors of prison life.

Morgan was also free to take his visitors on guided tours of the prison. Once he invited his brother to accompany him to the dungeon to inspect a violent maniac who, in the absence of a psychiatric ward, was locked in one of the cells. After peering at the poor wretch through the door, Morgan produced a key and suggested they have a closer look. The maniac sprang at him as soon as the door was open; Morgan clubbed him unconscious with the heavy padlock, which he was holding in his hand. Captain McAlister merely advised him to be more careful in the future.

Two rookie guards once found out to their own great embarrassment how secure Morgan's position was. Outside the east gate of the prison, across the street from the San Quentin district school, stood Sheppard's Hotel. Here, in 1877, a San Francisco gambler was running a game of faro. The two guards were trying their luck on a Saturday night when, being new to the prison, they were astonished to see Newt Morgan enter, dressed with his usual fastidiousness. It was nine o'clock, five hours after the convicts had been locked up for the night. Morgan bought a drink and threw down a gold piece on the faro table. He lost, finished his drink, and sauntered out. Eager to do their duty and bask in the favorable attention of the captain, the two guards followed Morgan outside, where they laid rough hands on him and demanded to know what he was up to. Morgan protested that he had Captain McAlister's permission; the guards laughed and tried to drag him back to the prison. Morgan twisted out of their hands and ran into the schoolhouse, where a dance was in progress. Captain McAlister was among the prison officers there.

Morgan, closely followed by the two guards, made his way across the floor toward McAlister. The dancers paused and watched curiously as the guards approached their commanding officer, on their stern faces only a trace of the self-satisfaction that comes with the knowledge of a job well done. Morgan whispered into the captain's ear; the guards waited confidently for orders to return the prisoner to his quarters or possibly to the dungeon. Instead, McAlister turned on them with anger at their impertinence and contempt for their ignorance. Before they could escape from the anger of the captain and the amusement of the ladies they saw Morgan take the hand of a young lady and prepare to join the dance.

It was another young lady, Nellie Maguire, alias Handly, who caused Morgan's style of living to be cramped, though not too severely. Not long after Nellie had been sent down from San Joaquin County with a sentence of three years for grand larceny it was discovered that she was pregnant. A solemn conference in the captain's office reached the conclusion that Nellie must not be permitted to give birth in prison. First, the event would cause substantial embarrassment to the officers and guards. Second, sentencing an innocent babe to spend two years in San Quentin would clearly be both illegal and unjust. An urgent message was sent to Sacramento to procure a quiet pardon for Nellie.

The problem of accounting for the child's fatherhood remained. The prison authorities would have happily gone along with a theory which, in the words of a reporter who was no theologian, would have been "a hideous verisimilitude of the Immaculate Conception." But parthenogenesis was too uncommon a phenomenon to carry much conviction. The prison officers were obliged to consider possible candidates for the biological fatherhood of Nellie's unborn child.

Apart from the officers and guards, only two men had access to the cottage in the female convicts' exercise yard where the act of conception was supposed to have taken place. One was the gardener, a superannuated German who was manifestly incapable of any exercise more vigorous than pottering around his flowers. The other was Newt Morgan. Morgan's capacity was as unquestioned as his opportunity, but Captain McAlister was reluctant to charge his favorite with the crime. Another father had to be found. He was discovered when Nellie was induced to sign an affidavit that one Alonzo McCloud, a deputy jailer, had seduced her in the Stockton jail. Nellie was pardoned, Alonzo McCloud continued in his employment at Stockton, but Newt Morgan was forbidden to enter the garden cottage again.

Morgan's wings were finally clipped, not by the prison officers but by the San Francisco *Chronicle,* which reported sourly on the gay life he was leading. By the end of 1877 the newspaper had made enough copy out of his case to convince even McAlister that it would be wise to put his favorite back in stripes. Into stripes Morgan went, and in stripes he remained until, three years later, he was pardoned by Governor William Irwin.

"History is replete with instances where the word of God, falling on the ear of the vilest of sinners, has conjured up some innocent memory of the past, and by appealing to the better feelings of his nature, recalled him to a better life." The quotation is from a report of the 1861 legislative committee, which went on to regret that San Quentin convicts were not offered opportunities for moral and religious instruction such as were given convicts in the eastern states. "No prayer is heard," they wrote, "no Bible is read, no exhortation to repentance is heard."

The spiritual regeneration of the San Quentin convict had not, in fact, been completely overlooked. The rules drawn up by Governor Weller three years earlier had included a paragraph directing the warden to arrange for Sunday services and to invite ministers in good standing to officiate. A Reverend Doctor Gilbert had volunteered to act as chaplain, and, beginning in December, 1858, regular Protestant services were held in the mess hall. The next year the Society of Friends began to send workers to the prison. In March, 1860, the first Mass was said by a Father Gallagher, and two months later Archbishop Joseph Sadoc Alemany himself preached in the mess hall. Alemany was later to preside regularly at the confirmation of convicts who had strayed from the Church in their misspent youth.

Although a room sixty feet square was set apart in one of the factory buildings for use as a chapel, no single chaplain was appointed during the 1860's because of the variety of religious beliefs held by the convicts. Instead, Sundays were parceled out to clergymen of the various sects. Dr. William T. Lucky, principal of the State Normal School, preached twice a month, Father Picardo of San Francisco once a month, and the Reverend Mr. Rush once a month. Father Picardo and Mr. Rush were paid honoraria of $50.00 a year.

It was not any of these clergymen, however, but the captain of the yard, R. G. Gilchrist, who, in November, 1868, suggested that the regenerative power of the word of God might be materially assisted by the establishment of a prison school. The suggestion was all the more surprising as the captain of the yard is traditionally the toughest, most cynical, and most "con-wise" of the prison officers. (Until 1938 San Quentin's table of organization boasted both a captain of the yard and a captain of the guard. The captain of the guard was responsible for the organization of the guard force, which was usually called the "guard line," and for the outer security of the prison. The captain of the yard was the principal officer inisde the walls, in charge of the cell blocks, the workshops, the yard, and the discipline of the prisoners. "New fish" were understandably confused by the multitude of officers whom they had to address as "Captain"; besides the captains of the guards and the yard, these included the turnkey, the chief steward, and the keepers of both front and rear gates. In the days of which we are writing the captain of the yard walked the yard with a whistle around his neck and a loaded cane in his hand.)

Like most prison captains, Gilchrist was a promoted guard, but he appears to have had a more liberal and humane view of mankind than most men whose sight has become adjusted to the limited horizons of prison life. For the light it throws on his personality, it is interesting to note that later in his life Gilchrist worked as an agent for the Society for Prevention of Cruelty to Children.

Captain Gilchrist's school thrived. The first donation of $20.00 from a San Rafael philanthropist was reinforced by money and books collected in San Francisco. By the time C. C. Cummings, a former superintendent of schools in Mendocino County, was appointed to the newly-created post of moral instructor in 1870, the school's 250 scholars were applying themselves to reading, writing, arithmetic, grammar, geography, mathematics, German, and Spanish. The classes met in the chapel for an hour and a half or two hours after Sunday services. The teachers were convicts, and were rewarded by being permitted to take part after classes in programs of selected readings, declamations, and lectures. After this came an hour's practice for the choir of twelve men, who sang to the accompaniment of a cabinet organ they had bought from their overtime earnings in the shops.

Almost half the prisoners committed to San Quentin could neither read nor write. Of these a large number, mostly Chinese and Mexican, spoke English imperfectly and wrote it not at all. Professor Cummings threw himself into this work, and by the end of the year he was able to report that his Chinese students had not only learned some English but had also displayed extraordinary talents for penmanship.

The library, which had grown along with Captain Gilchrist's school, now included about two thousand volumes of theology, history, biography, and science, as well as, by sufferance, some novels. In addition, San Francisco religious weeklies and the more sedate dailies were induced to send free copies. (One wonders how the convicts made out with the *Churchman,* the *Monitor,* and the *Evangel.*) Stamps, stationery, and lights were supplied by the California Prison Commission, a semi-official organization of clergymen and lay people interested in prison reform. The library was the scene of occasional grand balls given by the officers and guards, sometimes as a benefit for the library itself, and sometimes just for the sake of a good time.

A religious census of newly-committed prisoners in 1870 showed 202 Roman Catholics, 173 Protestants, 1 Mormon, 11 Jews, 1 atheist, 63 pagans, and 27 who claimed no religious training. (The pagans were presumably un-Christianized Indians and Chinese.) The convicts represented a field ripe for missionary efforts, but Professor Cummings' interest was primarily in the school and library rather than in the chapel.

Professor Cummings' successors were both pious and inefficient and did little to advance either the worldly or spiritual welfare of their charges. The Reverend Hiram Cummings—no relative of the professor—was a professional chaplain who came to San Quentin as a white-haired old bumbler whom the governor referred to familiarly as Poor Old Parson Cummings. His successor, William Hill, was pious, moralistic, and a willing tool of the warden's. The chief sufferers, particularly under Hill's regime, were the boys of San Quentin.

Administratively, boys are always a major nuisance in prison for two reasons. First, they are wild, unpredictable, and violent in their actions, and second, they are prime bait for the aggressive homosexuals, the wolves and jockers. So far as his capacity for stimulating bloodshed goes, a fresh, attractive boy might as well be a shameless wench of sixteen. Beyond this the presence of young boys in prison had acted as a burden on the public conscience and stimulated professional reformers to bedevil wardens and legislatures.

In 1858 John Weller had recommended that all boys under eighteen be kept in the county jails rather than sent to San Quentin. It wasn't an ideal solution, but it would have been better than what actually happened. Although a state reform school had been established at Marysville, suggestions of its abandonment were heard only a few years after its founding. San Francisco delinquents were sent to that city's Industrial School, but after about 1870 boys from the rest of the state were committed to San Quentin when they got into serious trouble.

In 1873 there were ninety-nine youngsters under twenty in San Quentin, about one out of every nine convicts. By 1881, when Hill was hired as moral instructor, there were two boys of twelve, two of thirteen, three of fourteen, three of fifteen, and thirty-three of sixteen, seventeen, and eighteen. The administrative solution had been to segregate these boys from the men by attaching them directly to the moral instructor. They were kept severely apart from the other convicts and marched under guard from their quarters to the mess hall, to the workshops, and to the schoolroom.

The schoolroom was on the second floor of a factory building. When Hill was appointed, the day-school enrollment was only eleven, rising to a maximum of eighteen. Although this seems a modest-sized class, Hill was apparently incapable of keeping discipline and was soon discouraged by the boys' indifference to scholarship. He agreed readily when the warden suggested they be put to work, either at caning chairs or in the newly-established jute mill. By July, 1882, there were only six boys left in school, and a year later the scholars all being assigned to the mill and the shops, the day school was abandoned. Hill looked on the change with cordial approval. He reported to the warden that many of the boys were becoming expert spinners and weavers, "and the constant attention which they must give to their work saved them from the curse indicated in the old couplet

"For Satan will find some work
For idle hands to do.

None of the boys' opinions of Mr. Hill and his regime has survived, a fact which is surely to be regretted. Hill was the last of the moral instructors, for in 1883, in appreciation of his services, he was given the grander title of chaplain.

Chapter VIII

DAWN OF RESPECTABILITY

OF THE six physicians who served San Quentin between 1860 and 1880, the two whose personalities stand out most clearly are the irrepressible Dr. Taliaferro and Dr. J. D. B. Stillman.

Dr. Taliaferro, who, it will be recalled, came of the family that pronounces their name as if it were written *Tolliver,* was a Forty-Niner, an amiable and gregarious man who early in his California career established himself as a prominent Democrat. Manly and unassuming in appearance, he was one of the most popular of the Virginia colony that settled in Marin. Although running on the Democratic ticket in a strong Whig district, he was elected to the state senate in 1851 to take his seat in a session which was also graced by the presence of General Estell. Dr. Taliaferro's senatorial style was witty in the fashion of the times, and his surviving speeches show a man who possessed both some oratorical grace and a firm belief in the Gospel of Progress. A sample may help to give the feel of the man. As a committee chairman, Dr. Taliaferro wrote:

> Your committee, to whom was referred the senate bill providing for the construction of telegraph lines within the state of California, would recommend that as this is rather a *flashy* subject, we should pass it like a flash. To a people so

progressive and goahead as we Californians are, the anni-
hilation of space and time should meet with the most particular favor. . . . And further, the powers and influences of
electromagnetism will be a fine theme of philosophical con-
templation to our Digger Indians. But, to be serious,
we recommend this bill to the most favorable consideration
of the House, and hope it will pass.

This is really rather deplorable, but one does not have to
stretch one's imagination very far to see the amiable doctor
presiding in the prison office, a bottle of black draught at his
elbow and a succession of pleasantries on his lips. Judging from
his large private practice around San Rafael, he was both a
popular and able physician, and one can hope that the convicts
appreciated his little jokes. We have seen him elsewhere in this
history in a more serious mood. On the whole, he seems to have
been a decent and humane man.

Dr. Stillman was a somewhat stiffer personality, but, like
Taliaferro, he was a humane man, and again, like Taliaferro, he
was articulate. His medical reports are clear and well written and
sometimes glitter with flashes of real style. "How we abominate
unsuccessful crime!" Dr. Stillman wrote, an aphorism that surely
deserves to be lifted out of the obscurity of state prison reports.
Noting that no societies to help ex-convicts had been organized
in California, Stillman wrote that "the earth below them is of iron,
and the sky above is brass." This is not bad, either.

Several of the other prison doctors did not lag far behind the
clergymen in their concern for the moral welfare of their charges.
Dr. Peter Campbell, who assumed the duties of visiting physician
in 1860, confessed that he was troubled by the treatment of those
"diseases, the results of libidinous indiscretions to which many are
addicted—these cases are in many instances rendered impervious
to the sanitary effects of medicines from the immoderate use of
spiritous liquors." This theme of the physical consequences of
immorality, which runs through the medical reports of the period,

comes to its finest flower under the careful nurturing of Dr. J. E. Pelham, who came to San Quentin in 1877.

Dr. Pelham lost no time in declaring a crusade against the habits which one of his predecessors had described as "those secret and most disgusting vices indulged in by the incorrigibles." Pelham addressed himself vigorously to the subject in his first report:

> The great evil presenting itself for remedial action in prison life is self-abuse, a vice that undermines the constitution and debases the moral instincts more than all other causes combined. It kills body and soul; and if the subject of this vice is so fortunate as to serve out his sentence, he returns to the community a fit subject to adopt crime as a profession for life. This disgusting vice exists as a primary cause of the principal diseases with which convicts are afflicted, and to repair the resulting injury is the principal study of the prison physician; and its eradication is also of primary importance in a moral point of view.... To meet and control this great vice, with the present system of management of the prison, is a herculean task, and will tax a physician beyond his abilities.

Dr. Pelham suggested that the best curative and preventive therapy for those poor devils who were addicted to this vile practice was the adoption of the Pennsylvania system of prison discipline, a system of complete solitary confinement. Dr. Pelham did not explain how he expected solitary confinement to discourage solitary vice; one is tempted to smile at the seriousness of his concern and to suspect that, in any case, he was more concerned with homosexual practices than with masturbation.

But until fairly recent years masturbation was not a matter for levity, even among the sophisticated. The records of the state insane asylum at Stockton give clear evidence that it was regarded by the psychiatrists of that day as a veritable scourge, a direct cause of insanity, and a dragon to be slain. A supporting opinion was submitted by Dr. W. A. Grover, physician and surgeon at Folsom Prison, in his first report in 1880:

> Seminal weakness is another serious disease which afflicts a large number of those sent here ... a formidable disease ... usually brought on by self-abuse and other vicious habits. It causes a long line of unpleasant symptoms, such as palpitation of the heart, nervous excitement, pain in the back and loins, nightly emissions, and general debility.

In the light of this general opinion, and in the light of the inevitability of masturbation and other "secret and disgusting" sexual practices in a community of men deprived of women, one can only agree with Dr. Pelham that he was indeed faced with a herculean task. It was not, however, too much for his abilities, which must have been considerable, for two years later Pelham writes:

> I have to report a great change for the better in the habits of the convicts in reference to the loathsome and degrading crime of self-abuse and its kindred associations, which I referred to in my last report as prevailing at that time. . . . This change is marked, and the number of cases now presenting for medical relief from the vice itself and injuries resulting physically and mentally therefrom have very materially lessened.

By and large, however, the prison physician was concerned less with disgusting vices than with an occasional knife or gunshot wound and a steady stream of colds, upset stomachs, diarrhetic bowels, bruises, and outbreaks of flu. The prison doctors all agreed that the climate at Point San Quentin was an extraordinarily healthy one, and that both the incidence of disease and the mortality rate among the convicts were lower than in any other similar institution they knew of. Statistically, by far the most common diseases were afflictions of the digestive and pulmonary tracts encouraged by the crowded life in the cell blocks. The greatest number of deaths were attributed to phthisis pulmonalis, or tuberculosis of the lungs.

The quality of their medical care has always been a popular cause for complaint among prisoners, just as among their brethren in the Army and Navy. How many of these complaints may be laid to the simple pleasures of grousing and how many are justified is a matter which has never been properly settled. While the patients complain of their treatment the doctors complain of goldbricking. At San Quentin men suspected of malingering were left in a room where the complete lack of furniture and the diet of bread and water were thought to have a healthy effect on their imaginary ailments.

Apart from such real threats as tuberculosis and such imagined terrors as masturbation, the most serious medical problem was the treatment of insane prisoners. Dr. Stillman has left a vivid, if somewhat highly colored, picture of the classic case of a murderer whose nervous system was so shattered by waiting to be executed that by the time his sentence was commuted there was little left to be saved.

> For the year past he has been as simple as a little child [Stillman wrote], with nervous tremors, and, at long intervals, paroxysms of clonic convulsions, after which he would go trembling for days, constantly upon his hands and knees about his cell floor, staring, when raised to his feet, with wild and bloodshot eyes, as if the avenging spirit was working some terrible purpose with the murderer.

Stillman did as Dr. Taliaferro had done, and sent the insane to the state asylum at Stockton, and, later, to Napa and Agnews state hospitals. At first this process had seemed satisfactory enough, but by 1863 Dr. Stillman had discovered that although it was hard to get a convict admitted to Stockton, it was easy for the doctors at Stockton to discharge him as cured and send him back to San Quentin. Stillman accordingly stopped sending them away, partly with the thought that they were no worse off at the prison anyway.

Dr. Taliaferro reported much the same story after his return in 1869. He, too, tried again to send the insane to Stockton, and he, too, saw them shuttling back and forth uncured. At San Quentin the insane were now kept in a sunless alleyway between two of the cell blocks, behind a sort of palisade but still accessible to any friend or mischief-maker who wanted to slip a knife or other contraband through the fence. This stockade came to be called Crazy Alley, or, less commonly, Crank Alley, Cranky Alley, or Nut Alley. Although Dr. Taliaferro earnestly recommended that some proper provision be made for the insane, the only immediate change was that the more violent prisoners were moved from Crazy Alley to the dungeon, where they stayed until they died or were discharged. Not until the 1920's were the insane moved into decent cells, but the name Crazy Alley clung, and continued to give a good measure of their treatment.

The care of the insane prisoners was a chronic scandal, and in 1882 the president of the California Medical Society protested vigorously to the assembled members against the twin evils of keeping the criminal insane in the dungeon and of sending them to a regular asylum. He recommended the construction of an institution for the criminal insane, a suggestion which, probably because it was so sensible, was not acted on until a prison ward was built at Mendocino State Hospital more than fifty years later.

Crazy Alley remained in precisely the same place for another forty-five years and contributed its share of pathetic stories to the folklore of the prison. There was, for example, Johnny Sansome, known to all as Samson, who regularly wrote letters to that "wicked trinity," the warden, the captain of the yard, and the captain of the guard, inquiring hopefully if they had yet confessed their sins and joined the church. There was old Frenchy, who collected bits of ribbon and string and scraps of tin to sew on his coat. Rain or shine, Ah Gin ate his food out in the alley, crouching on the stones with his jacket pulled over his head.

Crazy Alley also held a stagecoach robber who had sworn he would never say a word in prison. For years he kept his vow, even during violent spells when he attacked other prisoners, but finally the day came when somebody stole his tobacco. The stagecoach robber held out for several days, but at last he could stand it no longer and spoke for the first time since the main gate had slammed behind him.

These momentous words were: "Gimme some of your tobacco."

Although, as wardens of San Quentin, the lieutenant governors had managed to avoid becoming involved in any major scandals, and although the history of the prison under their administration seems almost tranquil by comparison with the wild days of Estell and McCauley, their management of the prison had been the target of sporadic sniping both from the press and from the legislature. At length, in 1879, the legislature removed San Quentin from direct political control, and, under the law of April 15 and an amendment to the state constitution, placed it under a five-man Board of State Prison Directors who were charged with appointing the warden and the clerk. By the same legislation, contract labor was outlawed; in the future, the convicts would be permitted to work only for the state itself.

Prison labor has always been tainted labor, particularly in the opinion of the unionized workman. If, as was the case at San Quentin, the convict laborers included many Mexicans and Chinese, a rational objection to having to compete with sweated convict labor was turned at full flood into the well-marked channels of California xenophobia. In spite of the plain fact that the prison factories never employed more than a total of five hundred men, the furniture factory was the largest on the West Coast, which gave some color to the outrage that legislators, union officials, and newspaper editors expressed at the awful threat that Mexican and Chinese convicts represented to the free American workingman. It was in response to this feeling that the Constitution of 1879 gave the contractors until the end of 1881 to wind up their affairs and turn their shops over to the state.

Along with the change of administration came another change which was to have a great effect on the welfare of the California convict. This was the establishment of a second state prison at Folsom, on the American River north of Sacramento.

Folsom prison turned out to be not exactly what John Weller had in mind when, in 1858, he pointed out how desirable it would be to have an institution which would undertake the reformation of "young men imprisoned, who are the victims of drinking and gambling, in whose breasts beat warm and generous hearts and honest impulses." The law under which Weller and his colleagues managed San Quentin was entitled "An Act for the Government of the State Prison Convicts, and to Provide for the Creation of a Branch Prison." With the latter phrase in mind, the directors suggested the purchase of a site for a branch prison at Folsom, where both granite and water power were readily available. They underlined their recommendation by offering in high irony an alternative proposal that the capitol plaza in Sacramento be fenced in, and the rooms in the basement of the capitol itself be fitted out as cells.

Eight years later, when neither Folsom nor the capitol had yet been turned into a prison, an assembly committee recommended that San Quentin be renamed a House of Correction, a euphemism for prison which was popular among the reformers of the time and which is still preserved in the names of some state penitentiaries. The incorrigible prisoners and repeaters were to be sent to a branch prison to be located on a site with a good title, a quarry, and water power, where the convicts could be employed in labor which did not compete with the free workingman. The description happened to fit Folsom exactly.

The ground for the new prison, a site of three hundred acres on the banks of the American River, two miles above the town of

Folsom, was acquired in 1868 from the Natoma Water Company, but the building of the prison itself took another twelve years. The work started in earnest in 1874, when a contract was signed for completion by 1875, but it dragged on until 1878, when the last of a succession of scoundrels posing as contractors was driven to the wall by his creditors. The contractor's equipment was all attached and sold by the sheriff to the board of prison directors, who put the foreman of the stonework in charge and grimly oversaw the completion of a hundred cells instead of the 328 called for in the plans.

On July 15, 1880, Thomas Pockman, who had been the superintendent of construction, was appointed first warden of Folsom. Between the end of July and the end of September two hundred prisoners were transferred permanently from San Quentin to Folsom. If the convicts welcomed the change, they soon learned better. The history of San Quentin has its diverting moments, but the history of the rock-bound prison on the American River is a record of almost unrelieved grimness.

During the twenty years from 1880 to 1900 San Quentin was turned into a giant gunny-sack factory and the convicts into sweated industrial laborers. At the same time the moral atmosphere of the prison took on a particularly unbecoming flavor of sanctimoniousness and brutality.

There were three main reasons for this change of temper. First, California was in the painful and not especially edifying process of becoming respectably middle class. The gold miners were gone forever, and in their place the land was populated with farmers, clerks, bankers, dentists, housewives, ministers of the gospel, insurance salesmen, schoolteachers, and many other supporters of a narrow and unadventurous view of life. In the south the boomer and the subdivider were hard at work raising orange groves and ugly white bungalows, while in San Francisco, the descendants of the Argonauts wore stiff collars and encouraged their young to marry sensibly, wear dark clothes, and put their money in the bank. A minor aspect of the new morality was a denial of any common bonds of humanity with the criminal classes.

Even in the days of Estell and McCauley a strong tradition of what might be called the sporting view of crime flourished both in San Francisco and at San Quentin. The tradition can be seen in the workings of Estell's capricious trusty system and even in the brief words of the visitor who wrote that "599 more ragged devils he had never seen in his life." There is a rough sort of compassion here, a recognition that during the days of the Gold Rush the distinction between convict and freeman was often due to nothing more noble than the luck of the game.

According to the high-spirited Major Horace Bell, the buoyant point in this liberal attitude came in 1856 when Alexander Bell took up his duties as chairman of the board of directors.

> When Aleck took command at San Quentin, he found that among the ragged rascals there confined, every fifth man was an old friend, each of whom claimed an indebtedness for small loans made when times were flush with him. Some had known him in Texas, some in the Army in Mexico, others had followed him to Ecuador, and had worked for him at Panama. He found Los Angeles friends, San Francisco friends, friends from Stockton, from Sonora, Mokelumne Hill, Santa Barbara, and friends and kinsmen of his Sonoreña wife.

But by the eighties and nineties the sporting view survived only in the writings of facetious newspaper reporters. The good citizen now saw clearly that the convicted criminal was a creature of another sort from himself, made of coarser material, brutal by his very nature, and, somehow, passed over by God in the distribution of moral understanding.

This view of the criminal found scientific support in the work of the great Italian criminologist Cesare Lombroso and his followers of the so-called "positive" school of criminology. The positive school has few supporters in these sentimental days in which we live except among such mavericks as the late Earnest Hooton of Harvard. Briefly, the positive school maintained that the criminal was a biological defective, an atavistic throwback to an earlier stage of human development. It was Lombroso who applied the techniques of physical anthropology to Italian convicts, demonstrating statistically that felons tended to have such characteristic physical stigmata as sloping foreheads, long ear lobes, and beetling brows. (As late as the 1940's Hooton was applying these techniques to American criminals, with such startling results as the discovery that "Old American" robbers are distinguished, in the mass, by low waved hair, high heads, median eye folds, and short ears and noses.)

In the United States there were few more fervent or, for that matter, more eminent supporters of Lombroso and the positive theory than the Reverend August Drähms, chaplain at San Quentin from 1891 to 1909. As the successor to Poor Old Parson Cummings and the earnest and humorless William C. Hill, August Drähms was a novelty, a scientist-clergyman. (He was also a past chaplain of the Grand Army of the Republic, and was said to have been one of the youngest boys to have carried arms for the Union.) As a prison chaplain Drähms does not appear as a very sympathetic figure. One of the more articulate of his spiritual charges described him in later years as an "ugly toad" and went on to support his opinion with recollections of the harshness and narrowness of Drähms's preaching in the San Quentin chapel. Another prisoner remembered him as a "parasitical sniveling hypocrite, a grafter and traducer of hopes of unfortunate convicts."

As a scientist Drähms was a good deal more respectable than as a chaplain. His major work was a book of the positive school called *The Criminal,* which was published in 1900 with a laudatory foreword by Lombroso himself. It is a better book than one expects, and it deserves some brief attention not only because Drähms was one of the most intelligent men at San Quentin in his time but also because he represented the thinking of the contemporary advance guard in criminology.

Drähms's method was to compare the detailed physical measurements of two thousand white male adult convicts with the corresponding measurements of Amherst College undergraduates. The results demonstrated to his satisfaction the truth of Lombroso's thesis that the criminal was indeed a biological degenerate. Drähms's scientific observations were generally detailed and precise. He wrote, for example, that

> the eyes of the habitual criminal are usually small and uneasy; in the homicide cold, fixed, and nystagmous; in the sexual offender, generally light, and projecting in their orbits. I have noticed the congested state of the eyelids as peculiar to this latter class, noticeably in the case of certain pronounced sexual offenders and congenital homicides.

Unlike most prison officers, whose books are usually extended celebrations of their own wit and wisdom in handling the convicts in their charge, Drähms is objective. He does not permit himself a single anecdote, and there is barely a clue that he is in fact a chaplain. The single passage in which he reports his conclusions as to the criminal and religion, however, bears directly on our larger topic. Drähms wrote:

> Careful inquiry convinces me that, so far as nominal Protestant prisoners are concerned (to which class my inquiry has been more particularly directed), not one-half of one per cent of the total prison population held actual membership in good standing with any Protestant Evangelical church at the time of committal to prison; and as to the habitual criminal, or recidivist, I have never known such an instance.

This, really, is the heart of the matter. The criminal, according to this view, is the man who, in one metaphor, stands outside the grace of God; who, in a slightly different metaphor, stands outside the Protestant Evangelical communion; and who, in a broader sense, is unfit for membership in the general society. The criminal has not willed to be a criminal; he cannot help himself because he is condemned to a life of crime by his congenital physical and moral inferiority. In the sense in which it became generally understood, the positive theory of criminality could not have been better suited to a prison administration that denied the convict any individuality at all. (In fairness to the memory of August Drähms it should be said that, even while preaching a narrow and mechanical theory of criminality, he also advocated shorter prison sentences, the indeterminate sentence, and parole, as well as coming out against capital punishment and sterilization.)

The growth of California as a respectably middle-class state was, then, the social milieu for the crimes that were committed against San Quentin's prisoners, while the positive theory provided its philosophical apology. The third reason for the brutalization of the convicts was the political and economic necessity for making San Quentin pay for itself.

The system of contracting with private manufacturers to put prisoners to work in factories inside the walls had not been successful at all. On the list of prison manufactures which had failed were iron safes, foundry and stone castings, plows and agricultural implements, boots and shoes, coopering, wagons and buggies, brooms, stockings, sewing-machine needles, shirts, needlework, house moldings, and packing boxes. Besides being inefficient and unprofitable, the contract system had stirred up California's increasingly powerful labor organizations to a positive mania of righteous outrage. As a result, that hydraheaded monstrosity, the California constitution of 1879, outlawed the private contract once and for all. The state was obliged to put the convicts to work on its own account, which meant that some industry would have to be found which would not compete with free labor but which would, at the same time, show a profit. In both the theory and practice of a capitalist economy this was a manifest impossibility, since any profitable industry would automatically find an entrepreneur. The answer to this riddle was found by Warden J. P. Ames, who proposed that San Quentin be turned into a factory where raw jute would be spun, woven, and sewed into sacks to be sold to California wheat farmers. Jute is an Indian plant that is the source of the fiber used in burlap and in the grain sacks commonly known as gunny sacks. The cultivation of jute had been one of the principal industries developed by the British East India Company, and developed with such success that every year California farmers alone bought millions of grain bags imported from the world center of production in Calcutta. The only jute mill in California was an establishment in East Oakland which employed Chinese. If San Quentin were to go into the jute business, hardly any white American workingmen would be thrown out of work; at the same time, California wheat farmers, who were to enjoy their greatest harvests of all time in the mid-1880's, provided a ready market for the finished product.

Unfriendly newspapers and politicians jeered at the economics of the project, but they did not discourage Warden Ames and his supporters in Sacramento. In August, 1880, the board of prison directors contracted with Messrs. Fairbairn, Kennedy, & Naylor of Leeds, England, for one hundred jute looms to be shipped from Liverpool at a cost of $1,000 apiece. Five hundred tons of jute were ordered from Calcutta, as well as a quantity of jute seed, which was hopefully distributed to interested California farmers. This first order was the nose of the camel under the tent; twenty years later the manufacture of jute bags was the only industry carried on at the prison, and for fifty years more the jute mill was the principal fact of life at Point San Quentin.

Chapter IX

RIOTS NEVER END ON SCHEDULE

JOSIAH P. AMES, the innovator of the jute scheme, had come to California as a private in Stevenson's regiment and had thereafter risen in politics through the state legislature to the bench of the San Mateo Court of Sessions. When, in 1879, he decided to run for warden of San Quentin, it was a logical extension of his political career. Although the new constitution had been advertised as taking the state prison out of politics, this notion would have been considered riotously funny even in an eighth-grade civics class. The choice of warden had been made a matter of election by the five prison directors, and the candidates for the post campaigned as heartily as if they had been running for county road commissioner. Ames bought off his chief rival, an ex-sheriff, with the promise of making him captain of the guard, while he ingratiated himself with the prison directors by offering them, illegally, the power of making all other appointments with the exception of keeper of the front gate, a post he reserved for his own brother-in-law.

Ames was accordingly elected and installed as warden in February, 1880, inaugurating the new era at San Quentin with a declaration that he intended to teach the convicts useful trades, to segregate newly-committed prisoners from the old lags, and to erect a separate building for the prison's boys. This was nothing more than the pious eyewash which is expected of every new warden; experienced observers of California politics passed quickly over Ames's professed penal ideas but noted with interest that 58 Democratic guards, comprising almost the entire guard line, were permitted to resign so that their posts could be filled with 58 loyal Republicans.

Thanks to the survival of Turnkey A. G. Hinman's letter book we are permitted a closer look into the fascinating workings of the patronage machine. Hinman himself owed his appointment to his friendship with his fellow townsman, State Senator James C. Zuck of Gilroy.

As soon as he was appointed, Hinman himself began to play a part in the distribution of patronage, receiving from interested politicians letters of recommendation for loyal but unemployed Republicans. (At San Quentin the turnkey was not a mere turner of keys but an officer who rejoiced in the title of captain and who had in his keeping the prison records. Hinman's correspondents were sometimes puzzled by the proper style in which to address such an exalted personage; one of them salutes him as "My Christian friend and turnkey.")

Relations between Hinman and Senator Zuck continued friendly, even though Zuck could lend Hinman only $60.00 when Hinman needed $100. ("There is a *great deal* of honor in holding office, but very little coin," Zuck explained.) In March Zuck wrote to Hinman, asking his friend to find out if Ames was allowing each senator to nominate a guard, as he said he would. Ames apparently was faithful to his word, for Zuck's nominee, one Clendennin, was afterward appointed.

This, then, was the system which obtained at San Quentin under the reformed constitution. It was part and parcel of a spoils system which really scandalized nobody except a few sensitive idealists and which would not have come to public notice at all if Ames had not been one of the most unbearable and irascible individuals ever to sit in the warden's office.

Judge Ames's crankiness was directed largely at those prison officers who were least capable of defending themselves. First was Poor Old Parson Cummings, who wandered around San Quentin in well-meaning bewilderment, blundering into the corral around the cell blocks when he had no business to be there, buying tickets home for discharged convicts, going to Sacramento to plead for pardons for other men still imprisoned, and even recommending to the warden an informal discharge for a prisoner who claimed to be unjustly convicted. All the officers and guards were accustomed to Ames's nervous mannerism of shaking his stick in the air whenever he gave an order, but Parson Cummings had reason to believe that the warden intended the gesture as a personal threat. Once, when Cummings complained to Ames that the boys in his charge had been fighting, Ames snapped back, "Why didn't you knock them down with your cane?" When the white-haired, seventy-year-old clergyman answered mildly that he wasn't at San Quentin to knock boys down, Ames roared, "If you don't do it, I'll have someone there that will!"

Ames embarked on a campaign to harass the chaplain until his life would become so miserable he would leave of his own accord. A number of humiliating incidents, some large and some small, were added to the chaplain's store of bitterness. When Cummings addressed Ames with the words, "Judge, I think . . ." the warden said harshly and in the presence of convicts and freemen, "You have no right to think, sir!" Later, Ames drove Cummings out of the house he occupied on the prison grounds to make room for a guard, and Cummings was assigned a tumble-down shack that would hardly have been fit shelter for the prison pigs.

Cummings' chief companions in humiliation were the prison doctor, L. H. Cary, and the superintendent of outside work, R. A.

Marden. Dr. Cary observed in the warden's conduct the clinical symptoms of what today would be called a manic-depressive psychosis: alternating periods of depression and boisterous activity. Dr. Cary took Parson Cummings' part in his quarrels with the warden, and earned Ames's displeasure on his own account by trying to get a convict released from the dungeon where he had been locked up for more than a year. Cary was a seriously sick man and had to dose himself with morphine to keep going; rightly or not, Ames called him a dope fiend. In May, 1881, after only fourteen months at San Quentin, Cary resigned.

Marden, the outside superintendent, had also been publicly humiliated by Judge Ames, who had once criticized him so cruelly in front of convicts that Marden had turned in his resignation. Marden had run afoul of the warden when he had noticed that the warden's house servants had small bundles hidden under their stripes when Ames himself returned them to the prison gate at night. With opium smuggling in mind, Marden suggested the men be searched, but Ames cut him off with "How dare you have my servants examined in my presence!" After this incident, Marden held his tongue when the warden's pet convict, R. B. Denson, presented himself at the main gate after hours, dressed in civilian clothes and redolent of whisky. Marden remembered the incident, however, and he also remembered that Denson had been seen driving a buggy with the wife of a prominent San Rafael citizen at his side.

Accounts of the experiences of these men as well as other rumors of queer goings on at San Quentin reached the ear of J. J. Owen, editor of the San Jose *Mercury,* who published a list of a dozen charges against Ames. The story was picked up by the San Francisco *Examiner,* and another scandal was set off. Although there had already been three official examinations of San Quentin during the year, Governor George C. Perkins called for another one and took the unusual step of calling on Owen himself to act as prosecutor.

Besides stimulating the circulations of the newspapers involved, the investigation revealed that an old lag returning after twenty-five years would have found much that was familiar. Although Ames was officially cleared of any serious misbehavior, this was thanks to Scottish verdicts of "not proven" in answer to such charges as deceiving a convict in the matter of a pardon and "refusal to heed remonstrances of the governor concerning habits of intemperance." The committee did find that Ames had given over to the prison directors some of his own prerogatives and that he was guilty of various financial irregularities. The directors also found out that Ames allowed convicts who were within ten days of going home to pass freely through the gates to the three saloons which were still doing business within a few yards of the prison boundaries. One saloonkeeper testified that a convict had run up a bill of $23.00 in his establishment, mostly for bottled goods, at $1.25 a bottle, which he carried back to his thirsty friends inside the walls.

There was other testimony which would have reminded our hypothetical old lag even more strongly of the days of General Estell. The local station agent claimed to have seen the prison clerk and the warden's favorite convict strolling down a street in San Francisco together. (The committee recalled the witness to the stand to test his eyesight. It was found to be not very sharp.) Judge Ames was described by Dr. Cary, Cummings, and others as frequently drunk, and one of the prison captains diplomatically could not remember whether he had once said, "The Old Man is pretty full again." A food contractor testified candidly that the beef supplied to San Quentin was of an inferior grade, from stags (by which he meant castrated bulls), and that, although he would not care to eat it himself, it was good enough for convicts and for export to the British Army. The committee also heard of the consternation of Mrs. W. Banks, wife of the prison engineer, who thought Ames had lost his mind when, in a towering rage, he had ordered everybody out of the officers' and guards' mess at mealtime in order to use the dining room for the punishment of prisoners.

The moral atmosphere of the whole affair is summed up in the following exchange:

Q. Do you receive any perquisites?

A. I know what you want to get at: You want to know whether I am a thief. I receive no perquisites.

The witness was Fulton G. Berry, the prison commissary officer, who had half-ownership in a $2,000 prison-built sloop manned by a convict crewman; who sold commissary goods to citizens of San Quentin village; and who bought meat so putrid that the smell of its cooking nauseated a supervisor in the wood-shop almost two hundred feet from the kitchen.

In spite of these various irregularities, Judge Ames's regime was by no means a complete loss for San Quentin. On March 1, 1880, shortly after Ames took over, all but 164 of the 1,446 prisoners were unemployed and during the day were either locked up or allowed to run loose in the yard. Ames persuaded the prison board to buy fifty more acres of clay land, and opened up the brickyard again. During the first years of his administration convict workmen not only began to erect the jute mill, built of San Quentin brick, but also put up a new brick wall, cemented over Major Love's old wall to keep it from tumbling down entirely, and built the guardhouse which still stands to the left of the main gate, containing the officers' and guards' mess ("the O and G mess") and living quarters for bachelor officers. Ames also painted the interiors of the cells and contracted with the San Rafael gasworks to supply illuminating gas. The guards were put into semi-military blue uniforms with brass buttons and slouch hats and required to attend regular drills and rifle practice. A Lowell gun battery was mounted at the post commanding the yard and the front gate. Ames had only one convict flogged before the whipping post was abolished in 1880, but a number of others were showered or locked up on bread and water in the dungeon.

The greatest day of Ames's administration was the formal opening of the jute mill on April 3, 1882. A delegation of fifty gentlemen from San Francisco, including representatives of the military forces and the chamber of commerce, watched the first twenty-five looms go into operation and marveled at the speed with which raw jute went in one end of the mill and emerged from the other as grain sacks. Missing from the crowd of well-wishers who sat down to a banquet at noon were representatives of the East Oakland jute mill, which had lost twenty-odd of its skilled Chinese workmen, seduced by the higher wages they were offered to teach their trade to the prisoners. The managers of the Oakland mill predicted darkly that the experiment would be a costly one for the state, but the supporters of San Quentin jute saw nothing but success coming from the combination of prison labor and an annual demand for several million sacks.

During its first year of operation the jute mill helped cut in half the $200,000 which the upkeep of San Quentin had been costing the state. Encouraged by this and other initial successes, the administration doubled the size of the mill and, in response to outside pressure, abolished even the profitable furniture factory, which had been operating under a sort of hermaphroditic state-account system. When finished, the mill contained two hundred looms, with the attendant breakers and carders, spinning and winding frames, finishing calenders, sewing machines, and baling presses. Every month an average of 370,000 pounds of jute were turned into approximately the same number of gunny sacks, which were sold at prices ranging from five to eight cents apiece. Ultimately, the mill became the focal point for infection that erupted in mass mutinies by the prisoners and in graft and corruption among the managers. Yet it never failed to show a profit.

Judge Ames was not present to see the growth of the mill or

to figure in the mutinies and financial scandals that revolved around the ugly brick building in the lower yard. George Stoneman, a Democrat, took possession of the governor's mansion in Sacramento in January, 1883, and immediately thereafter Democratic hatchetmen began to look thoughtfully at the broad Republican backs in San Quentin.

The only obstacle in the way of the immediate assassination of the Republicans was that Judge Ames had served only three years of his four-year term. He managed to hold on stubbornly for almost another year in spite of what he called "troubles and turmoil created by despicable political apostates and partisan foes." Governor Stoneman contributed the major part of this harassment by convoking a board of inquiry in July, 1883, firing the board of directors in August, and appointing men of his own who at length succeeded in making life so unpleasant for Ames that he turned in his resignation in October.

The expected Democratization of San Quentin took place early in November, several old San Quentin hands of the Democratic party returning to oust their opposite numbers of the Republican persuasion. Captain Charles Aull, who had been working temporarily as a Wells Fargo detective, and Captain McAlister, who had resigned in 1880 to make room for Captain John C. Edgar, arrived at the prison even before the appearance of the new warden, Paul Shirley, a former Democratic state senator. There was apparently little personal animosity; at any rate, on the night after Warden Shirley's arrival officers and guards of both factions and their ladies attended a grand ball in the prison library. Two weeks later Judge Ames, accompanied by Captains Edgar, Hinman, and Stegman, sailed into the political wilderness on the morning boat to San Francisco.

When Shirley's term expired in 1887, the board elected another Democrat, Brigadier General John McComb, who had been serving as warden at Folsom. McComb was a genuine pioneer who had come from New York on the ship *Oregon* in 1849. He was a newspaperman by trade and had been managing editor of the *Alta California*. There was a general exchange of officers between Folsom and San Quentin, with McComb bringing with him his intimate friend Ben Chambers, his son, John McComb, Jr., and the Folsom doctor.

Even though his military career had been limited to the state militia, McComb was intent on keeping things in "exhibition shape," which turned out to mean not only maintaining spit and polish but also providing an acceptable façade for investigators. A curious state senator discovered that McComb and Chambers had been cooking the prison books when a careless or vindictive clerk left both original and doctored pages in a copybook. Nothing came of the discovery except a sour note in the Senate journal that San Quentin's bookkeeping "would not be permitted in an ordinary grocery properly conducted."

When McComb resigned in 1891 he left little behind of a permanent nature except the introduction of electricity to light the grounds and a firmly established "con-boss" system, which he had also taken pride in developing to a fine point at Folsom. The con-boss system is based upon the premise that the toughest, meanest, and most feared convicts are the best taskmasters for the others. It is a system that befouled San Quentin for years.

William E. Hale, the elderly ex-sheriff of Alameda County and a Republican, induced two other sheriffs and a former United States marshal to withdraw their candidacies, and was elected warden to succeed McComb in April, 1891. Hale brought back as captain of the yard and ex-officio deputy warden John C. Edgar, who in this history was last seen aboard a steamboat bound for San Francisco. (Edgar's return was not by water, but by railroad. Although freight was still carried by water, passengers now had the choice of two railroads connecting with the San Francisco ferries in Tiburon or Sausalito.) Hale also appointed Lombroso's disciple, August Drähms, as chaplain.

Hale managed to be re-elected in 1895 in the face of the

opposition of the Democratic governor, James H. Budd, who was reported to be grooming a state senator of his own party for the job and to have three Democrats standing by for appointment to the board of directors. But because the director's term of service was for ten years the incumbent Republicans managed to hang on and carry Hale with them.

The eagerness of hitherto-respected public servants to take or keep possession of the warden's residence is a curious phenomenon in view of the certainty that their personal characters would be thoroughly muddied before they left office. It was, of course, a generally rough period in California politics, and the power and perquisites of the warden of San Quentin were not insignificant. Yet one wonders if Warden Hale did not wish a Democrat were in charge when the prison blew up under his feet in May, 1897.

The jute mill was a factory of a particularly repellent sort, where none of the workers was free to quit, and where, if a man failed to finish his daily task, or made bad cloth, or otherwise showed himself unskilled or recalcitrant, he was turned over to the disciplinary department until he promised to reform. Even by the standards of nineteenth-century factories, the mill was not a pleasant place to work. The great brick work rooms echoed with the slapping of power belts and the clattering of the looms that filled the air with jute dust until the men had good reason to think their lungs were lined with lint. There was no heat, and until the prison directors supplied the workers with gray-ribbed army blouses the men shivered in their thin prison stripes as they tended the looms and breakers or sewed sacks on cold winter mornings. Until a second unit was finished, the mill worked two shifts, and for a short time in 1890 three shifts. The three shifts proved unwieldy from the standpoint of security and, besides, required the importation of extra hands from Folsom, which meant more crowding in the cell blocks. In what finally evolved as its normal routine, about eight hundred men worked in "loom row" and "sack alley" from seven-thirty until four-thirty in the afternoon, with forty-five minutes off for lunch. They were guarded by the jute-mill police, a corps of guards who were armed with loaded canes. Besides the spinning and weaving of jute the mill saw stabbings, cuttings, clubbings, homosexual intrigues, assaults on guards, plots to escape, actual tunnelings through its brick walls, and conspiracies to murder and mutiny.

In their usual fashion newspapers and discharged prisoners described the horrors of the mill in terms of the wildest literary license. It was not a place a free man would have chosen to work in, but most of the convicts seem to have agreed with the convict writer Donald Lowrie that he did not find the mill the inferno it had been painted. Of all the troubles that started in the jute mill, practically none was brought on by working conditions in the mill itself.

Almost without a single exception every riot and mutiny that broke out between 1880 and 1950 was caused by food. The mill figured largely in these riots, but for incidental reasons. For the convicts, the mill was the center of their lives, a great place of congregation where unrest and rumors spread with electric speed and intensity, and where their leaders could organize revolts. For the management, jute and food were closely connected, for the control of the mess hall was the handiest method of enforcing mass discipline. Although Judge Ames had started the practice of paying each man in the mill ten cents per day, the legislature had forced the abandonment of the per diem pay, leaving food as the only medium of payment.

Paul Shirley improved the food in January, 1886, to soften the loss of wages, but by September the men were again complaining bitterly of tainted meat, filthy soup, sour bread, sloppy coffee, and spoiled beans served with cold fat. One day when the board was meeting at the prison, twenty men refused to go back to work after lunch, and, after much bad language and bad temper on both sides, managed to get a hearing before the board. The board listened to their complaints but chose to put more weight on Captain Edgar's advice that dissatisfaction with the food was only a pretext for making trouble for its own sake. Shirley told the board that he himself ate the prison food by choice because it looked "so tempting and nice," and reported that he was now serving the convicts pure coffee instead of a brew made from 40 per cent coffee and 60 per cent beans. The board sent the complaining convicts to their cells and forfeited their "good time."

July of 1896 saw convicts threatening another strike in the mill, claiming they had been served rancid pork, four-day-old bread, and meatless beans so hard they rattled in the pan. Captain Edgar hauled the leaders before the board, whose members proved surprisingly sympathetic and promised to see that the quality of the food was improved and the menu varied with regular servings of fruit and breakfast mush.

The revolting food was not entirely the fault of the prison administration; the legislature also bore some of the responsibility by its refusal to modernize the kitchen, which inspectors of the board of health found as dark as a cave and dripping with moisture. The inspectors also noted a leaky latrine in the tailor shop directly over the bakery. The food remained bad, partly through force of circumstance and partly through neglect. When the inescapable uprising finally occurred, it took the form of a great mutiny in the mill which was met with unprecedented violence by Warden Hale and his men.

The trouble broke out on Thursday, May 27, 1897. On the morning of that day the jute-mill gang of 720 men, more than half the total prison population, reported as usual, but when the machines started up they simply stood in their places, and lifted not a hand to spin or weave. The guards walked around, urging the men to turn to, but, as is always the case in prison troubles, even the most chicken-hearted prisoner feared the other convicts more than he feared the guards.

The machinery was turned off, and, in the unaccustomed silence, the convicts' voices turned into the howling of a mob, but the strike committee and the guards kept the men sufficiently in hand so that no appreciable damage was done, even though the mutineers could have completely ruined the plant, whose machinery was valued at a quarter of a million dollars.

The strike committee left the mill under a guarantee of safe-conduct to meet Captain Edgar and the warden at the captain's office. Warden Hale, white-bearded, sick, and trembling, heard the prisoners' demands: First was the discharge of the chief mess-hall steward and all convict cooks, with the choice of new cooks being left to the prisoners. The chief baker, a convict, was to be deprived of his good-time credit and brought before the board on charges of graft, making bread from maggoty flour, and encouraging his assistants to commit "unmentionable acts" while making the bread. Chaplain Drähms was to be replaced, as was Mrs. Van Dorn, the matron. The committee also protested the order forbidding the prisoners to receive gifts of fresh fruit, because fruit had been used as a vehicle for smuggling opium.

Although, according to the official account, Hale stood firm, it seems likely that, as other prison administrators have done in similar circumstances, the warden agreed to the prisoners' conditions with his fingers crossed, hoping to save the mill and get the prisoners to their cells without violence. If this was the case, he was successful, although at some expense of honor.

When the noon siren blew the men were marched, as usual, to the mess hall, but instead of the regular noon routine, the evening lockup bell was sounded, and, obedient to one of the prisoner's most strongly conditioned reflexes, the entire body of thirteen hundred convicts marched dutifully from the mess hall to their cells. The mutiny was over, broken by a combination of deceit and a brilliant stroke of applied psychology.

If the story of the mutiny had ended here, it would not have amounted to very much. It was remarkable so far only because of the number of men involved and the ease with which it had been put down without bloodshed and without destruction. But prison riots never end on schedule. The riot continued for two weeks longer, and it is clear that Hale and his officers were responsible for this evil.

As soon as the great mass of prisoners were locked up, the yard was filled with trusties carrying messages and officers and guards hurrying back and forth in preparation for a mass movement of men. The sixty-six cells along Kids' Alley were cleared of their youthful occupants, and four hundred of the strikers were crammed into these cells and into the eight-man tanks on the top floor of the stones. (Kids' [or Kid] Alley ran between two cell buildings, parallel to Crazy Alley and China Alley, and provided for the segregation of the boys from effeminate homosexuals such as Battleship Mag and Clara Bell—the "kid men"—in the yard. The men in the yard had a plainer name for it, which could be referred to in an official report only as the "alley of unmentionable name.") Another seventy men were packed into the fourteen dungeon cells. Gatling guns were trained on the tanks and on the dungeon entrance, a hundred rifles were borrowed from the San Rafael armory, ten extra guards were hired on the spot, and all off-duty guards were called up to form a cordon around the walls.

It is hard to tell from the accounts of these warlike preparations whether they were made before or after the prisoners began to shriek and howl and hammer on the steel doors of their cells. In either event, Warden Hale seems to have been thoroughly demoralized by the mutiny and to have reacted with the stupidity of a weak and panicked man. Furthermore, he was sensitive to the insinuations which had been made in the newspapers that under his administration San Quentin had turned into a pleasure resort to which convicted felons actually begged to be sent. Judging from his actions of the next few days, he was determined to break the back of the mutiny even after it had been, for all practical purposes, safely put down.

The uproar from the cells which started at six o'clock was described by a reporter as coming from men "shrieking like maniacs, rattling and pounding on the iron doors of their cells, working themselves into [a] hysterical frenzy, and cursing like demons of the pit." Shouting and pounding on their cell doors are the traditional way for locked-up prisoners to show their dissatisfaction, and the men in the tanks surely had every reason to feel frustration and anger.

Every hour when the watch called out the time and the ironic words, "All is well!" the uproar began again, becoming particularly violent whenever the men saw Hale or Captain Edgar in the yard. Hale, according to one account, "was literally driven from the spot by the obscene explosions that ricocheted about the courtyard from seven hundred pairs of lungs, and beat a hasty retreat through the prison gates." Frightened that some of the older cell doors might be battered down, Hale gave orders that any prisoner who showed his face outside a cell door would be shot.

The families of guards, local citizens, and reporters from the San Francisco papers gathered on the hills looking down on the prison as the uproar continued through the night and into the next day. The ration of bread and water was cut down from two servings a day to one, a half-loaf of bread, and a tin of water at eleven in the morning. Still the noise continued. Hale announced that he had the power, under the law, to trice men up by the wrists or thumbs and to inflict the cold-water punishment. The uproar continued. Hale had each cell opened and the beds and blankets, stools, candlesticks, tables, and all other furniture removed. The noise still went on.

The men in the dungeon had been left to themselves, five to a two-man cell, except when a trusty brought them their bread and water. At three-thirty on the afternoon of the twenty-ninth, when four guards were entering the dungeon, they were ambushed by the supposedly locked-up prisoners, who had broken through some of the brick walls inside. After a sharp scrimmage the guards escaped and returned with reinforcements. Two guards were hit in the head by bricks fired at them by the convicts. Captain Berlem, who was in charge of the assault, ordered the sentries on the wall to open fire on the hole through the bricks while he sent for guards armed with Winchesters. While the armed men covered them from the outside, Berlem and his guards entered the dungeon, subdued the prisoners, and removed them to tanks in the south cell house.

A noise truce prevailed for two more days until Monday, May 31, when the board of directors met and decided to enforce "the most strict discipline." Wholesale floggings and tricing up by the thumbs were discussed but voted down in favor of the fire hose. Governor Budd phoned from Sacramento to endorse the board's decision and to announce that any convict involved in further unrest could forget any hopes of executive clemency.

At six that evening, while all the extra guards stood to with instructions to shoot to kill, Captains Edgar and Berlem and forty guards proceeded to carry out the "strict discipline." The first assault was made on Kids' Alley. The cells were opened one by one and the prisoners brought out, searched, and ordered to make no further noise. As the party of guards moved down the long line of cells, a guard with a piece of chalk marked the cells from which noise continued to come. Then the guards returned, hauled out the men from the guilty cells, stripped them, returned them to the cell, locked the door, put the nozzle of the fire hose to the Judas hole, and turned on the water at full pressure.

The walls of the cells were brick and the doors were of solid boiler plate. As the water rose inside, some prisoners defiantly pulled the nozzle inside. Whenever this happened, the door was thrown open and the men inside knocked down with the full force of the water.

When the nine-o'clock lights-out bugle sounded, not a sound was heard from Kids' Alley except for the dripping of water. The back of the mutiny had been broken and rebroken, and the silence that followed did not mean peace but sullenness and cunning and desperation.

Warden Hale and Captain Edgar showed no mercy. Two days after the wholesale application of the water torture, which one newspaper jocularly called the "Kneipp cure," Edgar released only fifty of the mutineers. The rest remained naked and wet, their ration of bread and water cut even lower than it had been, some of them complaining of bronchitis and pneumonia. To inquirers who asked about the lost production in the mill, Hale explained that an inventory of three million sacks was on hand, enough to supply the market for an entire year. There was, in other words, no hurry. On June 3 half the remaining mutineers were returned to their cells. The mutiny was declared over, but when the jute-mill whistle blew at seven o'clock on Monday, June 7, 250 men were still on bread and water in the tanks. They remained there for another week as a memorable demonstration of the brutality of which incompetent men are capable when frightened.

Hale hired extra guards and announced that he was going to pay their salaries by cutting down the prisoners' tobacco ration from a pound per man per week to one-sixth of a pound. But neither the ferocity with which the riot had been put down nor Hale's measures to tighten up discipline afterward satisfied the San Francisco newspapers. Within a few months they were again referring to San Quentin as "a bower of beauty and ease" and the "Paradise of the Pacific for the shady elements of the world."

Chapter X

ED MORRELL'S STORY

UNTIL he became a noted outlaw Ed Morrell's life is obscure. We know that he was born in Pennsylvania and made his way to southern California, for in 1891 he was convicted in San Bernardino County of the crime of grand larceny and sentenced to two and a half years in San Quentin, where he was received as convict number 14486 under the alias of "Edward Martin." He was discharged in precisely two years, with six months off for good behavior.

Between his discharge from prison in March, 1893, and his arrest early in 1894, Morrell became thoroughly involved in the troubled affairs of the San Joaquin Valley, where the land agents of the Southern Pacific Railway were swindling the settlers with the help of the law. The "martyrs of Mussel Slough," seven settlers who were shot and killed in a disturbance in 1880, were still remembered fourteen years later, and feelings in the valley flared up at every new instance of the railroad's highhanded banditry.

An offshoot of this feeling was the formation of a band of robbers who called themselves the Outlaws and under the leadership of Chris Evans and the Sontag brothers led a sort of Robin Hood existence, holding up trains to take shipments of the Southern Pacific's money from the express cars and then escaping to hidden camps in the mountains. According to his friend Donald Lowrie, Morrell was in love with Evans' beautiful daughter. In any case, after Chris Evans was arrested, Morrell took Evans from the Fresno jail at the point of a pistol, relieving the Fresno chief of police of his own pistol in the course of the exploit. The policeman was shot by Evans, but it was the taking of his gun that led to Morrell's conviction on a charge of robbery and, in view of his prior felony, of a life sentence to the rock quarry at Folsom prison.

At Folsom, Morrell found himself singled out for the treatment reserved for notorious badmen in that notoriously brutal prison. Soon, he was hanging from a "derrick" in the dreaded Back Alley.

The derrick consisted of an overhead block and tackle hanging from a hook before each punishment cell. The prisoner's arms were extended behind him by a guard and two convict helpers, who fastened a pair of handcuffs around his wrists, and hauled his arms upward until only the tips of his brogans were touching the stone floor. This caused his head to be tilted down to the level of his waist. The convicts under punishment were stretched for five hours a day, two and a half hours in the morning and two and a half hours in the afternoon. Few men were conscious at the end of a stretch on the derrick, and fewer still could walk to their cells.

Another punishment that the Folsom guards found effective in dealing with difficult prisoners was the chloride-of-lime cell. Chloride of lime, which is used as a commercial bleaching powder, reacts with water to form hypochlorous acid, whose fumes are a powerful oxidizing agent. The prisoner under punishment was thrown into a cell whose floor had been covered with freshly dampened lime. The fumes not only suffocated the prisoner but burned raw the mucous lining of his nasal passages, mouth, and throat.

It is not hard to understand why Morrell became a prison outlaw and soon found himself en route to San Quentin as a desperate convict.

A year after his arrival at San Quentin Morrell took part in the jute-mill mutiny of 1897. A little later he became involved, to his great cost, with a bigamist, forger, and impostor who went by the name of Sir Harry Westwood Cooper. Sir Harry proposed that, since a new administration was about to take charge, he and Morrell and a few chosen friends might hasten their discharges by forging new commitment papers and substituting them for the originals during the confusion of the change-over. Sir Harry was a living refutation of the saying about honor among thieves; he not only betrayed Morrell in the matter of the forged commitments but also framed him on a charge of having guns hidden in the prison. In March, 1899, Morrell stood trial before the board of directors, who sentenced him to spend the rest of his life in a solitary cell in the Incorrigibles Department.

The establishment of the Incorrigibles had first been suggested by Warden Hale in 1894, but it was not until after the jute-mill mutiny that the directors ordered the work to go ahead. When completed in 1900, the Incorrigibles consisted of a double row of twelve sheet-iron one-man cells, six feet deep by four feet wide by five feet high, which shared the top floor of the old sash, blind, and door factory with the gallows room. For this reason the Incorrigibles was referred to colloquially as the Sash and Blind. The Sash and Blind was intended primarily as a place of punishment for the worst troublemakers in the yard, but, inevitably, it also became a convenient depository for emotionally disturbed prisoners, one of whom used to cry out plaintively hour after hour, "Come, come, come, I demand you to come! Won't you come now?"

Morrell was one of the first men to go into the Incorrigibles. He was locked up in a cell at one end of the row of cages; in another cell was Jacob Oppenheimer, whom the newspapers called the "Human Tiger" or the "Human Hyena," depending on how they were feeling toward him, and who, next to Morrell, was the most notorious prisoner in San Quentin.

The new warden, whom Morrell had been trying to outwit in the matter of the forged commitment, introduced the jacket or San Quentin overcoat, a form of punishment which was to be the terror of the dungeon and the Incorrigibles for thirteen years. Although Warden Martin Aguirre has also been credited with the invention of the jacket, it had actually been used at Folsom as early as 1884. It was a coffin-shaped piece of coarse, heavy canvas about four feet long. Along the sides brass eyelets were spaced four inches apart. Inside were two pockets for hands.

Aguirre ordered Morrell to be placed in the jacket until he gave up the location of the rumored hidden guns. Morrell was made to lie face downward on the canvas while guards laced a heavy cord through the eyelets in the back. The cord was cinched up as tightly as possible, tied fast, and Morrell left alone in his cell. Of the many descriptions of the torments endured by prisoners in the jacket, the most precise is the following, given by a convict to an investigating committee in 1912:

> After they put me into the jacket they played tug of war with me. The rope broke, and they got another. They lifted me a foot off the floor and let me fall several times. This was to knock the wind out of me and to use my natural weight to tighten the jacket. The pain begins in five or ten minutes. It's a suffering of the kidneys. It seems as if someone was crushing them in his hands, or as if they were jumping and trying to get away from you. Your hands begin to feel twice their size. The hands and arms all go dead, then come to life with sharp, keen pains. You have sharp pains in your stomach—sharp pains.

Morrell himself described to Lowrie how Warden Aguirre tormented him personally in order to induce him to give up the guns, threatening to tear his eyes out while he lay helpless in the jacket and kicking him brutally in the kidneys.

Morrell not only endured this punishment, but, according to both his own story and the official record, he conquered it.

Morrell himself claimed to have perfected an autohypnotic technique which not only released him from the agonies of the jacket but also permitted him to engage in such spiritual feats as wandering wherever he wanted to go. In Jack London's novel, *The Star Rover,* the character whom he calls by Morrell's name tells the narrator that his spirit frequently left his jacketed body and wandered around the streets of San Francisco. He had, he said, visited his mother twice, finding her asleep on both occasions. Though he could go wherever he wanted, he had no physical powers and could not open or close doors or make his presence known to people he was visiting. According to Lowrie, Morrell said that his "broken-down carcass" had been dead for years, while his life went on, on a higher plane.

The reader may take this as he pleases, but something extraordinary did happen to Morrell during the five years he spent in the Incorrigibles. Apparently moved by motives of simple decency, a new warden, Major John W. Tompkins, persuaded the board to revoke Morrell's sentence to the Sash and Blind and personally went to interview the prisoner. If he was expecting gratitude, he was disappointed, for, according to Lowrie, Morrell said, "I've been throwing people down and cutting their throats all my life. I'm no good. I don't know what honor is. But if you want to give me a chance to cut your throat, why, all right."

Although rebuffed by Morrell's manner, Tompkins told him, "I'm going to turn you out of here tomorrow and I'm going to give you one of the best jobs in the prison. You're not going to throw me down either. That's all." Morrell, blindfolded against the bright glare of the sun, was led down the long flights of stairs from the third floor of the old building. Lowrie, who was the trusty who took him to a bath and issued him a clean suit of stripes, saw a thin young man of medium height, with long, straggly blond hair and beard, and alert, steel-gray eyes that protruded slightly. He had lost seventy-five pounds in the Incorrigibles, and his limbs were severely emaciated, the joints of his knees and elbows standing out like huge knots through his yellow skin. In the prison barbershop "Old Frank," the veteran head barber, offered to shave Morrell with his own hands, but before he put the razor to Morrell's cheeks he called the attention of the spectators to the striking resemblance between the newly-released Incorrigible and Jesus Christ.

A week later Tompkins appointed Morrell head key-man, a position in which he was in charge of the prison keys and acted as chief assistant to the lieutenant of the yard, rivaling that officer in responsibility. Ironically, Morrell's duties included accompanying the dungeon officer on his rounds. Now, he ate at the Red Front, the eating room where the trusties dined on "outside" tableware at tables covered with cloths. Tompkins' faith in Morrell was justified, and the story of the Incorrigible who became head trusty spread outside the walls.

Unlike most other famous convicts, Morrell did not slip into obscurity after his sentence was commuted in 1908. He and his San Quentin friend Donald Lowrie began lecturing on prison reform, arguing primarily for the abolition of corporal punishment. They took a strait jacket and a portable derrick with them, demonstrating both devices on volunteers to the horrified fascination of the audiences, and very likely contributing to the abolition of corporal punishment several years later. Morrell's was not a voice crying in the wilderness, for he was heard before the state legislatures of California and Pennsylvania and, in 1918, before a committee of Congress. He became friendly with Jack London, who used Morrell's experiences in his novel *The Star Rover*. Later, Morrell collaborated with the young lady who was to become his wife in the production of his own story, *The Twenty-Fifth Man*. In spite of a rather purple style, it is an extraordinarily interesting book about a man whose life was clearly out of the common prison pattern.

Chapter XI

DEATH BY HANGING

UNTIL 1891 executions were conducted in the county jails of California rather than in its state prison. In San Francisco murderers were strung up in the yard of the old county jail on Broadway, events which are still well remembered by some octogenarians. Even at San Quentin convicts found guilty of murder inside the prison were taken to San Rafael to be dispatched at the hands of the sheriff. The sheriffs were relieved by law of this unpleasant duty in 1891, but the paraphernalia of rope and trap were not used at either Folsom or San Quentin until two years later.

The first man to hang from the gallows which Warden Hale had built on the top floor of the Sash and Blind was José Gabriel, otherwise known as Indian Joe, a friendless and simple-minded murderer of an aged farm couple. Hale, who had turned down a suggestion that the scaffold be erected in the yard for its cautionary effect, imported for the occasion a veteran hangman, Colonel J. W. McKenzie, who brought with him his three deputies. Indian Joe, who until the end insisted he was really just about to leave on a trip to San Diego, was hanged as scheduled, and the *Chronicle* observed justly that "the only point conclusively proved by Gabriel's execution is that the California law concerning capital punishment is swift and sure in the case of a murderer who has no friends or money. . . ."

The newspapers did not, however, have to wait long for a murderer worthy of them. In 1895 a young San Franciscan named Theodore Durrant was accused of the murder of two young women under circumstances which every city editor in the town recognized as being a gift from a kind Providence. Durrant was christened the Demon Killer of the Belfry and, until his execution in January, 1898, the newspapers followed his case with lip-licking attention to the least detail that might titillate their readers. It was a performance whose sheer obscenity makes such recent journalistic orgies as the reportage of the deaths of Barbara Graham and Caryl Chessman seem as flat and innocuous as a pious lecture by an Episcopalian canon.

Durrant was a young man of respectable, though rather foolish, family. He was a medical student, an assistant Sunday-school superintendent, and a pillar of strength in the Christian Endeavor Society. His sexual life was rather odd, but until after his arrest this was nobody's business but his own. (When he visited the Commercial Street brothels he carried a chicken or a pigeon and, according to Herbert Asbury, "at a certain time during the evening's debauch he cut the bird's throat and let the blood trickle over his body.") His crime consisted of murdering Minnie Williams and Blanche Lamont and hiding their mutilated bodies in the library and belfry of Emmanuel Baptist Church.

Durrant was convicted and sentenced to hang, whereupon he was installed in a cell in Murderers' Row, the first tier of cells on the north side of the Stones. As is always the case, the condemned men were by and large unfortunates who were either too poor or too simple-minded to escape the death sentence. One man, seventy-eight years old, claimed to have been an 1840's settler and probably was, but he was now so senile that he could no longer remember the name of the man he had killed, although he could mumble a story of justification to the high-minded and humane reporters who interviewed him. At length he was reprieved.

Every bit of information about Durrant's life that passed through the prison gates—and some that was sheer invention—was reported to the eager citizens of San Francisco, but until he was prepared for execution, the newspapers had a relatively hard time of it. Durrant's life on Murderers' Row was a generally monotonous routine, broken only by attendance at a Bible class organized by a pious murderer and by the visits of his parents, which were frequent. In view of the public interest in his prisoner, Warden Hale allowed Durrant's father to visit him even while the prison gates were under double guard during the jute-mill mutiny.

The uneventful life on the Row came to an end on the last day of June, 1897, when Durrant was transferred to the death-watch cell in the Sash and Blind. "I am going to take you up-stairs," Captain Edgar told him simply. Before he made what was expected to be his last walk across the yard Durrant was bathed and given clean underwear and a fresh suit of stripes. Accompanied by both captains and four guards, he walked across the garden that faced the Stones, down the stairway to the "tower yard," along the alley that ran beside the Sash and Blind, and up the outside staircase that took him to the door of the death-watch cell. At the last landing he turned and looked over the prison and the surrounding countryside in a manner that the attending newspapermen found profoundly affecting. The death-watch chamber was a cage built of slats only ten paces from the gallows, and furnished with a couch and a gas jet high out of reach. Here Durrant settled down to wait for his execution, but, to the joy of the newspapers, he was reprieved and was sent back to the Row.

Durrant's reprieve was also a reprieve for Warden Hale, who had been faced with an inordinate demand for tickets to the affair. One of those demanding admission was Mrs. Durrant herself, who professed her determination to remain with her boy until the end. Although even her husband thought this determination unseemly, there was a curious and unexplainable official reluctance to utter a simple administrative order that no members of the family would be permitted in the gallows room. As it turned out, Mrs. Durrant was persuaded to withdraw, but only on condition that her husband take her place. Thus it was that when Durrant was executed on January 7, 1898, it was both the best-reported and most bizarre execution that has ever taken place in California, or, I dare say, in any other state.

In the gallows room a stretched rope had been looped over a beam above the tall trap. About 120 spectators were gathered in the 60-foot long room when a door opposite them opened and the death procession entered. The procession was led by Warden Hale, who was followed by Father Lagan, the Catholic chaplain, who wore his priestly robes and carried a missal in his hand. Lagan had converted Durrant to Catholicism; later he was to make public his conviction that the boy was innocent. After the priest Durrant himself came, arms pinioned, supported by two guards. Then followed Captain Jamieson and the hangman, Amos Lunt, "mild of aspect, with a frank face, a steely but gentle blue eye—not a cruel man but firm." Durrant's father entered with the official procession and took a place in the front row of spectators. Although Mrs. Durrant was waiting in a room at the other end of the same floor, the Durrants had suffered a cruel disappointment: the warden had refused their request to have a kinetoscope made of the hanging.

Durrant, his accompanying guards, Father Lagan, and Amos Lunt mounted the scaffold. When Durrant protested his innocence and said he had been convicted by the newspapers, his father turned to the crowd and asked, "How's that for a brave boy?" While Father Lagan murmured in Latin, Amos Lunt adjusted the black cap and the hangman's noose. Warden Hale raised his hand, and the three guards concealed in a sort of sentry box cut three cords, one of which released the trap. As the onlookers surged forward, Durrant senior cried testily, "Stand back!"

Durrant's neck was broken by the fall, but the attending doctor continued to listen to his heartbeat for eleven minutes before declaring him dead. Afterward the doctor said it was the most perfect hanging ever carried out at San Quentin.

The most grotesque part of the execution was still to come. After Durrant's body was cut down, it was placed in a prison-made black coffin, but when it was learned that the parents had brought a casket, the body was transferred and carried to the room where Mrs. Durrant was waiting. The hangman's cap was taken off, revealing Durrant's face, almost black, the eyes half-protruding and the lids half-open. Mr. and Mrs. Durrant leaned down and kissed the lips of their dead son. Mrs. Durrant broke down and cried; her husband also wept as they tried to compose their son's features into a more normal expression. Everyone present is said to have turned away in sympathy with the couple's grief.

When the spectators turned around again both Mr. and Mrs. Durrant were sitting near the casket. Mrs. Durrant was smiling. They were chatting pleasantly together when the convict assigned to tend the room inquired if Mrs. Durrant would care for a cup of tea. "Thank you, I would," the lady replied.

Instead of bringing back merely tea, the room tender brought back a tray loaded with solid food from the kitchen. A table was laid a few feet from the corpse, and the two Durrants sat down and ate heartily. An eavesdropping reporter who professed to be shocked and disgusted by their appetite was careful to record in his story that he heard Mrs. Durrant say, "Papa, give me some more of the roast."

After they were through eating, the bereaved parents had the casket closed up and taken to a carriage which was waiting to take them to the Sausalito ferry slip. As a rival newspaper noted waspishly, the carriage had been ordered and paid for by the *Examiner*. The rope which had hanged Durrant was cut into souvenirs and sold at the going price of a dollar an inch. The bits of rope multiplied as miraculously as pieces of the True Cross, and if they could all be gathered together now, they would surely reach from San Quentin to the belfry of Emmanuel Church and back again.

In May, 1899, Warden Hale, who was old and ailing, resigned, leaving the post open for another 'nonpartisan" election. (The elimination of party considerations was achieved by choosing the San Quentin warden from the ranks of Republicans and the Folsom warden from the Democrats, or vice versa. Generally, the party in power took over the pleasant marine vistas of San Quentin, while the opposition was banished to the sweltering stone barrens of Folsom, a hundred miles from the fleshpots of San Francisco.) The choice of Governor Henry T. Gage, a Republican, fell on Martin Aguirre, a former Los Angeles sheriff, and the board of directors obliged with his election.

Quite apart from his other attributes, Aguirre was the most evil-looking man who has ever served as warden of San Quentin. The portrait of Aguirre that now hangs in the warden's office shows a swarthy man with a highwayman's mustache and only one good eye. If he looked like a pirate, the appearance was not deceptive.

Aguirre entered office like a buccaneer taking over a ship, bringing with him a full company of retainers from Los Angeles, including his brother, Joseph, who was installed as general overseer and acting warden. Captain Berlem was fired out of hand, but Captain Edgar hung on for a year before he resigned after quarreling with Aguirre over some of the sharp corners that the warden had cut.

The newspapers did not have to wait long for the first scandal. On December 10, 1900, C. J. Walden, the business manager of the jute mill, disappeared suddenly, leaving behind a fascinating story. Walden was neither a politician nor a run-of-the-mill accountant, but a former San Quentin convict who, on the occasion of his pardon, had exchanged his stripes for a neat business suit and taken up residence with his wife and children in one of the houses on the prison reservation. He did not even have to change his desk, for the job for which the state now paid him a salary of $140 a month—almost three times a guard's pay—was the same job he had filled during the seven years he had spent as a model prisoner. He was balding and sober in appearance, and his only known dissipation was joining other German residents of Marin County in Sunday shooting matches at Schuetzen Park, a mile from the prison.

Walden's disappearance reminded everybody concerned that his original sentence had been twenty years for the crime of embezzlement. The prison directors belatedly decided to look into affairs at the jute mill, but their investigation was hampered by the disappearance, by burning, of the mill books for the fifteen years from 1881 to 1896. Eventually they established the fact that Walden had been systematically embezzling the state, fraudulently charging tens of thousands of sacks to Miller & Lux and the Southern Milling Company, two of the mill's largest customers. The sacks had actually been shipped to a San Francisco junk dealer who sold them at a nice profit to himself and Walden. The junk dealer was taken to the courts and forced to make restitution, but Walden never returned.

A year later the newspapers were in full cry again, led by the *Call,* which opened the attack with a monster banner headline: *SCANDAL OF THIEVERY, FORGERY, AND CORRUPTION BURSTS UPON SAN QUENTIN PRISON, INVOLVING WARDEN AGUIRRE AS INSPIRING CRIMINAL AND GOVERNOR GAGE AS BENEFICIARY.* Even boiled down from the *Call's* virulent page-one prose, the charges were serious enough: Aguirre had, the newspaper said, employed convict forgers to doctor the prison books and bills; he had had furniture made in the prison shops for his brother and for Governor Gage, and, finally, Mrs. Gage and Mrs. Aguirre had charged dress goods bought at Levi Strauss & Co. to the San Quentin account.

The scandal broke in the last week of May; in August the Republican state convention was to meet in Sacramento to consider Gage's renomination. Gage had no choice but to bring a libel suit against the proprietors of the *Call*. The case was heard in court while the convention was going on, a circumstance which hardly strengthened Gage's hopes for renomination. On August 27 the assembled Republicans handed the nomination to George Pardee. On the same day the libel case was recessed. Eventually, after further recesses, it was dismissed. The next January the *Call* noted with a straight face a paragraph in Gage's farewell address in which the departing governor recommended that libel be made a felony.

Aguirre managed to serve out his full four-year term even though the smell of scandal became riper every month. In February, 1903, an assembly committee sat down at San Quentin to look into charges that men had been crippled and even killed in the jacket. The investigation followed the usual program for such affairs. Former convicts and current prisoners testified that men were jacketed for twenty-four hours at a time, that the cords were laced so tightly they cut into the flesh, that one man had suffocated from a gag, and that, speaking for themselves, they would rather be triced up by the thumbs than go into the jacket. One convict witness testified with unusual expertise; he had once served as a guard at Sing Sing, where, he said, the punishment was even worse than at San Quentin. The committee also heard that, though the jacket was not used on female prisoners, they were punished by inordinate sentences to dark cells.

With something of the formal grace of a ballet, the prison officials moved onto the stage, pirouetting gracefully behind the lead of Aguirre and Dr. P. F. Casey, who testified to the mildness of the jacket as a physical restraint and its wholesome spiritual effect. Aguirre denied that cathartics were ever forced down the throats of men in the jacket, denied that the jacket was ever cinched up tight, and asserted that the men who claimed to have been injured really suffered from "bad blood." The jacket, he said, was no worse than a woman's corset, and, considering the corsets of the time, he may not have been far wrong. A couple of brave committeemen allowed themselves to be cinched up briefly and reported no ill effects. The committee was divided on the degree of cruelty they found in the jacket, but there was a general feeling in Sacramento that Aguirre had got himself into too much trouble even for a loyal Republican. He was permitted to finish out his term, which ran until July, 1903, but he was not encouraged to renew his candidacy. (Although Aguirre himself dropped out of prison affairs entirely, brother Joseph turned up shortly as general overseer at Folsom, testifying to the political hardihood of the family.)

The newspapers were under the impression that Aguirre's successor was to be John C. Edgar, the former captain of the yard, who had testified for the defense in the Gage libel suit. Instead, the directors selected Major John W. Tompkins, Ed Morrell's liberator. Although Tompkins' term of office was to be no happier than Aguirre's, he was a man of an entirely different, and considerably more admirable, personality.

Tompkins had been Oakland's first chief of police and had also served as city clerk. His title of major came from service in the military forces of his native New York. In California he had risen to the comand of a quasi-military organization known as the Republican Alliance. Major Tompkins was a handsome, well-turned-out man with gray hair and a military mustache. His personality, as it was revealed in his management of the prison, was rigid and authoritarian. He was honest and had little regard for the extralegal perquisites that had traditionally been enjoyed by San Quentin officers. It was this last characteristic which, more than any other, led to the thoroughly unpleasant situation in which he embroiled himself.

Characteristically, Tompkins inaugurated his administration with a generous use of the ax, firing or accepting resignations from the incumbents of notoriously "fat" jobs and redefining the duties of other positions in such a way that the unhappy officers were faced with the terrible prospect of eight hours a day of reasonably demanding work. Tompkins fired other guards without preferring specific charges, simply informing them that he wanted to fill their places with more efficient men.

The wholesale clearing out of Aguirre's favorites was all to the good, but Tompkins was constitutionally too inflexible to adjust to the prison community, which is essentially political rather than military. By the end of 1905 Tompkins was not speaking either to his principal deputy, Captain of the Yard James Russell, or to Clerk J. M. Oliver, who was in charge of the business affairs.

The point at which the unhappiness of the employees boiled up into rebellion came when Tompkins began using convicts to spy not only on other prisoners but also on the 120 officers and civilian employees. From his corps of stool pigeons Tompkins learned that the aprons of the local saloonkeepers were washed in the prison laundry, that some guards were in the practice of bribing convict butchers in the commissary to save the tenderloin and sirloin for their own kitchens, leaving the round steak for the others, and that other employees were feeding their pigs with prison swill.

The guards fought back with countercharges. A prisoner named Harry Smith was identified as the chief of Tompkins' convict detectives, and was said to be immune from punishment, as were his assistants. The prison bandmaster and several of his musicians were said to have been thrown into the Incorrigibles for having objected to giving up a bunk in the Red Room, where they lived and practiced every night after the five-o'clock lockup, to a nonmusical stool pigeon. Tompkins' enemies tried to hoist him on his own petard, charging that an ex-convict whom he employed as his son's tutor traveled in a buggy driven by a guard. He was also said to have committed the heinous crime of boarding his son's pony at the prison stable. More seriously, his enemies brought forth evidence that he had kept a man in the jacket for 139 hours running, although the board had decreed a six-hour maximum. Tompkins was also said to have used the hose on noisy prisoners on New Year's Eve, which traditionally had been the one night of the year when the men could work off their hatred of the guards in an orgy of cursing, screaming, and raking of cell doors.

By the beginning of December, 1905, Tompkins had thoroughly alienated not only his own subordinates but also the board of directors, who ordered the prison pay roll held up while they investigated the charges made against the warden. A reporter who visited the prison wrote that "the very air seems to breathe suspicion. Warden Tompkins passes his officers with a nod. They are his equal in curtness. Everyone about the prison, from warden to convict, seems to be on his good behavior and fearful lest he make some move which will be interpreted as suspicious. The officers are now very careful not to be seen talking together frequently. The warden stands aloof."

Instead of eating at the warden's mansion, as was their custom, the board of directors ate in the officers' mess on the days when they heard witnesses. When the investigation began, the convict bookmakers in the yard were offering odds that Tompkins would go; a week later the odds were three plugs of tobacco to one that he would stay. But Tompkins was not his own best witness. He accused Captain Russell and Clerk Oliver of plotting against him, and said his desk had been ransacked and his house put under surveillance. He defended the stool-pigeon system, and, in the matter of discipline, not only defended the jacket but also recommended that San Quentin adopt the Folsom practice of "creasing" convicts who got out of line, which is to say, of shooting them. The odds on the yard swung against Tompkins, and across the bay the *Chronicle* predicted correctly that Tompkins would be gone within a week.

Tompkins left with full honors, including a banquet, a testimonial signed by ninety-six employees, an inscribed gold watch, chain, and locket, and a eulogy delivered by the foreman of the road gang. The warden's parting shot was in character: Of twelve guards he had fired only ten days before his resignation he said, "Well, they were a nice lot of cutthroats anyway, and I was too lenient with them."

Tompkins was succeeded by John C. Edgar, who had first been appointed to the guard line in 1880 as keeper of the front gate, who had advanced to the office of captain of the yard, and who had already come and gone according to the political fortunes of the Republican party and his own relations with the incumbent warden. Warden Edgar served without particular distinction until, in April, 1907, he was taken seriously ill and resigned, making room for John E. Hoyle, who was currently serving as clerk of the prison board and who was to become San Quentin's first modern warden.

Chapter XII

COMING OF THE NEW PENOLOGY

THE literature of the professional penologists is often quite un-intelligible to the outsider, even though the ideas that stand be-hind the awful jargon of the sociologists and their scholarly brethren are not particularly profound. The twentieth-century prison-reform movement which has been called the "New Pe-nology" is a gorgeously rococo structure erected on a foundation that consists of a few basic ideas: first, that criminals are created not by simple meanness but by a variety of causes, some rising out of the criminal's own nature and some out of the world in which he lives; second, that the object of a prison is reformation rather than punishment; and third, that in treating the criminal (the verb is used advisedly), kindness, decency, and the techniques of social case work are more effective than brutality and repres-sion. These are ideas which have become so thoroughly entrenched in our conventional wisdom that they are accepted by virtually all right-thinking citizens as representing the finest flower of enlightened modern thought. In California, at least, it would be hard to find a layman who is not persuaded that the New Pe-nology was brought to San Quentin by Clinton Duffy in 1940.

As we have seen in the course of this history, the facts are quite otherwise. With the exception of the contributions of Drs.

Freud and Pavlov and other modern psychologists, the broad features of the New Penology were laid out in the official preachments of San Quentin's officers almost from the very beginning. In 1858 John Weller spoke out for the idea of reformation rather than punishment and in favor of short sentences, the segregation of youthful offenders, the judicious use of the pardoning power, and a general attitude of kindness and sympathy on the part of the officers and guards. Although the legislative committee of 1861 expressed great faith in the reformative powers of religious conversion, in the 1870's James A. Johnson was advocating more worldly measures, such as individual treatment of each prisoner, "good-time" credit, and single cells. Drs. Taliaferro and Stillman had raised their voices against the whip, the water cure, and the dungeon, against the cruelty with which insane criminals were treated, and against the plight of the ex-convict. Captain Gilchrist and Professor C. C. Cummings had made themselves partisans of the value of education in the reformative process. The fact that the actual management of San Quentin did not often square with these high ideals is, for the moment, quite beside the point. The point is that even as early as 1880 the main ideas of the New Penology, which were becoming the common property of literate people everywhere in the United States, had reached San Quentin.

The formal advent of the New Penology to the United States may be dated precisely on October 12, 1870, when, at the founding meeting of the American Prison Association, the assembled wardens adopted a declaration of principles so advanced that many of its provisions have still to be put into general practice. While the New Penology was gaining supporters, however, the newspapers were engaging in recurrent campaigns against "coddling" prisoners, and the public was generally indifferent to their welfare.

With the beginning of the new century the general attitude toward prisons and prisoners began to change radically as humanitarianism became fashionable. Within the next few years articles about the New Penology became staple items in such magazines as the *Atlantic,* the *Forum,* and the *Literary Digest,* and even newspaper feature writers told their readers of the wonders that could be achieved in a prison run decently and reasonably. In retrospect, much that was written seems naïve, but as an organized social impulse it was a welcome contrast to what had gone before.

Still, the period between the adoption of the "nonpolitical" system of administration in 1880 and Hoyle's appointment in 1907 had not by any means been an entirely dark age whose history consisted only of rioting, medieval punishment, and official malfeasance. When Hoyle took office, the face of San Quentin had changed markedly since Judge Ames had assumed office as the first full-time warden.

The most striking legal innovation had been the passage in 1893 of a parole law. The idea of parole had been in the air since Ohio passed this country's first parole law in 1884. Seven years later the California prison directors had felt obliged to turn down a petition by San Quentin convicts asking permission to raise funds to hire a lawyer to draft a parole law like those in Ohio and New York. The law which was passed two years after this was not hailed with universal admiration, and, although it was administered cautiously, within five years it was under heavy fire in the press and legislature. The case that caused the greatest outcry was that of a paroled youth who crossed the line to Utah, organized a gang of desperadoes, terrorized the natives, and killed two or three of the posse sent to catch him. On the whole, though, it seems likely that the paroled men were more sinned against than sinning, being exploited and blackmailed by greedy employers who were delighted to be able to hire workers who were so completely in their control.

A second innovation of the nineties, which was hailed by its friends as a giant step forward and just as enthusiastically damned by its enemies, was the establishment of a reformatory at Whittier and an industrial school at Ione for the reformation of erring youths. These had been in operation only a few years when one of the prison directors denounced them as preparatory schools for San Quentin and Folsom, a charge which has been repeated frequently, and with some reason, ever since.

In spite of the operation of the parole law and the funneling off of the youngest prisoners to the new reform schools, a mounting number of prisoners continued to press against the walls. In 1904, fifteen hundred convicts were locked up in six hundred cells, with five or six men in some cells that had been built for one. On Sundays and holidays, when the men had the freedom of the yard, there was hardly any room for them to move about. The warden and the directors' perennial demand for more cells was finally answered in 1905, when the legislature made the first appropriation toward modernizing the prison by building three great concrete cell blocks to supplement the four old Spanish-type buildings. The first of these, whose construction was under way when Hoyle came to office, was to be known as the South Block, a great, gloomy, echoing cave of a building which was the largest cell house in the world when it was opened up in 1913 and is still the longest.

The decision to go ahead with the new buildings gave a final and definitive answer to the recurrent suggestion that San Quentin be abandoned. As late as 1894 the directors had urged that the prison be razed and the land sold at a profit for suburban home-sites, with Folsom to become the principal state prison. Now, huge crews of convicts, reinforced by fifty troublemakers transferred from Folsom, began the tremendous job of leveling Cemetery Hill south of the old prison.

The reorganization of the Women's Department in 1885 had not necessarily brought much relief to the unfortunate females who lived above the captain's office. The building itself was enlarged, and the women were put to work in their own workroom, sewing prison clothing, including the blue uniforms which they themselves wore. They were, for the first time, put under the care of a matron, but she was a woman of a coarse and brutal nature whose regime was not noticeably softened by the monthly visits of the Sisters of Mercy. The only diversion possible for a woman cooped up in the dismal world of the Women's Department was to have had the foresight to arrive pregnant, whereupon the directors would vote permission to take her to a hospital outside the walls during the period of childbirth and for a reasonable time thereafter. There were 27 women in the old yellow building when Hoyle took over.

San Quentin's first Roman Catholic chaplain, the same Father H. Lagan who officiated at Durrant's hanging, had been appointed visiting chaplain in 1888 on the urging of Archbishop Patrick W. Riordan of San Francisco, who was himself in the custom of frequently visiting the prison for the confirmation of fifty or sixty convicts at a time. The Salvation Army also became active in work with the prisoners, holding Sunday services in the yard and also helping the men going out on discharge or parole. They were later joined in this good work by the rival organization, the Volunteers of America. The Billy Grahams of the day added San Quentin to their itineraries, and the prisoners, always delighted with a break in the routine, turned out in gratifying numbers. On Christmas Day, 1899, for example, five hundred men listened to the noted Unitarian preacher, B. Fay Mills, before being marched off to a holiday dinner of roast pork.

Thanks to visitations by inspectors of the state board of health, sanitary conditions had improved somewhat, although the morning march of the bucket brigade to the Rose Bowl continued to be a daily feature of San Quentin life for years. The prisoners' bath, an open-air cold-water plunge, was moved into the upper yard, where it was more readily available for a convict's weekly bath. Some finicky prisoners preferred to stay dirty rather than enter the water where a thousand other men had washed off the dirt and sweat of the jute mill, bathed their sores, and left behind them the mingled germs of various loathsome diseases. Later, tubs were placed here and there, allowing some fortunate men to bathe in more decency.

It was also during this period that the newspapers began reporting the sort of human-interest items that are typified by the story that old Mary Von, doing life for murder, had asked the board for a set of false teeth so that she might once again eat solid food. The question of false teeth (or eyeglasses or wooden legs) nicely summarizes some of the attitudes toward the New Penology. To the ordinary reader of newspapers, that universal expert, providing false teeth for convicts is equivalent to turning a prison into a sybaritic paradise and weakening the very foundations of justice. To the warden, the number of edentulous prisoners is an administrative problem which is only partly solved by setting up a "toothless table" in the mess hall. In 1903 the plight of a starving man in Mary Von's predicament moved a state senator to note that "when a fellow needs teeth, he needs them bad," and to threaten to take up a missionary fund for the purpose of providing dentures for deserving cases. (As a matter of record, Mary Von finally got her plates in 1912, but enjoyed them for only a year before she died.)

The new spirit that was at large did not, of course, miraculously sweep away San Quentin's problems, some of which were reminiscent of the days of Estell and McCauley. In 1904, for example, the board found it necessary to report its difficulty in hiring competent guards for a salary of $50.00 a month plus board and lodging, an increase in pay of precisely nothing during fifty years. Also traditional was the sporadic warfare waged by the directors against the saloons that thrived illegally outside the prison gates. Although a state law forbade drinking places within a mile of a prison, the San Quentin saloonkeepers broke the law frequently, refusing even to pay their taxes and counting, with apparent success, on the benevolence of the local district attorney to save them from prosecution.

The greatest of the chronic problems, however, was opium. After the introduction of opium into San Quentin in the 1860's by the Chinese, the use of the drug spread throughout the prison until the number of addicts was estimated at from an eighth to a half of the population. The most alarming official figure was that of Dr. T. B. Eagle, who reported in 1896 that half the new prisoners received from the cities were addicts. There were attempts to make the traffic in drugs a crime, but they failed regularly in the face of a strong opposition. As late as 1889 the California legislature refused to pass a bill making the preparation and sale of smoking opium a felony.

Even though the traffic in opium could not be made a felony in the state at large, the wardens of San Quentin could and did make it a capital crime within the prison walls. The captains of the yard waged vigorous warfare against the drug, but, in spite of frequent reports that victory was theirs, the ingenuity of the smugglers always won out.

The most common and successful method of smuggling was to "plant" the opium outside the walls, where it could be dug up and brought in by trusties. In 1897 a man who had been discharged only a week earlier was found planting opium in the warden's garden. He had, he explained, bought the drug with his gate money and hoped to run his initial investment up to a decent sum. The judge could give him only 120 days in the county jail. A year later trusties working in the piggery tried to smuggle seven pounds of the drug in lard cans after a session of hog butchering. A few months later a guard was caught lowering half a pound of opium on the end of a string from his post on the wall. The trusty who had betrayed him had to be put in protective custody to save him from the infuriated convicts. Opium was also thrown over the walls at night, brought in by visitors, hidden in cigars and fruit, stolen from the dispensary, and acquired by any other means that seemed to have a chance of success.

The opium war was sometimes enlivened by open battles. When, in 1898, a vigorous guard named S. L. Randolph searched the cell of Jack Kane and Joe Keyes at the six-o'clock unlock, he discovered fifty-seven packages of opium tucked into various corners. Keyes knocked Randolph down, whereupon Kane leaped on the guard and tried to throttle him. Keyes, meanwhile, attempted to get rid of the evidence by throwing it into the yard, setting off a wild scramble among the men who had already left their cells. Both Guard Randolph and the opium had to be rescued by a squad of club-swinging guards. Randolph's intrepidity in exploits such as this led to his appointment as captain of the yard a few years later.

A typical sentence given by the board to a prisoner involved in the opium traffic was the loss of a year's good-time credit and sixty days of the ball and chain. One of the liveliest of these disciplinary sessions occurred when a thief named O'Donnell was being examined. Several cakes of opium lay on the table. Under the pretext of showing the board members that one of these cakes was really not opium, O'Donnell palmed another cake and, pretending to wipe his nose, got it into his mouth. The captain saw him chewing, took him by the throat, and forced him to spit it out. The board gave O'Donnell thirty days of ball-and-chain.

Finally, in 1899, the legislature made it a felony to bring opium into the prison grounds. Within two months San Quentin's addicts were suffering acutely from an opium famine. They stretched their remaining supplies by adopting the classic technique of the "mainliner," mixing opium with water in a spoon, heating it with a match, cutting open a vein with a sharp knife, and injecting the opium solution with a medicine dropper whose tip had been ground down as fine as possible. By September of the same year convicts told reporters that no opium had come through the walls in the past two months, and fifteen of their number lay in the hospital, suffering the agonizing symptoms of withdrawal. The board announced that the traffic had been destroyed.

With the disappearance of opium, the convicts were forced to find other stimulation. Someone discovered that a considerable charge could be derived from drinking a tea made from boiling a belladonna plaster in water. The doctor wondered at the increased demand for belladonna plasters until the ever-vigilant Guard Randolph investigated the curious case of a convict who told him a Bengal tiger had just jumped over the prison wall.

Two years went by before a considerable quantity of opium was again found inside the prison. A ring of smugglers led by one "hypo" had been engaged in planting and smuggling, selling the precious drug for $50.00 a pound. A year later the board complained that smuggling was again common on the "Hill Road," a public thoroughfare which ran through the prison grounds, and, after five pounds had been found in the barbershop, Warden Tompkins announced that he intended to keep the prison free from dope if it cost him a leg. But three months later fifty ounces were taken from Mexican prisoners who carried it in their tobacco sacks.

Although the new law was equipped with some real teeth— smugglers were sentenced to as long as eight years in Folsom— the traffic went on in spite of the efforts of Warden Edgar and Randolph, now captain of the yard. Just before John Hoyle took command of the prison twenty-five men employed in Sack Alley struck briefly to protest the dungeoning of twenty men found with opium on their persons.

There was also a chronic trade in alcohol, but whisky is bulky to hide and aromatic on the breath. The most ingenious of the whisky smugglers was an educated convict who wrote himself a prescription in Attic Greek, which he asked a friendly guard to have filled for him in San Rafael. Because both the guard and the pharmacist to whom he took the prescription were unlettered in Greek, the pharmacist was obliged to ask the help of the Greek master at the local military academy, who cheerfully rendered a translation: "One quart of alcohol. Please label bottle *For rheumatism. Apply at once.*"

These, then, were some of the aspects of the wildly chaotic mixture of paradox, contradiction, and anachronism to which John Hoyle fell heir when he took office in 1907.

In San Quentin's collection of portraits of its past wardens John Hoyle immediately arrests attention for his open face and air of good-natured intelligence. This appearance was not deceptive, for, according to a literary friend, Hoyle was "a most amiable man, bubbling over with good nature." He was a newspaperman from the far north of California, where, in Shasta County, he had edited *The Mountain Miner,* been active in fraternal affairs, and served as chairman of the Republican Central Committee. After a brief period of indoctrination as clerk of the prison board Hoyle was appointed warden to square a political debt. The circumstances of his appointment to San Quentin were less than promising, but, although Hoyle was never a formally ordained missionary of the New Penology, this was in effect what he became.

The general atmosphere of Hoyle's administration may be sensed from two seemingly unrelated events. The first of these is that on Hoyle's first New Year's Eve in office the convicts, for the first time in the memory of the oldest guards, refrained from their wild and destructive celebration. The second is that in January, 1912, a convict was shot in the leg when he attacked the contractor in charge of a work gang. The significance of the shooting was that it was the first time a prisoner had been shot by a guard since Hoyle had taken command five years before.

Hoyle's reforms were built around the general principle of keeping the prisoners busy at useful work in an atmosphere which was as much like that outside the walls as it could be made.

One of the most widely publicized features of the new order was the great show which the prisoners organized for New Year's Day, the Fourth of July, and other holidays. Although a convict ensemble calling themselves the Iron Gate Minstrels had performed in earlier years, it was not until Hoyle's time that minstrel shows, vaudeville, plays, and orchestral concerts became regular features of San Quentin life. As the years went on, the "Cons' Own Show" became more and more elaborate until the New Year's Day show came to take up a full day.

To a cynic some of Hoyle's ideas seem a trifle soft-headed. The distribution of 3,600 Easter eggs is a case in point, while the production in the prison of *Alias Jimmy Valentine* by H. B. Warner's company has a suspicious air of press agentry to it. Yet the Easter eggs served in the mess hall were the only eggs enjoyed by the prisoners during the year. The spontaneous gesture of kindness, even though it was often sentimental, came naturally to Hoyle. When during his first Christmas in office Hoyle saw that the men had with massive irony hung dirty stockings from their cell doors, he sent a guard into San Quentin village to buy all the candy in the grocery and had the stockings filled before breakfast.

The most sweeping of the planned reforms, the classification of prisoners according to the nature of their crimes and of the men who had committed them, had been proposed by the board of directors in 1904 while Hoyle was serving as its clerk. The plan, as Hoyle worked it out in the warden's office, would involve the complete segregation of three classes of prisoner, each class to have its own living quarters, mess hall, exercise yard, and a distinctive uniform. First-termers arriving at the prison would be assigned to the second class until they had either shown that they deserved promotion to class one or demotion to class three. There were various proposals for uniforms, the most imaginative plan calling for the first-class convicts to wear civilian clothes, the second-class men to wear a sort of cadet uniform, and only the untouchables of the third class to remain in stripes. The plan was endorsed by the directors, but when stripes were finally abolished in July, 1913, all the men went into the now-familiar blue-gray uniform, and segregation remained a hopeful plan for the future. Hoyle himself had more than one reason to be glad to see the stripes go. For years he had been suffering under invidious comparisons between the physical appearance of Folsom men and San Quentin men, to which he good-naturedly explained that it was only the ring-around stripes worn at Folsom that made the men look plumper than their San Quentin colleagues, whose stripes ran up and down.

A more successful reform than the attempt at segregation was the enlargement of the prison school. The school had been ordered abandoned in 1893, with no audible protest from Chaplain Drähms, and though it had been revived in 1906, it was still under Drähms' management. The average attendance was fourteen students. Hoyle did not find Drähms a congenial subordinate and finally got rid of him by abolishing the office of chaplain, an awkward stratagem made necessary by the virtual impossibility of firing a Civil War veteran from a state job. (There was a hint later from one of the directors that Drähms had been selling pardons.) Eight months later the chaplaincy was resuscitated and the position filled by the Rev. William H. Lloyd, who had been chaplain at Folsom. One of Lloyd's first activities was to interview all the prisoners under twenty-four and assign the illiterates to day school. The day school got off to a promising start with 112 students, who were required to attend until they could pass an eighth-grade examination. Half attended for two hours in the morning and the other half for two hours in the afternoon. Lloyd was assisted by three convict teachers. A night school was also organized for the older prisoners, who were assigned according to race into a colored, a white, and a Spanish-Italian class. The academic standards of the night school can be judged from the fact that the colored class was taught by a bright

Negro boy who was himself enrolled in the day literacy classes.

As the chaplain's department gained new strength, invitations went out again to prominent inspirational speakers to address the men. The prisoners were consequently treated to such lecturers as the Rev. Charles Brown, who delivered his famous Lincoln's Birthday address, Mrs. Maud Ballington Booth of the Volunteers of America, and Z. P. Smith, founder of the Golden Rule Club. Five hundred of the prisoners were said to have been so impressed by Brother Smith's prospectus that they took the pledge "to do good, be good, and make good."

More important, with the help of the Women's Christian Temperance Union and the California Club, Hoyle managed to arrange the discharge of Matron Van Dorn, who was universally disliked. Although the WCTU failed in its campaign to have women represented on the board of directors, the lot of the women improved a good deal. Besides bettering the women's living conditions, Hoyle was capable of the sort of gesture on which more than one reform warden has built his reputation. In the early spring of 1910 Hoyle issued a mysterious order forbidding anyone to pick wildflowers on the hills above the prison. Then, on a Sunday, the 32 women convicts, dressed in fresh blue uniforms, were escorted from their crowded quarters by the matron and two male guards. For several hours they hiked over the hills, plucking wildflowers to decorate their cells. (The newspapers were careful to note that among them was Emma Le Doux, who had stuffed the drugged body of her husband into a trunk.) The walks continued on one Sunday a month.

The use of the parole law increased tremendously, with about two hundred men a year going out on parole. At any given time about 10 per cent of the San Quentin population would be finishing their sentences outside the walls. In the period around 1910 the directors, who also sat as the parole board, reported that the rate of parole violation was only about 10 per cent. This was an astonishingly low figure, but, alas, it rose several per cent when more parole officers were hired, allowing closer supervision of the men. It is also interesting to note that, although the public at large has a picture of the average convict spending long years of his life behind the walls, as early as 1909 the average time served by all prisoners except lifers was just over two years and nine months. The figure has changed by only a few months in the fifty years since then.

Even that chronic shame of San Quentin, the incarceration of lunatics and cranks in the foul shadows of Crazy Alley, seemed about to yield to the modern spirit. At Folsom a gang of convict workmen was set to work on a stone structure that was to be operated by the state lunacy commission as a hospital for the criminal insane. It was to be known as the Folsom State Hospital, but the convicts called it the Bug House until, in 1942, another generation of convicts tore down the partly-finished stone walls.

At about this time there was another change in San Quentin's population. Since Civil War days the prison had been boarding federal prisoners not only from the Pacific Coast states but from as far away as China and the Philippines. Most of them were civilians convicted in federal district courts, but about a third were Navy prisoners convicted of crimes too heinous for summary punishment in the ships' brigs. During 1908 and 1909 about fifty United States convicts were on hand, but beginning in 1910 the federal government began sending all but a few short-termers back East to the first federal prison at Leavenworth. Navy prisoners, however, continued to come to San Quentin for some years more. All this was not, of course, Hoyle's doing, but it is part of the emergence of the modern look in American prisons in which he was playing a leading part.

Hoyle concerned himself not only with the welfare of the convicts but also with the welfare of that forgotten man of prison administration, the lowly guard, hated by the convicts and despised even by the man on the street. One of Hoyle's first acts had been to recommend a raise in pay for his men, the restoration of their commissary privileges, and a cash food allowance for married guards, some of whom were forced by sheer poverty to eat free meals in the guards' mess in order to cut down the food bill at home. Drunkenness was still one of the commonest causes for dismissal; Hoyle suggested that providing the guards with a gymnasium and a billiard room might keep them out of the saloons that continued to flourish outside the gates until the local district attorney was at last persuaded to arrest their owners.

There was, then, every reason for the newspapers to indulge their local pride when in 1910 the new South Block was opened for their inspection. Not only was the San Francisco Bay area about to possess the most modern prison in the country, but its warden was known nationally as one of the three or four leading men in his profession. His admirers credited him with breaking up the con-boss system, with governing by withholding privileges rather than by the strait jacket and the chloride-of-lime cell, with fighting for a system of segregation, and, in general, with turning San Quentin from about the worst prison in the United States into one of the best. But only two years later John Hoyle was to start down the same road of riot, investigation, and scandal which so many of his predecessors had unwillingly taken.

On the morning of Saturday, June 8, 1912, nobody at San Quentin had any good reason to expect trouble. There had been no mass demonstrations for several years, and during the months just past the convicts had been thought to be in an excellent mood. Warden Hoyle was closeted in a routine directors' meeting when, at eleven-thirty, the nineteen hundred prisoners in his charge began to file into the mess hall for a meal of soup and stew. Fifteen minutes passed in normal mealtime fashion, the men bending silently over their tin plates as they shoveled away the food. Then, at eleven forty-five, a convict said loudly, "Pass the vinegar," and the riot was on.

Leaders at seven tables throughout the huge hall jumped to their feet and pulled the tops off the tables, spilling the remains of soup and stew onto the floor. Howling for the blood of the steward and his cooks, men threw their food at the walls and dumped the buckets of the convict waiters. The twelve guards on duty in the mess hall reacted according to their natures. Some fled, some hid, and some tried to break up the riot. Guard Redmond, who rushed into the midst of the rioters, slipped on the greasy floor, and was covered from head to foot with soup and stew before he escaped. In the kitchen, Steward Frank B. Moulton waited not upon the order of his going, but fled precipitately through an open window. Moulton was luckier than a convict waiter who, to escape the anger of his fellows, threw himself through a closed window, taking sash and glass with him and landing in the yard outside with a broken ankle.

Hoyle rushed into the yard from the directors' meeting, saw Captain Randolph restore order, and had the prisoners marched to the cell blocks. The men were ordered to disregard their cell assignments and enter the first empty cells they came to. This maneuver and the lockup afterward were handled entirely by trusties. Two hours later Guard Redmond, wearing a fresh uniform, returned to duty in the yard. As soon as the men in the cell blocks saw him they began to rake the bars and hammer on the doors. Hoyle reluctantly ordered the fire hose, but when the men saw the guards fastening the hose to the hydrant they became quiet again. Hoyle had four of the leaders of the riot locked in dark tanks, and punished the rest by serving only beans for supper.

If any newspaper readers saw the riot in terms of college-boy restlessness they were soon disabused. The riot was repeated at the noon meal the next day. The unarmed mess-hall guards were again attacked, and even the redoubtable Captain Randolph was knocked down. A young Navy prisoner named Harold Lynwood started out the door into the alley. According to one account, he was leading a mass movement of rioters; according to another, he was simply removing himself from the riot. From a guard post overlooking the alley a guard named Harold Grubb raised his rifle, fired, and shot Lynwood through the heart. In the kitchen, the steward's crew defended themselves by turning the live-steam hose on the rioters. Again extra guards rushed into the mess hall, and eventually the men were locked up safely. This time thirty-four men went to the dark tanks, where they would live for six months on "poverty fare."

The dead boy, Lynwood, had been young and well liked. He had been convicted, not of a crime of violence, but of impersonating an officer. The guard who killed him was thoroughly disliked; he had served for years as a keeper of the Incorrigibles, where his name had become synonymous with stupidity and abuse. There was howling that night, and the fire hose had to be used on Kids' Alley, but the guards themselves took up a collection to allow Lynwood's mother to bury her son outside the cemetery on Boot Hill.

On Tuesday Steward Moulton resigned for reasons of health. In his place Hoyle appointed a veteran guard, William J. Duffy, who was popular with the prisoners and who had once demonstrated remarkable coolness when he had disarmed a giant convict who had just murdered another man. ("I'm ashamed of you," Duffy had said. "Give me the shiv.") Duffy was also the father of a fourteen-year-old boy named Clinton.

Life at San Quentin appeared to go back to normal after the riot. On the following New Year's Day there was no raking of the bars, and the prisoners were treated to a monster program produced by the San Quentin Minstrel and Vaudeville Company. It started off with a grand minstrel show, followed by olio acts, "German" comedians, Spanish dancers, an artistic club swinger, a female singer, buck-and-wing dancers, a close-harmony quartet, several skits, a comic monologue, a "Laughable Afterpiece," and movies of the Flynn-Johnson fight. Afterward Hoyle stood in the exit to the mess hall, calling the men by name and wishing each one a happy New Year as the prisoners filed out. In February the sixty-nine-year-old but indefatigable Sarah Bernhardt and her troupe presented on an improvised stage in the yard a play written by her son and called *A Christmas Night Under the Terror*. Nine prisoners took part as supernumeraries. A French-born convict read Bernhardt a testimonial in her native language and, for the benefit of the audience, translated the flowery tribute into English. But not even these cheerful events could cover the deep scars left by the June riots, nor, to change the metaphor, could they brighten the shadow of the new storm that was about to break around John Hoyle's head.

The charges of cruelty and mistreatment which were presented to a legislative committee in March, a month after Bernhardt's visit, had little to recommend them in the way of originality. Public accusations had been brought against Hoyle and Captain Randolph by Dr. E. E. Duncanson, a graduate of the medical school of the University of Michigan, who had spent three years in San Quentin on conviction of abusing his stepdaughter. The girl later retracted her story, and Dr. Duncanson left San Quentin with a tale of neglect and mistreatment on the part of the prison authorities, topped off with the charge that the prison doctor had threatened to sterilize or castrate him but, foiled, had merely tortured him with a pressure enema.

Other convict and ex-convict witnesses appeared in Duncanson's wake, testifying largely against Captain Randolph and the keepers of the Incorrigibles, Guards Grubb and Wambold. The investigators heard of jacketings, of castor oil, of blackjackings, of chloride of lime, and of the rainbow-colored meat that had touched off the June riots, which the newspapers, in their unaccountable fashion, called the "bread riots." They also heard that whenever the stew began running low the convict cooks were ordered to "play the hose in the barrel." The *Bulletin*, which on provocation could go into hysterics six times a week, and did, told the story in tones of righteous horror, and demanded Hoyle's expulsion. Colonel Dennis M. Duffy, president of the board and one of Hoyle's strongest supporters, retorted that the newspaper's real motive was to harass the directors until they voted to parole the curly-headed grafter, Abe Ruef, who had been convicted of corrupting virtually the entire San Francisco city government.

In Hoyle's defense, the clerk of the board, Mark Noon, submitted an impressive sheaf of affidavits impeaching Dr. Duncanson's truthfulness. The administration then trotted out a parade of 19 reliable convict witnesses, including as many unfortunate doctors, lawyers, and bankers as they could round up in the yard. The former superintendent of an orphans' home, imprisoned for lascivious conduct, testified that he had never seen any prisoners unkindly treated, and that the food was splendid. His story was corroborated by a disgraced police captain and, in a lawyerlike and almost interminable presentation, by San Quentin's reigning celebrity, Abe Ruef himself, who was now employed as prison librarian.

Of Warden Hoyle one of these educated witnesses said, "If Jesus Christ were to supersede Warden Hoyle, the majority of the convicts would find fault with His administration." It was a fair comment. Even Hoyle's enemies pictured him as a decent and kindly man; even Captain Randolph's friends admitted he was a narrow-minded disciplinarian without a nerve in his body. (Once, an ex-convict had tracked Randolph to a saloon, with the intention of shooting him. Randolph walked up to the man, saying, "Why don't you shoot?" so unnerving the assassin that he dropped his gun hand and shot Randolph only in the foot.) To Hoyle's enemies this suggested the picture of a weak and amiable man permitting his brutal subordinate to run the prison as his private torture chamber. To Hoyle's friends, Randolph's sternness and efficiency were a concession to the practical realities of keeping order among almost two thousand criminals. There was no question that the food was often bad (the meat, the commissary officer admitted, tended to become "flabby" in the summer), that Captain Randolph understood justice better than mercy, and that Grubb and Wambold were permitted to run the Incorrigibles pretty much as they pleased. Yet the main argument in Hoyle's defense was unanswerable. In 1905, two years before Hoyle became warden, 250 men had been punished in the jacket; in 1912 only seven men had been jacketed during the entire year, and in the first three months of 1913 none at all.

When it came, the committee's report was a complete victory not only for Hoyle but also for Captain Randolph and even the steward's department. The only criticism ventured was that Hoyle was "altogether too merciful and kindhearted to maintain the best prison discipline, as many prisoners take advantage of his abundance of human sympathy to the detriment of proper order." The committee confessed manfully to having been prejudiced against Randolph, but, now that the scales had dropped from their eyes, they saw that he was invariably just and fair. The food, "flabby" meat and all, was found to be "overabundant and of excellent quality." Even the friendly *Chronicle* was struck with wonder.

In June, when Hoyle's appointment ran out, he was reappointed without opposition. A month later he took the men out of the hated stripes, leaving only parole violators in striped shirts. Instead of the civilian clothes and cadet uniforms called for in his ambitious plans, however, the men went into their blue-gray uniforms, and the segregation of the various classes remained a hopeful plan for the future.

Then, suddenly, at the beginning of November, barely four months into his new term, Hoyle resigned. He gave as his reason undue interference by the board, and there was no doubt that there had been friction over the handling of an investigation into graft. The newspapers all knew of a deeper and darker reason which they were not free to print—"the sinister shadow of a story that won't be told." Whatever the story was, it had to do with the breaking up of the close friendship of Hoyle and Colonel Duffy. It was Duffy who had saved Hoyle from his enemies in the cruelty investigation and it was Duffy who had persuaded Hoyle to stay on after Governor Hiram Johnson had appointed some new and hostile directors. What had happened between the two men nobody would say. Colonel Duffy himself was a thorough gentleman, saying of his former friend that Hoyle was the best warden California had ever had. It was a judgment with which nobody except the *Bulletin* showed any disposition to quarrel.

Chapter XIII

WAR, WOBBLIES, AND THE GREAT AIRPLANE PLOT

THE PENDULUM of public opinion is notoriously irregular, but once they were committed to prison reform, the press, the politicians, and the public at large continued for a number of years to look with favor on the New Penology. In spite of World War I, the years between 1910 and 1929 were years of confidence in the eventual triumph of progress, and Californians, like Americans everywhere, were happily innocent of the disillusionment ahead of them.

In prison affairs the spirit of the times was expressed by James H. Wilkins in 1918:

> Crime itself is on the wane, mainly, of course, because some of the main incentives thereto are in a fair way to be removed. Opium and its products are practically unobtainable by addicts, alcohol is on its last legs, dives, deadfalls, and the other houses of crime are being cleaned up. It is a long cry before our prisons, jails, and other like institutes of detention will bear upon their rusty gates the legend "Closed for want of inmates." But we are heading in the right direction, and in that direction I trust society will persevere.

Wilkins was no naïve idealist but a newspaperman and politician who, since the 1880's, had served two terms as prison director and who had seen at firsthand the great jute-mill mutiny and the Aguirre and Tompkins scandals.

Even though John Hoyle had retired to the management of a San Francisco hotel, San Quentin remained firmly pointed in the "right direction" under his successor, James A. Johnston (not to be confused with an earlier warden, James A. Johnson, without the *t*). Johnston was a newcomer to prison work, who, in 1912, had unexpectedly been asked to give up his position on the state Board of Control by Governor Hiram Johnson in order to bring the New Penology to Folsom. He had distinguished himself by abolishing corporal punishment at Folsom, and his administration of San Quentin seemed to show every symptom of success.

Johnston's first major contribution was to establish camps to which well-behaved prisoners were assigned to build state highways. As an incentive, besides escaping from the confining atmosphere of San Quentin, the prisoners received an extra day's credit for every two days spent at camp. The first of these "honor camps" was established in the beautiful and rugged logging country in the north of the state. Six months later the experiment was declared a success; only six men had tried to escape, and all of them had been captured. The road camps became permanent establishments and were on all counts a considerable improvement on the old San Quentin road gang, whose most notable achievement had been a road from the Tiburon ferry through San Quentin to San Rafael.

Johnston also wrote a long-overdue law separating the functions of Folsom and San Quentin. Repeaters and parole violators were henceforth sent to Folsom, while San Quentin became the receiving point for all newly-convicted prisoners. In line with these reforms, the building plans went ahead, and there was real reason to hope that within a few years each of the young, reformable first-termers assigned to San Quentin would enjoy a modern cell of his own, equipped with plumbing, electric lights, a comfortable bunk, and decent ventilation.

The progress of World War I provided more opportunities than usual for the inspirational functions which, as we noted in Hoyle's administration, are one indicator of a reform-minded prison regime. The general tone was set by the secretary of the San Quentin Agricultural Club, who in August, 1918, begged Secretary of the Interior Franklin K. Lane to "give men who missed their footing in the battle of life a chance to do their bit for America." Although the law denied convicts, and even ex-convicts, the opportunity to redeem themselves at Château-Thierry or the Argonne, they did their bit. A collection of $1,150 was turned over to Warden Johnston to buy Liberty Loans, while, on a humbler level, the prisoners were urged to deposit half their tobacco ration in red-white-and-blue barrels, some of which were actually sent to the troops in France. In the female department, 28 women emulated their free sisters by volunteering to sew and knit for the Red Cross. The newspapers did not take long to get the message: as the *Examiner* put it, "The sword unsheathed for democratic ideals glints with reflections even into prison cells."

Johnston was an able administrator, but he had a weakness for the inspirational side of the New Penology, which continued strong even in peacetime. Among the speakers whom he lured to San Quentin were William Jennings Bryan, the two Booths—Maud Ballington of the Volunteers of America, and Evangeline of the Salvation Army—the Rev. Billy Sunday, and assorted educators, theosophists, and secular uplifters. On Mother's Day, 1919, twelve hundred convicts wearing white carnations heard a Salvationist brigadier preach on "Mother," an address that stimulated the heaviest day's mail in history. (The whiteness of the carnations was apparently a tribute to the sorrow the convicts had caused their mothers rather than a sign they were all orphans.) A few years later sixteen hundred men who had volunteered to test the theories of Dr. Emile Coué were given booklets of instructions and Coué rosaries of twenty knots. (Dr. Coué was an exponent of positive thinking who flourished in the twenties.) Prof. Damascus Garcia Gavieres Gallur, a musician with a genuine talent for personal publicity, enrolled his entire prison band, and through the Big Yard was heard the murmur of "Day by day, in every way, I am getting better and better."

For some reason which defies logical analysis, the modern wardens of San Quentin have all shown an affinity for show people. Johnston began the custom of turning over the production of the all-day New Year's show to professional entertainers from San Francisco. The Big Show has somehow acquired a halo of sanctity during the years and even now seems to be considered as a major contribution toward the rehabilitation of its audience. At various other times Johnston invited a widely-assorted panel of musicians, actors, athletes, and movie stars to the prison, chief among whom were Douglas and Mary Pickford Fairbanks, the royal couple of Hollywood. ("It was a gray day of wind and rain and more rain, but 'America's Sweetheart' brought a ray of cheer and brightness," Johnston reported in his book, *Prison Life Is Different*.) The movies which were shown the prisoners were selected personally by the warden, who inflicted on his captive audience such morbidly wholesome films as *The Little Minister, Rebecca of Sunnybrook Farm, Penrod and Sam, Orphans of the Storm, The Ten Commandments,* and *Peg o' My Heart*.

The encroachment of the modern age on the prison was seen dramatically in the grotesqueness of The Great Airplane Plot. The postwar growth of aviation caused exceeding nervousness to Warden Johnston, who noted the numbers of planes, both civilian and military, that swooped down to take a look at San Quentin. For a while Johnston suffered these visits patiently, but he was forced to take action in April, 1923, when the guards reported that a plane had dive-bombed the yard with a package that was never recovered. With the possibility of aerial drug smuggling in mind Johnston proceeded to set up his defenses. He conferred with the Air Corps commander at Crissy Field, who ordered his pilots to avoid the prison by two thousand feet. The guards on the walls were instructed to take the numbers of low-flying planes, and, for the newspapers at least, Johnston talked of installing antiaircraft batteries. These precautions paid off before the month was out. A light biplane with a man standing on the wings flew low over the prison, setting off an air-raid alarm and bringing warning shots from guards. The plane returned in spite of the hostile reception; this time the defenders opened fire with a machine gun, breaking the propeller and sending the plane into a dive into the nearby marshes. When an armed party of guards reached the scene of the crash they discovered that the man they had seen on the wing was not a dope smuggler but a daredevil movie cameraman taking footage for a film. Unhurt, he had already set up his equipment on land and was grinding away while the pilot slopped about in the marsh, checking the damage to his craft.

To one group of prisoners the Coué strings, white carnations, and Liberty Loan drives were nothing more than a capitalist plot to befuddle the working classes. These convicts were the Wobblies, members of the Industrial Workers of the World, who had been convicted of the offense of "criminal syndicalism" as defined by a hysterical wartime law. Before the war organizers of the IWW had roamed the lumber camps and grain fields of the Pacific Coast, enrolling migratory workers whose membership was scorned by the craft-oriented American Federation of Labor. There were never very many Wobblies in California, but, particularly after the Russian Revolution of 1917, they were blamed for every outrage not otherwise accounted for, from hayrick fires to infernal machines. When caught, they were promptly convicted and sent to San Quentin with sentences of one to fourteen years. (The indeterminate sentence law of 1917 established maximum and minimum terms for the various crimes, the actual time to be served being set by a board of terms and paroles.)

Johnston had several reasons for wishing the Wobblies had been sent somewhere else. In April, 1918, the San Quentin educational program came under fire when the *Examiner* revealed breathlessly that one Dublin Bob, who had allegedly taken a University of California extension course in chemistry at San Quentin, was the inventor of the phosphorous bomb believed to be used by the Wobblies. The newspaper scolded Johnston for letting such unpatriotic types study chemistry, obliging the warden to point out to the editor that the university did not attempt to teach chemistry by correspondence to anybody at all, in prison or out. This was a minor incident, however, compared to the distress the Wobblies caused Johnston by declining to be treated like ordinary convicts.

They were for the most part big, heavy-muscled Poles, Swedes, Germans, and Russians, who spoke English with thick accents and carried around dog-eared copies of such incendiary writers as Plato and Nietzsche. They remained loyal to their curious beliefs and declined all favors, even refusing to apply for parole because to do so would be an admission of guilt. They were, consequently, blamed for every disturbance in the shops, most notably for a jute-mill strike in October, 1918, when five hundred of the eight hundred men in the mill quit work after a fist fight between a convict and the superintendent. In 1922 and 1923 the Wobblies adopted the strategy of passive resistance, deliberately inviting Johnston to put them in the dungeon. There were repeated strikes, with up to sixty men choosing to go into solitary on bread and water rather than submit to unjust and tyrannical work. The atmosphere of the times thoroughly endorsed the harshest measures Johnston was willing to take.

The Wobblies were a temporary phenomenon of the sort that has been noted in every country of the world that has jailed political prisoners together with felons. The Red scare lasted through 1924, when sixty "criminal syndicalists" were committed to San Quentin. The next year there were only two, and in 1926 none at all. One by one they went out as their terms expired until, according to Robert Joyce Tasker, who had done time with them, "they were no more than a memory—a breed of steadfast, principled men—a group as noble as had even been known in the midst of the misery that is prison." This is perhaps a sentimental and romantic view of the Wobblies, but it is a necessary and proper antidote to the opinions of the man on the street.

After the last Wobbly was gone, one political prisoner was left whose activities overshadowed all the rest. This was Tom Mooney, convicted of the 1916 Preparedness Day bombing in San Francisco in which ten people had been killed. Although Mooney's guilt or innocence can still start an argument in a San Francisco bar, there are good grounds for believing he was framed. After his death sentence had been commuted to life imprisonment Mooney was set up in a cell in the Stones, where he pounded a typewriter in a twenty-two-year fight for a pardon. He was, on the whole, treated well, being assigned to "bonarue" jobs in the officers' mess and the dairy ranch. ("Bonarue" is an all-purpose adjective said by inmate philologists to derive from *bonne rue* and meaning first class or desirable.) Mooney himself was energetic, determined, and resourceful in his own cause, and his organized friends outside the prison bedeviled the authorities expertly. San Quentin was thoroughly glad to bid him good-by after his pardon by Governor Culbert Olson in 1939.

Of scandals in the more formal sense there were practically none during these years. Two officials had been dismissed in 1913, the prison doctor, for incompetence, and F. L. Arbogast, who doubled as steward and hangman, for appropriating prison coal for his own house. In 1920 there was an abortive scandal in which the San Francisco journeyman tailors charged that guards had clothing made in the prison tailor shop. Johnston replied that this indeed did happen, but that the clothing was uniforms for guards who could not otherwise afford to buy them out of the $80.00 monthly salary. In 1922 the Protestant chaplain was fired for kiting out a manuscript containing the life story of the notorious murderer Bluebeard Watson. Except for a few other minor incidents, the surface of San Quentin showed a deceptive blandness.

Johnston resigned in November, 1924, to go into private business. (Later he was to return to prison work, most notably as warden of Alcatraz.) In eulogizing his administration one newspaper wrote innocently, "San Quentin today is a sort of university and health center combined." Of course it was nothing of the sort, as events were to demonstrate very soon.

The new warden's qualifications for the job were that he was the state printer, a former composing-room trouble shooter for the Hearst newspapers, and son-in-law of Governor Friend W. Richardson, who, as a candidate of the Old Guard, had taken over Sacramento from Hiram Johnson's Progressives. Frank Smith took office with a great flourish of trumpets for the New Penology, announcing that he intended to establish an academic and vocational high school accredited to the University of California. Although he denied reports that he was going to found a college, he explained that his high-school faculty would be drawn from the nineteen inmates with academic degrees, including Ph.D.s from Melbourne, Wisconsin, and Moscow universities, an L.H.D. from Edinburgh, and assorted masters and bachelors from such institutions as Harvard, Columbia, and California. The students were to be divided into freshman, sophomore, junior, and senior classes, and would attend school part time, working at their regular jobs the rest of the day. Besides expanding the school, Smith intended to industrialize the prison, providing jobs for three thousand men in the jute mill, the new furniture factory, and the road camps. He showed his humane earnestness by moving the thirty-three inmates of Crazy Alley into decent cells in the new block. Except for a certain air of ballyhoo about the school there was nothing at all in Smith's plans to which any decent person could take exception. Nor was there any reason to expect that Smith's regime would be remembered for its violence rather than its liberality.

The trouble this time was not food but the racial hatred that had been growing in the crowded cell blocks and mess hall. As early as 1914 there had been signs of serious racial distress when more than a hundred Negro prisoners went on a hunger strike to protest the enforcement of segregation in the mess hall. In 1923 there had been a near-fatal knife fight involving three whites and three Negroes. When, in 1925, racial troubles broke wide open it was strangely not whites and Negroes but whites and Mexicans who were at one another's throats.

In San Quentin's early days racial feeling was directed mainly against the Chinese, who, as we have seen, represented a clannish group of aliens who were generally regarded as disgusting in their personal habits. The small number of Negroes were not merely tolerated but often enjoyed some status as prison characters. The Mexicans were looked down on as "Mexes," "greasers," and "chili chokers," but they were tolerated as long as they kept their own company. During the early years of this century the racial complexion of San Quentin began an important change. The Chinese, who had once represented one prisoner out of six, declined rapidly in numbers while the Negroes increased. (The Chinese were also no longer regarded as filthy but merely as exotic; Warden Smith and his officers and guards were willing and honored guests at an elaborate banquet the Chinese prisoners organized for their New Year celebration.)

By 1925 there were 247 Negroes and only 61 Chinese out of a total of just over 2,300 inmates. The number of Mexicans was impossible to determine, since they were then counted as white, but the 1925 prison census shows 412 men born in Mexico, to which must be added an unknown number of California-born men of Mexican stock. The Mexicans and Mexican-Americans together may have amounted to as much as a quarter of the prison population.

The race riots of 1925 began only six weeks after Johnston turned over the prison to the new warden and the officials and guards who followed in his train. The new guards (in the prison lingo they were called "fish bulls") were uncertain of themselves, officious, and, in the eyes of the prisoners, ridiculous. The guards did not create the trouble that came, but they were responsible for the climate of unrest in which it broke out with such sudden violence.

The trouble started on February 17 with an insignificant and inconclusive quarrel between a Mexican and a white man. That evening the Mexican was trapped by a crowd of whites underneath the "dog shed" in the Old Prison yard. The Mexican drew a knife and dared the whites to get him. The guards broke up the mob before anybody was hurt, but the next day the Mexican was ambushed at his job on the top floor of the shops building and beaten to death by eight or ten whites. The word flashed across the prison yard and through the jute mill, where open warfare broke out. Men were cut and clubbed along Loom Row and Sack Alley, and when the quitting whistle blew, the men were searched one by one for the homemade knives stashed in their boot tops or under their shirts.

In spite of this precaution a riot broke out as soon as the men reached the upper yard. Armed with knives, lead pipes, iron bars, and rocks, twenty-four whites attacked fourteen Mexicans, who were similarly armed. When guards moved in, swinging their clubs, the rioters disarmed them and used the clubs on each other. The general alarm was sounded, and the gun guards at the wall posts began to fire cautiously. Thirty minutes after it began the riot stopped. The body of a Mexican well known as a brawler was later found behind a large rock. He had been beaten and trampled to death. The men involved in the fight were all locked in the dungeon.

In early March, as the February rioters were being returned to the dungeon from the bathhouse, a white man was shot and killed by a guard. There are two versions of the killing. The official version was that the prisoners had picked up rocks and attacked the four guards escorting them. The other version was that the dead convict had merely stooped down to pick up a contraband cigarette butt when a trigger-happy guard, whose aim was better than his judgment, shot him dead.

Race war broke out again at the end of April, this time, curiously, with the knife murder of an Indian by a Mexican. The murderer was himself wounded by a guard. The next day there were two revenge killings and a knifing in the jute mill. In the morning, as a Mexican walked past one of the machines, a white man jumped out, stabbed him fatally, and disappeared before the guards could identify the killer. After lunch a white man was killed, presumably by a Mexican, under similar circumstances. Still work went on in the mill until, later in the afternoon, the dead Indian's cell partner was knifed. After this there was a general shakedown of the jute mill, which yielded 130 knives. That night the guards talked uneasily of a plot to murder all the Mexicans in the mill. Twenty-one more men went to the dungeon, and Warden Smith canceled all visits and entertainments.

Reports of San Quentin's race war, in which six men had died, were heard far beyond the prison walls. Even as a doubled guard force shook down the entire prison for weapons, hundreds of Mexicans demonstrated before the United States consulate in Mazatlan. The Mexican ambassador in Washington demanded an immediate investigation. Governor Richardson came down from Sacramento to direct the inquiry in person. As a result, two convicts were transferred to Folsom. One of them, Spud Murphy, the keeper of the prison ball field, was suspected of organizing a general riot.

After the riots were over, San Quentin seemed to return to normal. In July Professor Gallur and his twelve-man band began to play at meals. The professor's program included "I'll See You in My Dreams," as the processional, as it were, and "Cheatin' on

Me" as the recessional. The band also played every Sunday morning for a bizarre social affair that was known as the Jockers' Ball. (A jocker is an aggressive homosexual, one who goes out of his way to "make a punk" of young and attractive convicts. Jockers are also known as "wolves.") While Professor Gallur led the band in dance music, hundreds of jockers and queens waltzed and foxtrotted under the 300-foot-long iron roof in the Big Yard. A veteran guard remembers the Jockers' Ball in these words: "You either danced with your girl or she found someone else who would. It was the damnedest sight I've ever seen." (Effeminate homosexuals are invariably referred to in the feminine gender.) Dancing, Frank Smith explained, is good exercise and music keeps up morale.

In spite of the appearance of what passed for normality, racial trouble broke out again in November. This time a white prisoner attacked a Mexican as the men were lined up in the yard to march to their cells for the evening lockup. A wall guard fired a warning shot at their feet, which ricocheted, wounding two Mexicans. It was a minor outbreak compared to the mass violence earlier in the year, but incidents such as this made it increasingly clear that the reformative powers of simple decency, "science," education, and a squashy religiosity had not proved entirely adequate to the realities of San Quentin.

Frank Smith turned in his resignation in January, 1927. The immediate cause was not the riots but the failure of his father-in-law to win re-election as governor. The new prison board, now representing the Republican Progressives, kept Smith on the job until July, when, with a great profession of nonpartisanship, they appointed a Democrat, James B. Holohan. Holohan, like many earlier wardens, was a former sheriff. Sophisticated observers recognized that the New Penology had, for the time being, run its course. For the next thirteen years San Quentin was to be not merely a Big House, but the Biggest House in the world.

Chapter XIV

FINKS AND MILLIONAIRES

A VISITOR to San Quentin not long after Holohan took charge described him as "a very quiet man, between fifty and sixty, slightly stooped, with most of his upper teeth missing, [who] might have been the leader of a Salvation Army band." This was a minority view, for to most of the reading public he appeared to be a prime specimen of what is generally recognized as the Gary Cooper type of Western lawman: tall and handsome, kind to women and children but a terror to bad men, quiet and shy but a dead shot with either hand. He had, in fact, killed only one man during his years as sheriff and marshal, but that killing had occurred under such dramatic circumstances that it gave him forever afterward the reputation of being the fastest draw in California. When an East Indian involved in a celebrated series of trials known as the "Hindu conspiracy cases" had gone berserk in the courtroom and shot one of his countrymen, Holohan had drawn his pistol and, in the astonished instant before the courtroom became filled with a mass of panic-stricken spectators, shot the Indian neatly and fatally through the neck. This single lucky shot sustained him throughout his career as a Democratic politician, but the minority view was closer to the mark. As an executive, Holohan's abilities were better suited to a Salvation Army band than to a prison which was to grow until it held nearly half as many convicts as all the prisons in England and Scotland combined.

In the ten years between 1924 and 1934 San Quentin's population almost doubled, rising until six thousand men were crowded into the three thousand living spaces in the cell blocks and improvised dormitories. (The all-time record was set on July 7, 1934, when the count reached 6,397.) As the rigors of life on the outside increased during the Great Depression, a steady stream of new fish came through the main gate, each one presenting the captain of the yard with an insoluble bunking problem. Two huge new cell blocks, the West Wing (finished in 1927) and the East Wing (1930), held two men in each of their 1,020 single cells. Emergency quarters for several hundred more were found in such unlikely and ill-suited places as the basement of the mess hall. At exercise periods and on Sundays the Big Yard was packed so tightly with men that there was hardly room for them to move. The sound of rifle and machine-gun fire was familiar to everyone around the prison, who found nothing unusual in ten or twenty shots a day to keep the men in line. Among the guards on the wall and the gun galleries there were prize-winning sharpshooters who could knock the book out of the hands of a man reading in the jute mill or spray gravel over the feet of a man stepping out of a chow line. To avoid disaster, San Quentin clearly needed a warden with intelligence and energy above the average. "Big Jim" Holohan's endowments in both these particulars were mediocre, and the heads of the various departments soon discovered that their best tactic with the warden was to repeat on their daily reports the soothing phrase, "nothing to report."

Holohan's contribution to prison administration was to revive and extend the ancient con-boss and fink systems of management. The con bosses were in actual charge of the men and it was literally true to say "the cons ran the joint." There was a boss in each shop, in each office, in each cell block, and even in the yard.

The boss of the yard slept in a private room in the back of the captain of the yard's office and exercised so much power he was sometimes thought to be a bigger man than the warden himself. "Fat" Talbott, who was chief clerk to Captain Homer E. Breakfield in 1934, was called upon to deny to the newspapers that he was boss of the entire prison, but in the course of the interview he admitted to holding the key function of assigning jobs. Talbott and the other con bosses slept in single cells or rooms, wore tailored ("bonarued") denims, were served from the guards' kitchen, and were generally exempt from the prison routine.

The finks or stoolies comprised a much larger class; according to one ex-prisoner half the men in San Quentin had been stool pigeons at one time or another. The motives for informing against prisoners or guards were various. To a small corps of regular finks it meant extra privileges, but for the great mass of occasional stoolies the motive was either revenge or homosexual jealousy. The inevitable result was a corrosive atmosphere of hatred, suspicion, and distrust.

There were two other groups of prisoners who stood out from the common ruck. The first of these were eight Los Angeles financiers who lived on a tier of the Stones that came to be known as "Millionaires' Row." Exposed as swindlers when the bottom dropped out in 1929 they had been sent to San Quentin for embezzlement and grand theft. Prominent among them were three former officers of the Richfield Oil Company, including the chairman of the board, the president, and the secretary, and a savings-and-loan company official named Gilbert H. Beesmyer who had made free with $8,000,000 of his depositors' money. (Beesmyer was later to learn the bitter truth that one should not hit people where it hurts. In 1939, six thousand of the swindled depositors hired a lawyer to prevent his impending parole.) Associated with the "millionaires" were others who had been prominent in the world outside: a former public defender, an Oakland commissioner, an Alameda County sheriff, the former chairman of the Los Angeles board of supervisors, and Kid McCoy, the boxer. Like Beesmyer, who was bookkeeper in the commissary, most of these men held such bonarue jobs as library attendant, clerk, and hospital orderly.

Less favored by the authorities but almost as well known were the prison intellectuals who were identified with the *San Quentin Bulletin,* an occasional literary magazine which began publication in 1925. The best-known writers to see print in the *Bulletin* were Richard Krebs, who was later to become a best-selling author under the name of Jan Valtin, and Richard Joyce Tasker, whose *Grimhaven* remains one of the two or three best books about an American prison. The *Bulletin* was discontinued by administrative fiat in 1936, the general feeling toward it being expressed by Clinton Duffy's judgment that it was the "personal plaything of the prison intellectuals." (For the record, it should be noted that the earliest known San Quentin publication was a semimonthly magazine called *The Index,* published in John Hoyle's administration. Although printed by hectograph, it was well written and attractive.)

Still remembered by old-timers are other prisoners who distinguished themselves by one peculiarity or another which became formally recognized by such names as Ace-in-the-Hole Whitie, Two Left Feet, Sleepy, Patty the Pig, Society Red, Madame Titanic, Dirty Girty, The Ox, The Mahatma, the Seagull, who daily raided the garbage cans, and Shithouse Rosie, the yard tender at the Rose Bowl. Nicknames were democratically bestowed on convicts and guards alike. Along the guard line there was no trouble in identifying Whispering Annie, Crying Joe, Gunrail Humpy, King George, or Grandma. Captain of the Yard Breakfield was universally known as Vinegarface, while Stingaree was the epithet earned by Captain Rivera Smith, who was Holohan's executive secretary.

In a modern parallel to the Roman saturnalia, when slaves

were treated like masters, the usual prison rules were suspended
once a year for the annual field day, which was usually held under
the general direction of the Olympic Club of San Francisco. (Only
Frank Smith barred the gate to the Olympians, apparently because
his predecessor, James A. Johnston, who had inaugurated the field
days in 1914, was a member of the club.) The day's events were
built around a track and field meet, with such added attractions
as an old men's race, a tug of war between teams recruited from
the mill and the shops, clowns, and a holiday dinner. The main
event was the tug of war, on which more tobacco was wagered
than on any other event of the prison year. The tug of war
aroused such passion that old-time guards remember that sometimes it took as long as twenty minutes to pry a contestant's hands
loose from the rosined rope. There were other pleasant diversions,
including, in 1929, a contest to catch a pig named "Parole." The
annual field day was also the occasion for the founding of the
Wall City News, a one-page sporting sheet which touted the
coming holiday.

The inspirational quasi-religious activities which had flourished
under the reform wardens continued, though somewhat abated.
The changing times were reflected in 1929 in the announcement
of a former cowboy, movie stunt man, and bandit that he was
in the process of organizing the Church of God Evangelistic
Troupe, which would include among its personnel a young lady
vocalist from Sister Aimee's Angelus Temple and two San Quentin convicts, one of whom billed himself as the "flying tramp"
and the other of whom claimed to be in a position to bank-roll
the venture.

The great common solvents of the prison's varicolored population were the Big Yard and the general, or "mainline," mess,
where all but the favored few ate in two huge mess halls. The
technique of serving the entire convict population at one serving
had changed somewhat from previous times. As the men entered,

they filled up the narrow tables that faced all in one direction. At each place the waiters had placed an aluminum coffee cup and a round metal plate on which the main dish had already grown cold. The main dish was typically beef stew, with little beef, corned-beef hash of dubious corned beef, or a couple of "jute balls," which were made of coarsely shredded meat and bread. The men could either fall to immediately or wait for the "dump men," who went up and down the aisles with buckets into which finicky eaters were privileged to slide their food. While this was going on, the waiters formed long lines before the steam boilers in which beans were cooking. Each waiter filled his galvanized water bucket with "red ones," and then proceeded to his assigned tables to fill up the plates of those who called for beans. There was a certain amount of hazard to this operation, as exasperated waiters had been known to dump the contents of their buckets over the heads of men who were too insistent in calling for more red ones. Beans were served twenty times a week, there being only two meals on Sundays. The quantity of food collected by the dump men was later to astonish an investigating committee, who noted that on one occasion sixteen 50-gallon drums of beef stew had been delivered from the mess hall to the piggery.

Although there were no mess-hall riots in Holohan's time, misbehavior at mealtime led directly to the captain of the yard's disciplinary court. Until it was torn down in 1959, the captain's command post was the ugly yellow building that, thanks to the most prominent feature of its undistinguished architecture, was simply known as the Porch. Every day saw the captain or his lieutenant dealing out prison justice to the "beef line" of misdemeanants, who straggled out into the "Garden Beautiful." Also summoned to the Porch by "ducats" were men being moved from one cell or job to another. (In San Quentin a "beef" is not a complaint of injustice but a charge of wrongdoing. A "ducat" is a pass directing a prisoner to report to an office.)

In numbers, the most common offenses were against the regime of work in the jute mill. All new men except those with unusually good connections were assigned to the mill for six months to a year as part of the breaking-in process. After this they would normally be transferred to more desirable jobs, but the threat of being returned to the mill was held over the heads of those who showed signs of being refractory. For the men assigned to weaving burlap at the looms the amount of work which each man had to do was called the "task" and varied from 85 yards of cloth a day in winter to 105 in summer. Skillful prisoners who could make their week's task in four and a half days were given the freedom of the yard on Friday afternoon and Saturday, but others never made their task, thanks to natural clumsiness or the impact on their nerves of the constant racket, the atmosphere full of jute dust, the monotony, the nerve-racking breaking of the warp and of the machines themselves, the frequent minor fires which had to be put out as a matter of course, and the pressure of making task. The captain of the yard's daily report for these years is filled with the names and numbers of unfortunates who were deprived of their privileges or sent to the dungeon with the notation "no task" or "bad cloth." (At the end of the working day a sharp-eared visitor can still hear from guards and prisoners alike the heartfelt comment, "Well, I've got it made," an unconscious tribute to the impact which the mill left on the prison.)

For more serious offenses there remained the dungeon or solitary confinement in a cell. Although the word "Dungeon" gave way to "Solitary" in the captain's book in July, 1931, the old dungeon continued to be used for such crimes as fighting, stealing, attacking an officer, refusing to work, persistently failing to make task, making a bootleg brew called "raisin-jack," kiting letters, and being caught committing any of the sexual offenses possible between men. The captain's clerk recorded these crimes in precise and damning detail with every profanity uttered or committed by a prisoner faithfully recorded.

The greatest change in the means of punishment came with the completion of the North Block at the end of 1934. The top floor of the North Block held the new Death Row and a row of solitary punishment cells that were first known as Siberia but are now more commonly referred to as the Shelf. Included were four dark cells whose temperature could be adjusted individually, inevitably leading to charges by convicts that they had been roasted or frozen at the whim of a keeper. The old dungeon was ordered closed, but, to the real or feigned astonishment of the directors, it continued in constant use until 1940.

Corporal punishment had been officially forbidden, but as the 1930's progressed there were ugly rumors outside of beatings with fists, clubs, and rubber hoses, of the use of chloride of lime in the dungeon, and of unnecessary shootings. These rumors turned out to be faithful echoes of the facts.

Yet, in spite of the food, in spite of the overcrowding, in spite of the jute mill, in spite of the dungeon, in spite of the beatings, in spite of the general atmosphere of naked hatred, in spite of the fears of the more perceptive guards that the top could blow off any minute, Warden Holohan could point to a record of seven years without a serious riot. Interviewed on his success in February, 1934, Holohan modestly credited his guards and employees and a policy which he described as restrained liberality, education, expansion of road camps, privileges for good behavior, and swift punishment for bad. His self-satisfaction must certainly have been construed by the gods as *hubris,* for only two months later Holohan was on the griddle after a sensational escape which one newspaper claimed had been engineered by John Dillinger so that the escaped convicts could recover $100,000 worth of loot cached in Texas and rehabilitate the Dillinger gang's fortunes. Less than a year later Holohan lay in his own blood on the floor of the warden's mansion so close to death that only a remarkably tough physical constitution saw him through. But before we examine this tragedy, let us fill in some more details in the picture of Warden Holohan's big house.

Goldbrickers and jailhouse lawyers trying to "make pogey" ("pogey" is the hospital) often damned the slender, scorpion-tongued chief medical officer as a monster in human form. Dr. Leo Leonidas Stanley was tough, shrewd, irascible, skeptical, and profane. He was also a terrible sentimentalist. The newspapers sometimes pictured him as something of a modern Frankenstein, and they may have had good reason, for he was inquisitive, ingenious, and pragmatic. In the world of San Quentin, which often seems to be made up entirely of square pegs and round holes, Dr. Stanley was a curiosity, a man doing a job which might have been tailored for him. He may not have been the ideal prison doctor envisioned by the prophets of the New Penology, but it would have been hard to improve on him for his time and place.

Unlike medical men who have taken a prison berth as a last refuge from drink, drugs, women, or simple incompetence, Stanley was a prison doctor from the beginning of his career in 1913 until his retirement in 1951, with time out during World War II for service as a Navy medical officer with the rank of commander. He did not choose the profession, but was chosen by the circumstances. As many other young, poverty-stricken married interns have done, Stanley took an institutional job to tide him over until he could afford to dive into the uncertain waters of private practice. Four months after he had been appointed assistant to Dr. H. N. Kierulff, his chief was allowed to resign. Warden Hoyle asked the young doctor to take over the hospital; the next year Warden Johnston appointed him chief. Stanley stayed on for thirty-eight years, outlasting five wardens and surviving almost unscathed through the jungle warfare of prison politics.

At the beginning of his career Stanley's chief medical concern was tuberculosis. There were two reasons for this, one of which was that his young bride had been discovered to be tubercular. The second was that, as it had been in the nineteenth century, tuberculosis was the worst killer in the prison. A typical year had been 1885, when, of 29 deaths, 18 had been from pulmonary disease. A few years later Dr. Durant tried the experiment of transferring tubercular Mexicans from the jute mill to the road gang, where, he reported, "they sometimes pick up, but in nearly every case the relief is but temporary, and they soon sicken and die." For the Indians and half-breeds a term in San Quentin was notoriously equivalent to a death sentence. Consumptives were sometimes sent from the coastal climate of San Quentin to the hotter and drier atmosphere of Folsom, but at the time Stanley took charge the problem was as severe as it had ever been. He estimated that a quarter of the prisoners gave medical histories suggesting tuberculosis; of the sixty active cases, twenty were locked up in cells in one of the old buildings.

The general consensus of the medical men was that it was not the pleasant but frequently damp climate that was to blame but the conditions of prison life—the horribly overcrowded cells, where five or six men breathed each other's foul breath and drank from the same tin cup, the tiny window or the absence of any windows at all in the great concrete walls of the cell houses and the workshops, the all-pervading jute dust in the mill, and the universal habit of spitting on the floor. Following the best medical practice of the time, Stanley established an open-air ward on the roof of the old hospital building. The patients were crowded bed to bed, but they could take the sun and the fresh air. Even though tubercular prisoners from Folsom were sent to the San Quentin hospital, the number of patients in the open-air ward dropped in half by 1922. By 1938 the tuberculosis death rate had dropped to almost one-eighth what it had been in the 1880's.

Not all of Dr. Stanley's tubercular patients were grateful to him. On one occasion he barely escaped with his life when three men with the curious names of John Doe (a Negro), Blackie White (a white man), and Heinie Housman (a German), attempted to murder the doctor for his zealousness in smelling out tobacco and other contraband. They drove him into a corner, Housman carrying the Indian club with which the patients were encouraged to take light exercise. Apparently over-eager to finish Stanley off, Housman threw the club at him but missed. The intrepid doctor picked up the club, clouted Doe on the head, kicked White in the groin, and, after beating Housman over the head, marched him across the Garden Beautiful to the captain's office, where he was left to the mercies of Captain Randolph.

Apart from tending to the tubercular and to such routine chores as handing out aspirin, sewing up cuts, and plucking out diseased appendixes, Dr. Stanley's professional energies were largely devoted to investigating the subtle and fascinating relationship of disease and crime. Although tender-minded social workers and even prison people are often heard to say that all criminals are "sick," they are clearly using the word in a special sense. To Stanley, disease meant physical disease. Early in his career it became apparent to him that many of his patients had been sentenced to prison as the result of diseases which had disabled them for lives inside the law.

The insane and the paretics, for example, are clearly not responsible for their actions. As he reported in his book, *Men at Their Worst,* Stanley found that two out of three prisoners had suffered some sort of venereal disease which he believed to be the chief cause of mental disturbance. Twenty per cent of the inmates were feeble-minded, 35 per cent were alcoholic, 25 per cent had a family history of tuberculosis, and 12 per cent were malformed or crippled. By the time they reached prison, most of these men were beyond medical salvation, but Stanley did what he could to remake revoltingly ugly faces and encourage the voluntary sterilization of the feeble-minded and syphilitic. (California has a compulsory sterilization law on the books, but it is so hedged about with safeguards that it has rarely, or possibly never, been used.)

The chief croaker's greatest notoriety came from his researches into glandular rejuvenation. Stanley had read of the experiments of Dr. George Frank Lydston of Chicago, who had experimented with rejuvenating aged men by transplanting bits of testicles into their bodies. Stanley was fascinated, and realized that he was in a unique position to contribute original experimental work. Three or four times a year the bodies of executed men were not claimed by relatives. What was simpler than removing their testicles before sending the bodies up for burial in the cemetery on the hill? Then pieces of these glands could be implanted into aging but otherwise healthy convicts to see what effect this operation would have on the symptoms of senility. Beginning in 1918, Stanley and his assistants embarked on an ambitious research project aimed at proving or disproving Dr. Lydston's theories. They started performing twenty, thirty, and even forty implantations a month. Before they were through, they had carried out ten thousand testicular implantations or injections, using human material when it was available and animal testicles when the human variety was in short supply.

Dr. Stanley describes in *Men at Their Worst* the success of the technique upon a senile convict seventy-two years old. A few days after material from the testes of an executed Negro youth had been implanted in old Mark Williams, the old man's eyes had brightened, his appetite was improved, and, according to the nurse, he showed the "jazz and pep" of a young man. Dr. Stanley also noticed that for the first time the old man laughed at his jokes. Later, Stanley perfected a technique of injecting the testicular matter hypodermically, thus bringing the benefits of implantation without the surgery.

The newspapers had such a field day with the various experimenters in glandular rejuvenation that in any sophisticated gathering the mere phrase "goat glands" is still sure to be met with knowing smiles, even among those who are too young to remember what the original excitement was all about. The public interest was, of course, directed entirely to the possibility that the operation could give a man beyond his prime the ability to engage in sexual intercourse with pleasure to himself and his partner. The best remembered of the quacks who grew fat on the profits made from aging young bucks was the outrageous "Doctor" John R. Brinkley, who covered the country with advertising from a 500,000-watt station just across the Rio Grande. Stanley had nothing in common with "Doctor" Brinkley except an interest in glands. He was himself a physician of good repute who was carrying out work of scientific respectability, paralleling the work being done in Paris by Dr. Serge Voronoff. (Stanley once demonstrated his technique for Voronoff, who, he reports, said, "Oh, zat is fine! Your operations are for zee poor man and mine for zee rich man!") Furthermore, Stanley was interested in heightening the general physical well-being of his patients rather than in reviving their sexual capacities, for which there was no legitimate outlet in prison. Yet it was impossible to do one without the other. Stanley's scientific papers on the subject frankly cite the attainment of erection and ejaculation after the operation. In any case, both the convicts who volunteered for the operation and Dr. Stanley himself seem to have been pleased with the number of cases where there were such clear signs of success.

Like Voronoff, Stanley had to suffer the frequent attentions of the press, which, at first, were good-natured. In 1922 three convicts upon whom Stanley had performed his operation went over the walls to the almost inexpressible delight of the papers. The rewrite man on the *Chronicle* did not have to look far for a figure of speech; they had gone, he said, "in a lifelike imitation of Rocky Mountain goats." But the newspaper columns took on a darker tone when, in 1928, a busybody in an undertaking establishment discovered that the body of a just-executed murderer named Buck Kelly had been castrated.

The Buck Kelly scandal was a three-day wonder. The *Examiner* played it as a page-one story which changed its color completely from day to day, leaving a somewhat bewildered readership. The first story noted solemnly that "Dying in disgrace, [Kelly's] body was dishonored after death," the dishonoring consisting of the removal of his heart, brain, and testicles. The paper hinted at an obscene autopsy performed by Stanley and his professional colleagues and quoted Holohan to the effect that Stanley had made a serious mistake. Stanley prudently remained silent. Two days later the *Examiner* had reversed its field completely, declaring on page one that "Clarence 'Buck' Kelly, a menace in life, performed in death the only useful service to society of his existence." Behind the change was a statement by the dean of the University of California medical school that the dishonored testicles had been transferred to a charity patient who had been "deficient from birth." The newspaper approved of this humane act, approved of Stanley, and called off its dogs.

Stanley's resilience and energy were his salvation in more than just the Buck Kelly affair. In 1933 Stanley fell afoul of Warden Holohan in a misunderstanding that would have meant the end of the San Quentin career of another man.

In the fall of 1933, when Holohan fell seriously ill, he appointed the experienced and prison-wise chief surgeon to act as warden while he took several months' rest. Stanley attacked the job with his usual vigor, firing drunken and lazy guards, setting clean-up crews to work, improving the clothing-distribution system, changing some of the administrative procedures, and presiding over two executions, as well as performing his usual surgery and supervising the move of the hospital into its new quarters. Stanley also had shoots of ivy set out at the base of the walls and prepared to turn the old quarry into a salt-water reservoir that could be used as a swimming pool.

The dismissed guards and their friends carried word to the sick warden that the doctor was engaging in activities which could only discredit Holohan's own performance as warden. Holohan came back in December, had the ivy torn up, ordered work on the swimming pool stopped, and asked for Stanley's resignation as deputy warden. Stanley resigned and went back to his duties as chief medical officer in the fine new hospital outside the walls that was still known as the Hen House, even though the last woman convict had left it late in October.

Chapter XV

SAN QUENTIN CHANGES

FROM the very beginning women convicts had been an embarrassment to the wardens. Even in the early days the state records show that both the wardens and the governors were eager to get rid of them as soon as possible, usually by way of a pardon. The ideal solution would have been to instruct the judges to sentence a woman to prison only under the most extreme provocation; preposterous as this may sound, it is pretty much what has always happened in most civilized communities.

In 1907 John Hoyle took over a prison containing almost two thousand men, but only twenty-seven women, a ratio of about seventy to one. In spite of a general conspiracy to keep female criminals out of prison, some women continued to shoot their husbands, poison their lovers, play the badger game, and engage in other activities which it was difficult for the rest of society to ignore. By 1922 the number of women had risen to fifty. Although the newspapers hailed this as an all-time high, statistically it was close to nothing. But, small as their numbers were, the presence of the women weighed heavily on the warden's patience and periodically stirred the public into orgies of sentimentality.

Part of the trouble is that many of the women who manage to get themselves committed to prison are not professional criminals

but middle-class housewives whose crime has consisted in dispos-
ing of unwanted or irritating relatives, usually their husbands.
These murderers can often be described accurately as "attractive,"
"motherly," or "soft-spoken." There were comparatively few like
the giant Negress Belle Nailer, who attacked the turnkey with
a kitchen knife, cut his jacket to bits, grappled with him on the
floor, and spent a good deal of her time in a dark cell in the
women's quarters. Besides run-of-the-mill thieves the old building
held such well-behaved characters as old Mary Von, the trunk
murderess Emma Le Doux, and Cordelia Botkin, who had mailed
a box of poisoned chocolates across the country to her victim
in Delaware. Except that their crimes were heinous, they were
not professional criminals in the sense that the habitual thieves,
bunco artists, second-story men, and hoodlums on the yard were
criminals.

The piecemeal improvements of the women's department which
took place now and then from 1885 onward really did little to
make the women's life more than barely tolerable. Although
women seem generally to adjust themselves to prison life better
than men, San Quentin offered them a minimum of amenities.
Where the male convict had at least the daily routine of moving
from his cell to the jute mill to the mess hall to the yard, and so
on, the woman's life was circumscribed by the walls of her cell
building. These walls had been extended until they joined the
main walls of the prison, forming an enclosed exercise yard. The
flower garden where Newt Morgan had seduced Nellie Handly
had disappeared, and the exercise yard was nothing more than
a concrete pit, where troops of huge rats scurried at night.
Although the women were supposed to work in the sewing room,
making clothes and flags, they were bored with their lives, jealous
of each other, and the constant despair of the guards and matrons.

Since the days of Scotch Mary, Dolores Martinez, and Nellie
Handly, the sexual life of the women convicts had been restricted
by the purer morals of the new century. Love letters—some of

them addressed to anybody in pants who found them—often made their way to the Big Yard, but so far as consummated affairs went, the women's quarters might almost have been a nunnery. But not quite. Clinton Duffy tells the story of the unsuspecting but not unwilling deliveryman who was dragged into a private room by two playful women convicts. This story takes its place in the San Quentin folklore beside the story of a fortunate woman prisoner named Red Carter who in one version managed to become friendly with the convict electrician. Making the best use of his opportunity, the electrician found or built a trap door through the floor of Red's cell. Whenever his duties brought him to the women's quarters, the electrician improved the occasion by slipping through the door, an arrangement which he and Red found of mutual benefit. Although the amount of electrical work required in the women's department may have puzzled the captain of the yard, the trap door was not discovered until, after Red's discharge, two other women were found in a vicious fight to decide who would inherit the trap door and the electrician.

Official efforts to brighten up the women's lives had to stop a good deal short of providing an electrician in every cell. Occasional entertainments were given the women beginning in 1916 with a phonograph concert. Later, the entertainments became more elaborate, including movies and, on Christmas Day, 1922, a fashion parade. The Salvation Army and the Volunteers of America provided such female necessities as mirrors and curling irons and candy.

After seventy years the state of California finally realized officially the practical outrageousness of locking women up in a tight little prison inside the walls of San Quentin, and in 1924 plans were announced for the construction of a women's building on South Point, outside the walls. The building was to be in the best tradition of the New Penology, with individual cells, large windows, plenty of closet space, including built-in hatboxes, a volleyball court, and a profusion of flowers. Although there were some murmurs that the new women's department looked more like a pleasure resort than a prison, the plans met with general approval, and in 1927 everyone concerned was happy to see the women march out the gate and down to their new house on the point. They stayed here until the fall of 1933, when they were moved to a newly-built cottage-type institution in Tehachapi, north of Los Angeles. (Dr. Stanley, who had long kept a greedy eye on the building—though not, heaven forbid, on its occupants—promptly took possession of the vacated Hen House for his hospital.) At first Tehachapi was run as a detached department of San Quentin, but it was liberated in 1937 and has since then been known as the California Institution for Women.

The Battle of Ross Landing in 1862 was the last attempt at a mass jail delivery that San Quentin has seen. This is not to say that the ninety-nine years since then have been innocent of escapes, but the breaks and attempted breaks have been small-scale affairs, involving one, two, three, or four men, and they have often been more distinguished by their ingenuity than by their violence. Only rarely have they been successful.

No matter how sharp-eyed and conscientious a guard may be, he can never hope to outwit all the prisoners in his charge. The guard is on duty for eight hours; he then turns his mind to other things—his son's grades in school, the price of whisky, the World Series, the novels of Aldous Huxley, a run of striped bass, the immortality of his soul, the seduction of the sergeant's wife, or whatever it is that represents to him the reality of the larger world outside the walls. To the prisoner dedicated to escape there is only one reality, and between his conscious and unconscious mental activity he can devote twenty-four hours a day to finding a solution to the problem. There is always a solution.

One of the most dedicated of San Quentin's would-be escapers was Jacob Oppenheimer, Morrell's companion in the Incorrigibles, who was known to the public as the Human Tiger. Oppenheimer had been sentenced for the rest of his natural life to a steel cell in the Incorrigibles after he had taken a leading part in a mutiny. After four years in the 6-by-4-by-5-foot cell Oppenheimer succeeded in undoing the twenty-six bolts on the ceiling, and, if Guard J. D. Jones had not been alert, there was a bare chance he might have made his way to the yard and possibly to freedom.

In another desperate and farfetched attempt Oppenheimer saved pages from the *Christian Advance* until he had enough to roll into a tube eleven feet along. While Jones had his back turned Oppenheimer pushed the tube through the grilled door of his steel box, lighted it at the gas jet, and set fire to his mattress. From the corner of his eye Jones had seen the tube going back into the cell. The guard pulled his revolver, ordered Oppenheimer to stamp out the fire, and had him put in the jacket until he confessed that the fire was part of a plot to escape.

(Oppenheimer, who was pictured in the papers as a monster because of the several murders he had committed both in and out of prison, was a lover of poetry who wrote a book of verse on toilet paper while in the Incorrigibles, an item which is now in the possession of a San Francisco collector. He died bravely on the gallows at Folsom in July, 1913, after a final speech of encouragement to the California women who were agitating against capital punishment. He also had a nice talent for gallows humor. During his last night in the death-watch cell he asked the guard to play a phonograph record called "Somebody Else Is Getting It, Right Where the Chicken Got the Axe.")

Oppenheimer's attempted escapes were planned in the face of the greatest obstacles the warden could devise. The average convict on the yard had many more opportunities, some of which were put to good use, and some of which were not. There were prisoners who almost drowned themselves in barrels of swill destined for the piggery, those who had themselves nailed up in boxes going outside the walls, and one man who went into hiding under a bathtub in the women's department. The last feat was hard to understand because it was not, apparently, an attempt at voyeurism but at escape. There were also those who made good use of stolen clothing. Among these was a room tender who escaped in a guard's civilian suit, another who got only as far as Schuetzen Park wearing female dress, one who was captured wearing a guard's uniform, and another who was stopped as he walked away wearing the outer garments of a visiting Episcopalian priest. The last man was given away by the gray uniform trousers that showed under the stolen garments. He was addressed afterward as "Father" by his admirers on the yard.

There were recurrent attempts to tunnel under the walls, or to go over them in a heavy fog and for the latter reason only trusted prisoners were issued passes to take them to jobs beyond the "fog line." The boats that visited the prison continued to be watched hungrily by would-be escapers, even as they had been in Estell's day. The stern-wheeler *Caroline,* which carried away the bags from the jute mill, also occasionally carried away an impatient prisoner, but the most celebrated water-borne escape occurred in 1925, when six convicts, led by two naval prisoners, killed a guard, overpowered the captain of the tug *Frances J.,* and sailed into the bay with the intention of making a run to freedom through the Golden Gate. The hero of the affair was an Army pilot from Crissy Field who tracked them from above until they were forced to beach the boat near Richmond, where a party of police was waiting for them.

There were also escapes touched with imagination or madness. The simplest of them all was the successful escape of a cripple who hobbled away in full sight of the guards, all of whom were confident that he surely could not be serious. In later years there was a prisoner who tried to walk away under water, wearing a homemade snorkel outfit consisting of a rubber football bladder, a rubber tube, and a tin can. He drowned. Another prisoner once presented himself at the distribution office wearing a belt from which hung a collection of brown sticks connected to a dry battery he was holding in his hand. He declared he was going to blow himself up if he were not permitted to depart in peace, but when another convict snatched the battery from his hand the brown sticks were revealed to be cut-up sections of broom handle. Finally, in this paragraph should be recorded the poignant distress of Professor Gallur when his entire clarinet section escaped with forged passes and Dr. Stanley's automobile.

Every prison has had one break which is remembered forever afterward as the Big Break. At San Quentin the Big Break was not any of the mass excursions of the 1850's and 1860's, but a small affair in 1935 in which only four prisoners took part. Yet it has every right to its pre-eminence, for these four men almost killed Warden Holohan and succeeded in kidnaping and taking with them the entire parole board.

The beginning of 1935 found San Quentin at one of the lowest points in its modern history. As we have seen, the most persistent and inescapable source of trouble was overcrowding, every cell and bunkroom holding twice as many men as it should. There had been a succession of nerve-tightening incidents: the captain of the yard had been stabbed; a convict had been shot in the yard; there had been an attempt to burn down the jute mill; there had been more fights than usual in the yard; and prison-made pistols had been used in an attempted escape. For six months the newspapers had been predicting trouble at the prison. According to Clinton Duffy, who had been hired as assistant to Captain "Stingaree" Smith, the warden's executive secretary, Holohan was tired, depressed, moody, and on edge.

At noon on January 16 the parole board recessed to have their customary lunch with Holohan in his mansion on the hill. The board members were Frank C. Sykes, a San Francisco contractor; Joseph H. Stevens, a Sacramento banker; and Warren Atherton, a Stockton lawyer and professional Legionnaire. Also present was the secretary of the board, Mark Noon, a veteran prison official. The five men were sitting quietly over their salad when four convicts, armed with .45-caliber automatics, burst into the room and ordered them to put up their hands. Sykes, who had his back toward the kitchen door through which the prisoners had entered, rose from his chair and started to turn. One of the prisoners poked a pistol into his chest and pulled the trigger, but it missed fire and Sykes was left unharmed. The officials were ordered to change clothes with the convicts; four of them did so, but Holohan turned his back on Rudolph Straight, the convict leader, and walked into the next room to use his telephone. Straight fired a shot that missed, and then knocked Holohan to the floor with the butt of his pistol. He beat and kicked Holohan without mercy and would have surely killed him if one of the other convicts hadn't grabbed his arm and said, "That's enough. Get up."

Mark Noon, a gun in his back, was forced to telephone for the warden's official automobile, which arrived with a guard lieutenant and sergeant aboard. Noon was then forced to telephone the main guard tower. He told the officer in charge, "The whole prison board is coming out in the warden's car with Noon and two guards. We are all covered with guns. Don't shoot at the car or we'll all be killed."

The Chinese houseboys working in the kitchen were all locked up in pantries and closets, but one of them escaped and ran to Mrs. Holohan, shouting "Fire! Fire!" in his excitement. When she entered the dining room she found her husband apparently dying, while the members of the board stood around helplessly, dressed in convict clothes. Mrs. Holohan took her husband's head in her lap and wept. This was how Duffy and Dr. Stanley found her when they arrived almost simultaneously at the mansion.

The guards outside the mansion had heard the commotion and given the alarm. Captain Ralph H. New had come on the run, gathering guards on the way, and by the time the convicts and their hostages emerged the house was ringed with armed men. The convicts fired two shots, the guards started to close in, but

Noon shouted, "Don't shoot back. Don't try to stop them. They'll kill all the board members."

The guards stood by helplessly as the convicts herded the hostages into the car, ordered Lieutenant Harry Jones to drive them and Sergeant C. L. Doose to stand on the running board. Meanwhile, Captain New had raced to the rear gate and blockaded the road with a car, but when the convicts' car drove up, Noon leaned out and shouted again to let them through.

New gave the highball to the guards in the back gate tower, and the big Studebaker, loaded down with four civilian hostages, two guards, and four convicts, went through.

Outside the gates the sergeant was thrown off the running board of the speeding car, breaking his leg. Lieutenant Jones was ordered to head north and then east, but the keeper of the drawbridge over Petaluma Creek had been warned and had already raised his bridge. The Studebaker whipped around, and Mark Noon was let go with instructions to warn the pursuers, who were closing in from all directions, that the board members were in mortal danger. Most of the posses heeded the warning, but the escape car speeded west for twenty-five miles until, in the isolated farmland near Tomales Bay, it encountered a shooting posse that wounded two of the board members but none of the convicts. This, however, was the end, for another bullet hit one of their tires. As the car slowed down, bouncing on a rim along the country road, the convicts ordered Jones to step on it. When Jones could go no faster, they threw him out of the car and one of them took over the wheel. They managed to keep going for another four miles, when they sighted a dairy barn.

"Let's take over the creamery and fight it out!" one of the convicts shouted. They crashed the car through a fence and into the side of a shed.

In the end the hostages were in more danger from the law than from the convicts. As Atherton, wearing convict denims, stepped shakily from the car, a policeman raised his gun and shouted, "I'll kill you, you dirty dog."

Sykes and Stephens, both bleeding from bullet wounds, screamed, "Don't shoot! That's Atherton!"

Three of the convicts were ready to quit, but Straight, their leader, walked out of the building, a gun in each hand. The district attorney of Marin County shot him through the head.

After the convicts had been returned to prison and the wounded board members taken to a hospital, one large question remained to be answered: Where had the convicts obtained their guns? During the wild ride to the coast they had told the hostages the name of a guard, who, they said, had sold them the guns for $250 apiece. This story turned out to be sheer spite. The guns had been smuggled into San Quentin by an ex-convict who had hidden them under the dashboard of a car belonging to an innocent civilian employee.

Straight died the night of the escape, and two of his companions went to the gallows in May. The only survivor was the man who had saved Holohan from Straight's murderous assault. Holohan recovered and returned to work, but, as he told Duffy later, he would have resigned as soon as he could if it wouldn't have looked as if he were giving in.

The problems Holohan faced after the break were not particularly eased by his self-appointed advisers of the press and public who took every opportunity to instruct him how to run his prison until their attention was diverted by the Hauptmann trial and the pursuit of Public Enemy Number One, Alvin Karpis. Holohan hung on stubbornly, but by the winter of 1936 his troubles had mounted to the point where he was forced to admit he had had enough. His decision to resign had been hastened by widespread interest in the curious discovery by the Secret Service that a ring of counterfeiters had been successfully operating from the prison photoengraving shop. The investigation of the counterfeiting scandal also turned up evidence that a prisoner had acquired a quantity of chloral hydrate to dope the coffee urn in the guards' dining room, that whisky could be bought on the yard for $5.00 a pint, and that potassium cyanide was available for would-be suicides.

In 1937 Holohan returned to the state senate, where his principal achievement was the law substituting the gas chamber for the scaffold. It was an achievement which his successor as warden fervently wished he had foregone.

Because the scandal that drove him from the warden's office is virtually all that is remembered of him, it is easy to picture Court Smith as a Neanderthal man who returned San Quentin to the man-killing jail it had been in the days of Ames, Hale, Aguirre, and Tompkins. This is not at all true. Smith was a big, slow-spoken, easygoing man who owed his reputation for toughness largely to the fact that he had been warden of Folsom during the Thanksgiving Day riot of 1927, when 1,300 rioters left thirteen convicts and guards dead. Like Holohan, he had entered politics as a sheriff and a United States marshal, and, also like Holohan, he was unusually large, standing six-feet-six and weighing two hundred and fifty pounds. He and his captain of the yard and deputy warden, Ralph H. ("Roughhouse") New, six-feet-two and two hundred and thirty-five pounds, made an impressive pair.

When he came to San Quentin, Court Smith told reporters the secret of managing convicts was to keep them contented, and that he thought San Quentin's men needed more athletics. Within a few months he had had several softball diamonds laid out in the lower yard and had also abolished the literary *Bulletin* but had retained the *Sports News*, or "Green Sheet," which was the successor to the *Wall City News*. Another change to which there were few objections was to break up the group of favorites with bonarue jobs who ate in the guards' mess. But the greatest change that took place during Smith's first two years at San Quentin was the substitution of the gas chamber for the gallows.

In this Smith was the victim of two great ironies. The first was that he was bitterly opposed to the gas chamber as a slow and cruel method of execution. The second was that it was forced on him by ex-warden Holohan, who as state senator wrote the gas-chamber law which he himself had wanted as warden. The differences between the two men in this matter went back to 1932, when Smith, as warden of Folsom, accompanied Holohan and Dr. Stanley to the Nevada state prison to witness the execution by hydrocyanic-acid gas of a murderer named Everett T. Mull. Holohan came back singing lyric praises of poison gas. Smith had found it unbearable.

Once the gas chamber bill was passed there was no help for it. A contract was let to Captain D. B. Castle, who had put his professional experience as an exterminator to work in building the Nevada gas chamber. At first the plan was to locate gas chambers at both San Quentin and Folsom, but later San Quentin was selected as the site for all executions in the state. In March, 1938, the gas chamber arrived at San Quentin from Denver, where it had been built at a cost of close to $5,000. The city editors of the San Francisco papers were delighted with this novelty and, when Smith announced that the gas chamber would first be tried out on the scrawniest pig in the hog ranch, they sent their funniest reporters to cover the story.

For several days the papers carried stories with jolly references to smoked ham and jokes about little pigs who were trying to avoid the executioner by stuffing themselves with food. The first experimental pig was despatched in decent privacy, the only release to the press being the information that he had died in a little more than three minutes. Then the papers were invited to send a reporter to cover the execution of a second pig.

There was no laughter at all when the reporters peered through the plate-glass windows at the dying pig. Court Smith turned his back while forty newspapermen and guards watched the twenty-five-pound pig struggle inside a wooden crate. The *Chronicle*'s man was so affected that he wrote, "Capital punishment in what I personally consider its most hellish form since civilized courts sentenced men to be hanged, drawn, and quartered was demonstrated yesterday in San Quentin prison."

Smith was given several months' grace before he had to face his first execution of a human being by gas. (Men who had been sentenced to die by hanging were still executed in the old gallows room.) In the first week of December, 1938, came the day that could no longer be put off. As it turned out, Smith was obliged to kill two men at the same time. It was an execution in which the warden might have found some satisfaction. The condemned men had killed Smith's successor during the "Bloody Sunday" uprising at Folsom in September, 1937, but Smith had a bad case of nerves and told reporters he wouldn't look at the two men after they had been strapped into the death chairs. By the time the two murderers were dead, the reporters wished they hadn't looked either. The gas had taken twelve minutes to kill one of them and fifteen and a half to kill the other.

Thanks to such widely-publicized executions as those of Barbara Graham and Caryl Chessman, the details of a San Quentin execution have now become so familiar to the general public that they have lost their horror to all but the young, the idealistic, and the naïve. This is a splendid example of the general truth that most men will accept without protest any act that has been turned into a routine.

The gas chamber is actually outside the walls of the prison, in a corner of the outer walls a few yards from the guards' mess and across the street from the employees' snack bar and barbershop. The witnesses enter from the street; the condemned man and his guards from inside the walls. Behind the chamber, hidden by a partition, is the machinery room where the guard assigned as executioner prepares the sulfuric-acid solution and, eventually, pulls the bright red lever that drops the cyanide into the acid.

The condemned person is brought down on the elevator from Death Row late in the afternoon of the day before execution. He is held in one of two death-watch cells, tiny rooms furnished only with toilets and mattresses. Here he spends his last night under the sharp eyes of two guards. His last dinner is cooked to his order in the guards' kitchen. After dinner he is visited by the chaplains and the warden. He can spend his last night sleeping or chatting with the death watch.

Until recently all executions were held on Fridays because that happened to be the most convenient day, but from this grew a spurious tradition about "Black Friday." They are always scheduled for ten o'clock, but sometimes a last-minute stay will move an execution into the afternoon. (There is a telephone on the wall of the execution room with a direct line to the governor's office in Sacramento.)

Fifteen minutes before the hour of execution the condemned man is given a fresh suit of clothes—a white shirt and blue jeans without any pockets that might collect poisonous fumes to injure the men who will remove the body. The chief medical officer tapes a stethoscope diaphragm to his chest and examines him to make sure he is aware of what is happening. This is important, for if a murderer or rapist or kidnaper were to depart in an uncomprehending mental fog it would deprive the law of the sweetness of its revenge. Not long ago one condemned man had to undergo two series of electric-shock treatments before he was judged to be sufficiently in touch with reality to be killed.

When the warden gives the signal the death march starts from the holding cell. Supported by guards, the condemned person walks barefoot over a narrow carpet that leads directly into the gas chamber. Everything is now scheduled to go like clockwork, but this doesn't guarantee that it always will. When Juanita "Duchess" Spinelli, the first woman executed in California, started down the carpet Duffy had to ask her to wait, because it was not until then that he noticed no witnesses were present. While the witnesses were ushered inside the unfortunate woman stoically faced the open door of her execution chamber. Then she was allowed to go ahead. (There was another odd thing about this execution. Duffy had heard a rumor that a newspaper had equipped its reporter with a subminiature camera to try for a photograph of the "Duchess" dying, Ruth Snyder style. The warden had asked the twelve official witnesses to crowd around the guard rail outside the observation windows to make the photographer's job as hard as possible. They did, and nobody ever found out if there was a photographer in the room or not.)

Once inside the chamber, the guards swiftly strap the condemned person into one of the two chairs. A long tube is fastened to the stethoscope diaphragm. It takes about half a minute from the time the death march enters the chamber to the time the door is locked shut. Even now there can be hitches, as the hideous one that occurred when one man broke his straps and ran around the inside of the chamber until the guards unlocked the door, captured him, and strapped him down again. After the door is locked, the executioner dilutes the acid, lets the solution run into the vat under the death chair, and tests the chamber for airtightness. Then the warden nods. The executioner pulls a red lever, which causes a rod to rotate. There is a hook on the end of the rod, and as the rod turns, the hook lowers a cheesecloth bag of cyanide pellets into the sulfuric acid. The acid and the cyanide react to form hydrocyanic-acid gas which soon fills the chamber. From the outside the warden, the medical officers, the official witnesses, the reporters, and the curiosity-seekers watch the condemned person die. It takes longer than most people expect. Then a fan is turned on to drive the cyanide fumes up the tall flue that rises high above the walls like a crooked cross. Contrary to the popular notion and to some newspaper stories, the gas is colorless.

As Chessman did, most of the condemned men go quietly and

with as much dignity as they can. Some, like the multiple-killer Stephen Nash, grin and wink at reporters or shout a last message against the plate-glass windows. A few go hard. One of these was a twenty-seven-year-old Negro named Robert O. Pierce who had been convicted of the murder of a cabdriver. Pierce somehow managed to get a fragment of broken mirror into the death cell, and, as he knelt to receive the Protestant chaplain's last benediction, he cut a three-inch gash across his throat. He clawed, kicked, and screamed as four guards dragged him into the chamber where his partner in crime waited quietly. As he was dragged in witnesses heard Pierce say, "I'm innocent, God, you know I'm innocent. Please, Lord, I am." After a moment, "All right, God, if you want to let me go, I won't curse you." The blood from the gash in his neck was spreading over his white shirt as he was forcibly strapped into the chair.

As the door was locked, the witnesses heard him scream, "God, you son of a bitch, don't let me go like this!"

Chapter XVI

THE MAKING OF A FOLK HERO

COURT SMITH'S troubles started in earnest with a plague of strikes that plunged him into the middle of the scandal that was to end his wardenship. The first strike was a relatively small affair that took place in May, 1938, when the two hundred men working in the tailor shop sat down at their jobs because they were allowed no time in the yard between the end of work and the beginning of dinner. When the strike continued into the next day, Captain New sent twenty-five men to Siberia, and Smith offered the remaining men a compromise solution. The prisoners voted to accept the warden's offer and went back to work.

As an administrator, Smith's main effort was devoted to economizing on his food budget, in the hope that he could astonish the governor by returning unspent money to the general fund. This, of course, led to trouble in the mess hall. Smith sometimes cut a rather clownish figure when faced with this sort of trouble. The story is still told in the guards' mess about the time Smith went into the yard to break up a food strike. The men greeted him with cries of "You bastard! You fruit! You son-of-a-bitch!" and with even less refined prison epithets. ("Fruit" is a term of scorn, implying effeminacy.) Hearing the word "fruit," Smith thought he grasped the men's complaint and with a great show of magnanimity promised to serve fruit three times a week at breakfast. The hysterical laughter that followed almost broke up the strike.

The worst of the food strikes occurred in February, 1939. On Wednesday—corned-beef-hash day—four thousand of the 5,300 prisoners refused to eat the despised hash and hung around in the yard, booing the men who entered the mess hall. They also passed up their usual supper of coffee, beans, and bread, even though rice pudding had been added as bait. Forgoing their meals was not so great a sacrifice as it sounds; the men had just stocked up with candy and cookies at the monthly canteen day. The next morning 2,700 men stayed in their cells rather than march to the mess hall. They were fed bread and water while the warden worried that something besides food was stirring them up. The strike petered out the next day, but Smith had a new worry in the shape of a grapevine rumor that the jute-mill men were planning to strike over their working hours. When the next strike occurred, however, it was again over food, the protest this time being over the quality of the chili con carne served at a noon meal in February, 1939. Captain New acted quickly, sending 27 of the leaders to Siberia for a "stretch on the spot."

"The spot" was the invention of William G. Lewis, the balding, steel-spectacled keeper of Siberia. For a long time Lewis had been troubled by the problem of keeping his charges occupied. In 1937 he found the solution: a dull gray circle, less than two feet in diameter, was painted on the floor in front of each cell. After this, whenever a man went to Siberia he spent two four-hour shifts a day standing on the spot. He was not permitted to move at all, even to shift his weight from one foot to the other or to move his head. He was allowed a two-minute toilet break in the morning and another two minutes in the afternoon.

Although Lewis said he never struck a man who hadn't squared off to fight, men who refused to stand on the spot were beaten with a billy or a rubber hose. The only chance to be delivered from Siberia came on the occasion of Captain New's weekly inspection, when he walked down the line of cells while Lewis pointed out the men who had proved themselves worthy of being released in the morning.

When the food strikers were sent to Siberia, the cells were already occupied and Lewis was obliged to double up the convicts, both in the cells and on the spots. Captain New arrived to tell the men they could look forward to six months on the spot and added some pungent advice on the foolishness of bucking the system. When he was gone, the men sat down on the spots in protest. Lewis and his assistant, Fred Sullivan, tried to bully them to their feet, but when the men talked back he called the Porch to ask for reinforcements.

In the 'tween-gates passage a guard named Timothy Bell was frisking inmates as they passed in and out. ('*Tween gates* is a passageway between the two gates through which working parties must pass to go outside the walls. After they enter one gate they are counted and frisked before being passed through the other. This is why the two gates through the wall are known as the inner and outer count gates.)

Bell was a heavy-set, slow-spoken man who had been at San Quentin for three years. Before that he had worked in a department store in Oakland and had owned a general store in the mining town of Twain, where, among other things, he bought gold from the men who, in those depression years, could still find a little profit in working the already worked-over river beds.

Bell's career at San Quentin had not been much more successful than his career in business. He had once been suspended for fifteen days and just barely escaped being fired for letting a prisoner come too close to him while he was carrying a gun. In addition, the "beef book," in which guards' misdemeanors were recorded, showed that he had been responsible for seven mistakes in the count. Officer Bell was clearly not a very efficient guard, but his shortcomings were due more to his native slowness than to any intention to beat the rules. He was allowed to remain, assigned as day extra guard, or relief man.

At about two-fifteen, while Bell and Guard Jack Watt were shaking down prisoners, the lieutenant of the guard, Chester E. Trafton, called out to the two men, "Get your clubs. There's trouble in Siberia." Bell took his billy from the hook where he had hung it and accompanied Trafton, Watt, and another guard across the Garden Beautiful to Four Box, the yard office, where they were joined by Sergeant Pete Richardson. The five men rode the elevator to the top floor of the North Block, which houses both the Row and Siberia. They arrived in Siberia at about two-twenty, to find four other guards already there. In his usual post on the other side of a wire grille stood a gun guard armed with a .38-caliber revolver.

When Bell arrived and looked down the long corridor he was surprised to see the men doubled up on the spots. Although some of the other guards later disputed his recollection, Bell didn't hear any sounds of rebellion from the prisoners. As the reinforcements arrived, Lewis shouted, "Into your cells!" The prisoners went quietly.

While Bell, billy club in hand, looked on, Sullivan and Lewis went to the far end of the row of cells and ordered out the first man, a convict named Philip Rosen. Rosen came out, dressed in the ragged jeans, shirt, and slippers that were supplied to men in Siberia. He put his hands around his head as Sullivan began to beat him with a foot-long steel spring encased in leather. This device was so made that if it were held at one end it became a club, while, if it were held at the other, it became a strap. Sullivan whipped Rosen for three or four minutes, beating him methodically from the head down to the legs. Rosen jumped around a good deal, but he didn't try to resist.

When Sullivan was through, Rosen went back to his cell and Lewis whipped Rosen's cell mate with a rubber hose. The hose was about twenty-two inches long. There was conflicting testimony later on as to whether it was loaded with lead. The handle of the hose had been wrapped with jute twine, and then it had been shellacked. When Lewis was through he passed the hose to another guard who whipped the first man in the next cell. Whether by accident or intention, the guard hit the man on the head so hard that he knocked him to the floor. Lewis said, "That's enough," and the man half-walked, half-crawled back to his cell.

Bell continued to look on as Sullivan and Lewis worked their way down the long line of cells. Although the instruments were passed back and forth, Sullivan was partial to the club, Lewis to the hose. After a man had been beaten for a while, he would be asked if he would stand on the spot. If the man said "Yes," he was struck two or three more times until he remembered to say "Yes, *sir*." When Lewis and Sullivan were about halfway through somebody said, "There's no use for one man doing all the work." Sullivan handed the hose to Bell. Bell asked Sergeant Richardson to hold his billy club while he went to work on his first man with the hose.

Bell didn't particularly care for the beatings and decided to do his duty and no more. He had noticed that the other men had been hitting the prisoners about ten or twelve times each, so he counted out about the same number of blows. Later, he explained, "I tried not to hit them any more, but I wanted to hit them as many times, or approximately as many times, as the other men did." The men were now being beaten two at a time; while Bell used the hose, another guard used the strap. Bell beat about ten or twelve men in all.

When all the men had been beaten and sent back to their cells, Lewis walked up and down the corridor to see how the prisoners had taken their punishment. He heard one man talking to his cell partner and shouted to Bell, "This man hasn't got enough. Come back down here and hit him a few more." Lewis brought the man out, and Bell struck him four or five times.

After this the prisoners were quiet except for some cries of pain.

Bell described it as "groaning and moaning, and perhaps some of them were hollering a little in agony." The guards walked into the little office at the end of the row of cells. When Bell lighted a cigarette, Sullivan bummed one from him. The men smoked and talked casually about what had just happened. Bell picked up the strap and looked at it curiously because he had never seen it before. When he was through with his cigarette, he and Jack Watt went back to their job shaking down prisoners 'tween gates.

A couple of weeks after the beatings Bell got into conversation with a friend who was superintendent in the shops. The friend suggested it might be a good idea for Bell to write down the details while they were fresh in his mind. Although he was not a markedly literary type, Bell covered two and a half pages on the back of an old letter. When he explained what he had done, his friend said, "Hold on to that. You may need it."

As it turned out, he did.

It was not the mass beatings but the mainline food that first aroused the curiosity of John Gee Clark, whom Governor Culbert Olson had appointed to the parole board and then made director of penology. Clark was a lawyer from southern California, a former assistant probation officer, a two-term assemblyman, and a good Democrat. The only surprise about his appointment was that he had not, as expected, secured a judgeship. (He was later rewarded with a superior court appointment in Los Angeles.) Although he came up the road of party politics, Clark was not a routine politician, and when, as had happened often in the past, rumors of rotten food at San Quentin were heard in Sacramento, he ordered an investigation.

To say that the food was bad leaves too much to the imagination. Lettuce paid for as United States Number 1 consisted of small, squashy heads with burned and rusty leaves. Turnips were porous, cottony, woody, and moldy. Other vegetables and fruits were received in such an advanced state of decomposition that not even the prison steward had the nerve to put them on the tables.

In May, 1939, the state prepared to file charges against the Oakland branch of a nationally-known meat-packing company for supplying more than 2,000 pounds of ham "consisting wholly or in part of putrid and decomposed animal substance."

To Court Smith's credit it should be said that he improved the food after his attention had been firmly called to its inadequacies. He appointed a new steward who, on the last day of July, served a meal that caused the prisoners to demonstrate approvingly by banging their cups on the tables until the steward came out of the kitchen, mounted the bandstand, and acknowledged their applause. The meal he had arranged was simple enough—hamburger steak, lyonnaise potatoes, bread, tea, and coffee with sugar and cream—but to San Quentin it was a banquet.

But the trouble at San Quentin had gone too deep for Smith to save his administration with such belated improvements. While the food investigation was going on, rumors of darker and more serious irregularities reached Clark: rumors of the beatings in Siberia, rumors of unnecessary shootings, rumors that men were given the heat treatment in the dark cells, rumors that the old dungeon was still being used, rumors of inadequate medical attention, and rumors of irregularities in the sale of jute bags. At the track meet that was held on the anniversary of California's admission as a state, September 9, Clark spoke briefly to Officer Bell. During this conversation he apparently discovered that he had a witness who was slow but honest and willing to tell the story of the March beatings in Siberia.

After looking further into Bell's story, Clark, in his capacity as director of penology, filed a bill of twelve specific charges against the entire board of five prison directors. Although Court Smith was not named as a defendant, he was the subject of many of the charges; the eleventh described him as an incompetent who knew nothing of prison developments outside California. The directors girded up their loins for battle by holding brief hearings of their own designed to show that San Quentin was in firm and able hands.

The full-dress investigation ordered by the governor opened at the San Quentin employees' recreation hall on November 3. The hearings went on until the last week of February, 1940, moving from San Quentin to San Francisco and the state capitol in Sacramento. Almost fifty witnesses were heard, including all five directors, twelve guards, and nineteen convicts. By the time the hearings were over, they had filled eighteen volumes totaling 2,834 pages of the court reporter's transcript, and, it seemed, several million column inches in the San Francisco papers.

The directors were defended by George T. Davis, a San Francisco lawyer who had already sprung Tom Mooney and who in later years was to take part in the defense of Caryl Chessman. Although most of the testimony was sober and straightforward, when it was not nauseating in its detail, Davis handled his defense with characteristic flamboyance. As a dramatic production the high point came during Davis' cross-examination of Bell, who had appeared as principal witness for the prosecution. After Davis had obtained permission to require Bell to demonstrate his technique upon a seven-foot straw dummy dressed in prison dungarees, the following exchanges took place:

DAVIS: Now, go ahead and give us some idea of what you did.

BELL: Suppose you hold it [the dummy] right there.

DAVIS (*helpfully*): Give us an idea of how you went at it. Beat the dummy's body approximately to the same extent and the same length of time that you used in beating up any of those prisoners out there in that beating.

(*Bell hits the dummy with a rubber hose. Davis yelps with pain and looks ostentatiously at his hand.*)

DAVIS: Did you see that, Governor?

GOVERNOR OLSON (*puzzled*): Yes.

DAVIS (*accusingly*): The witness deliberately struck my hand with that hose!

EDWARD P. MURPHY (a lawyer for the prosecution): No, I will object to that.

DAVIS (showing his hand): Do you see that? (Turning to Bell) You did, didn't you, Mr. Bell?

BELL (slowly): Oh, now—

DAVIS (hectoringly): You deliberately struck my hand with that hose, didn't you?

BELL: No, I didn't.

DAVIS (relentlessly): Did you strike it?

BELL (stubbornly): I don't know.

GOVERNOR OLSON: Well, now, listen—

DAVIS: Observe it then, Governor, please. I just ask you to do that, because this witness has attempted—

OLSON (impatiently): If you had your hand down the back—

DAVIS (injured innocence): I had my hand right there, and so the witness deliberately struck my hand with the hose. Now, Governor, I am asking you to take cognizance of that fact.

OLSON (who knows Davis well): I don't think the witness intentionally hit your hand.

DAVIS: I know he did, and I will show you the mark on my hand.

MURPHY (solicitously): Is it black and blue yet?

DAVIS (to Olson): If you want to feel it, you can feel the raise right now.

Olson brought the incident to an end by instructing Bell to hit the dummy, please, and not the counsel. After he was through cross-examining Bell, Davis ordered Bell's arrest for perjury, the point at issue being the witness's statement that the hose in Siberia had been loaded. The county district attorney and the sheriff were conveniently at hand, and one of the directors had forehandedly provided himself with a warrant for Bell's arrest. Bell was taken to the justice of peace at San Rafael, who released him on his own recognizance. Court Smith sent him back to duty until the matter was settled.

Apart from a few irrelevancies such as this, neither the prosecution nor the defense had provided much for anybody to smile at, even though one newspaper persisted in regarding the proceedings as a circus. The testimony of all the witnesses, both willing and unwilling, added up to the first clear picture that either the governor or the public at large had ever had of this aspect of San Quentin and, before many months had passed, turned the prison upside down.

There were no immediate repercussions, largely because the board of directors had secured a court order restraining Olson from firing them. Court Smith was reappointed in March, and was so encouraged by this that he promptly fired Officer Bell. Olson waited until July to move, but when he moved at last he moved decisively by throwing out the entire board of prison directors. The new board asked Smith for his resignation and called in the assistant secretary of the parole board, Clinton Duffy, who, they thought, could manage the prison while they looked around for a man to fill the job permanently. Duffy was available partly because he was virtually the only man who knew anything about running San Quentin who had managed to keep clear of the cross fire in the investigation.

Duffy records in his book, *The San Quentin Story,* that his first act after his appointment was to call his wife; his second was to walk down the street to "Rough-house" New's house. He knocked on the door. New opened it.

Duffy said, "I've just been appointed warden."

"I've heard that," New said.

"All right," Duffy said, "I'm making some changes, and as of this minute you're through."

To the newspapers, to the public at large, and to the Democrats in Sacramento, it looked as if a new broom were sweeping San Quentin clean. In the interests of historical accuracy, it is necessary to add that not everybody shared this opinion. To Dr. Stanley it was just another quarrel between politicians. Although the new board diplomatically passed a resolution praising Stanley's ability and willingness to co-operate, the doctor suspected that they were privately delighted when he was ordered into the Navy as a reserve officer shortly after Pearl Harbor.

Court Smith stayed on through the summer of 1940, drawing warden's pay and sitting behind the big desk in the warden's office while Duffy ran the prison from a small office outside. Until Smith's resignation became effective August 31 the new board had allowed him to remain as a "consultant," although they had made it clear that they would continue his pay and would not be offended if he departed promptly. Smith, however, stayed close to the warden's telephone, waiting for a call from Sacramento that would tell him he was again in charge of San Quentin. He waited in vain, but his reluctance to go was not merely stubbornness, for the courts had not yet passed on the legality of Governor Olson's firing of the old board. The Duffy family consequently remained in their modest house while Duffy set in motion the changes that were to propel him into the front rank of American prison wardens.

First came the tying up of the loose ends left over from the brutality scandal. Six of the guards who had beaten convicts in Siberia were fired, and the spots were painted over for good. Timothy Bell, fired by Smith, was hired again, to remain in service as a guard in the hospital and education buildings until he died of a heart attack in the summer of 1959. The great iron doors at the entrance to the dungeon were torn off their hinges, and the dungeon itself was turned into a storeroom for the prisoners' canteen. Duffy ordered that prisoners would no longer carry their numbers in large black figures on the back of their shirts. The food was improved, and, in the yard, the prisoners circulated a petition asking that Duffy's appointment be made permanent.

At length Court Smith departed, to spend the rest of his long life in the suburbs of law enforcement, first as an agent for a state tax board and finally as chief house officer for San Francisco's St.

Francis Hotel, where the accommodations are a long, long way from San Quentin prison. The Duffys moved into the old warden's mansion on the hill, a huge white building consisting of two identical halves joined like Siamese twins, and a few days after his forty-second birthday Clinton Duffy became both in name and fact warden of the country's largest and most notorious penitentiary.

Duffy has told his story to a large audience in *The San Quentin Story,* while his wife has recently added some domestic notes of her own in *Warden's Wife.* Besides these two books since 1940 a large number of major magazine articles, two movies, and uncountable newspaper pieces have been devoted to Duffy's work. Although, as we shall see, neither the books nor the articles tell the full story, there is no disagreement about what Duffy set out to accomplish.

Briefly, Duffy believed that criminals could be rehabilitated through a *mens-sana-in-corpore-sanc* program built around education, sports, religion, and psychiatry. The prison educational system, which ran from literacy classes to University of California extension courses, was strengthened by taking instruction away from inmate-teachers and hiring a faculty of instructors on the payroll of the local junior college. Vocational classes in the trades were expanded during the war years, and both labor and management were prevailed on to help place the graduates.

In December, 1940, the old "Green Sheet" gave way to the *San Quentin News,* a paper of professional quality which is available to interested subscribers outside the walls. Duffy wrote a weekly column for the *News* in which he combated the prison grapevine with the motto "facts, not rumors." Every cell was tied into a radio network that carried selected commercial programs as well as intramural news and announcements. For listeners outside a radio program called "San Quentin on the Air," built around convict talent, was carried by the Mutual network for five years, during which time it won the highest Hooper ratings of any Mutual show produced on the Pacific Coast. Part of each show was a chatty three-minute talk by Duffy in which he ranged from prison reform to such allied subjects as child rearing.

The inspirational functions that have always been an important part of San Quentin's reform administrations were not by any means neglected. Duffy, who is a past master of a Masonic lodge, actively encouraged a number of worthy organizations and recommended attendance at the various chapels. The prison chapter of Alcoholics Anonymous flourished, as did a curious organization called the Seekers, which might also have been called Anything Anonymous. A hobby shop was organized and the men were encouraged to spend their free hours making hand-tooled leather purses, models of prairie schooners, and the like. A committee of prisoners representing the various departments began to meet in a gesture toward self-government; the committee's powers have always been severely limited, but it has been active in such good works as organizing mass blood donations and carrying on charitable drives.

While the highway camps remained a bright part of the state prison program, the harvest camps that were established during the war came under heavy fire for the fantastically casual way in which some of them were run. A more successful innovation was improvised by Duffy as the result of a midnight call for men to fight one of the great forest fires that lay waste to large areas of California every summer. Since Duffy sent out San Quentin's first fire crew in the middle of a night during the war, hundreds of men have gone out each year, practically unguarded, to wield double-bit axes, brush hooks, McLeod tools, and shovels with such good effect that they are generally recognized as being among the best fire crews in the state.

Although other wardens have entered the yard (Frank Smith is said to have walked unguarded to the mill to investigate a disturbance) Duffy made a regular practice of strolling alone through the Big Yard, notebook in hand, and often ate in one of the big mess halls, dramatizing his availability and keeping the kitchen staff on its toes. Discipline was enforced by granting and withholding privileges such as the movies and the canteen. In general, as Duffy told a social-work conference only two months after his appointment had been made permanent, "we are not running a summer resort, but if you want men to respond like men, you've got to treat them like men."

In view of the decisiveness with which Duffy changed many of San Quentin's old ways it was not surprising that his work met with a gratifying public response. He became a popular speaker at meetings ranging from professional conferences to women's clubs, to whom he carried the message of the new San Quentin. But, although Duffy has always enjoyed a good press, he has not lacked critics. These included, to begin with, the old-line guards at the prison who were not at all in sympathy with their warden's philosophy and who felt themselves directly menaced by such new orders as the banishing of loaded canes and clubs. There were also people outside the prison world who were not enchanted by Duffy's evident talents for publicity. These lines of criticism were apparent in the first national magazine article devoted to Duffy's work, a piece by Gerald Breckenridge which appeared in the *Saturday Evening Post* in November, 1941. It was a sharp and objective piece of work which reviewed the Olson investigation and Duffy's first year in the warden's office. Breckenridge described Duffy as a "smart, ambitious, publicity-conscious executive with his eye on the main chance," and wound up by saying there was even money offered in California that Duffy wouldn't last.

Speculating about what might have happened is always a fascinating but not very useful occupation. The attack on Pearl Harbor changed the situation completely, and in the years that followed Duffy was provided with the opportunity to make some of the changes that have already been described. So far as the war itself went, the first reaction from inside the walls was characteristically wild and unrealistic. Fourteen men doing time for robbery, kidnap, and murder presented Duffy with a petition to the President, asking Mr. Roosevelt to let them prove their loyalty by sacrificing themselves as human torpedoes. This sort of foolishness was soon followed by more useful contributions, as San Quentin's industries turned to war purposes and the men inside were encouraged to make the same patriotic gestures as their countrymen outside the walls, giving blood by the gallon, buying bonds, and saving fat.

In the prison shops the convicts turned out stirrup pumps and sirens for civil defense, first-aid kits and hospital supplies, and in their cells built model planes for aircraft identification classes. Even the hated jute mill took on new life; the gunny sacks now went to the Army to be used as sand bags while jute cloth was made for camouflage netting. The task was raised to 110 yards a day without serious complaint. Submarine nets were made by hand on a huge concrete slab poured by the Navy. Incendiary-bomb extinguishers, cargo slings, ammunition cases, and mattress covers were among the other war products which San Quentin produced and which led to Duffy's appointment as a consultant to the War Production Board. (Other professional kudos included Duffy's election as vice-president of the American Prison Association and as president of the Wardens' Association.)

It is a cynical but necessary observation that most realistic prison wardens would probably be delighted to exist in a perpetual state of war. As George Orwell pointed out, periodic and not too violent warfare solves a good many troublesome social problems, promoting a sense of solidarity among the populace and providing for the ready disposal of excess production. Thus it was in San Quentin between 1941 and 1945. The prisoners were in spirit absorbed into the general population rather than being rejected, they were praised for their industry rather than being regarded as dangerous competitors, and first-termers convicted of all but the most heinous crimes were permitted to apply for parole to the armed services. Many did, many were accepted, and some died. Between 1939 and 1942 the prison population dropped almost a full two thousand, to 3,700. The war years were halcyon years in San Quentin, and the ending of the war could not help but come as an anticlimax.

The history of San Quentin after the war cannot be understood without first understanding something of the great change that had taken place in the entire state prison system in 1944. As early as 1940 John Gee Clark had backed an assembly bill that would have placed all the California prisons—San Quentin, Folsom, the new minimum-security prison at Chino, and the women's prison at Tehachapi—under a central administrative bureau, but the suggested organization had been firmly opposed by the Olson-appointed board of directors. It was not until two years later, after Earl Warren had succeeded Olson, that a ripe scandal broke in the newspapers, rivaling the battle of Tarawa for page-one space and generating enough steam for the reformers to push through the change.

This time the scandal did not involve San Quentin but Folsom. A convict named Lloyd Sampsell, who was known to the newspapers as the "yacht bandit," was arrested while visiting a lady named Jacqueline de la Provetiere in her apartment in San Francisco. The newspapers were interested because Sampsell was supposed to be incarcerated in a Folsom harvest camp near Sacramento. It turned out that this wasn't the first time Sampsell had enjoyed Mrs. de la Provetiere's hospitality; in fact, as the red-haired woman told reporters, Warden Clyde Plummer of Folsom had authorized the visits because he believed she could help with Sampsell's rehabilitation. She had returned the convict's visits, wandering hand in hand with him through the orchards surrounding the prison barracks, discussing poetry, of which they were both fond.

Governor Warren lost no time in ordering an investigation which turned up testimony that other Folsom prisoners had been seen in bars and poolrooms and in the company of ladies. The investigators also found out that the chief inmate nurse at Folsom, who carried the key to the drug closet, was a narcotics addict. (As a postscript to the scandal, Lloyd Sampsell, who had started it all, was sent to Death Row five years later, convicted of killing a loan-company cashier during a holdup.)

Warren's investigating committee found San Quentin in far better condition than Folsom, but spoke critically of some aspects of Duffy's management. Administratively, the prison was an efficiency expert's nightmare, with several dozen department heads reporting directly to Duffy. The committee found "certain weaknesses" in some of Duffy's appointments. Discipline was not tight enough, and negligence seemed to have contributed to a recent escape. Duffy did not seem to the committeemen to have been paying sufficient attention to classification and segregation. Vestiges of the con-boss system were still to be seen. Further, the committee had observed with distaste the guerrilla warfare that was going on between the chaplains and the psychiatrists, and between the Protestant and Catholic chaplains. Finally, they deplored Duffy's practice of inviting interested groups of citizens to tour the prison after lockup, and of allowing as many as six hundred outside visitors to attend the broadcasts of "San Quentin on the Air." It was not, therefore, surprising that when Warren called a special session of the legislature to pass the prison reorganization bill, Duffy was found in the opposition, together with the members of the Olson-appointed prison board.

The reorganization bill was passed overwhelmingly on the last day of January, creating a Department of Corrections which would establish and oversee uniform policies for all the state penal institutions, and a three-man board called the Adult Authority, which would set terms under the indeterminate sentence law and grant paroles. For the first time appointments to prison jobs were taken out of the category of political spoils and put under civil service. There were immediate rumors of a general shakeup, with one rumor that reached the papers having Duffy going to the minimum security prison at Chino, to be replaced at San Quentin by none other than the late captain of the yard, Ralph New. This development was, to put the matter conservatively, unlikely.

As soon as the bill was law, Governor Warren announced that he had asked a committee of eminent penologists to conduct a nationwide examination aimed at choosing the best possible candidate for the job of director of the Department of Corrections. Although many people suggested to Duffy that he apply, he preferred to stay at San Quentin. The successful candidate was Richard A. McGee, a forty-six-year-old professional prison administrator who was well known in prison circles although he was virtually unknown to the public at large. A former president of the American Prison Association, McGee had been warden of Riker's Island Penitentiary, deputy commissioner of corrections for New York City, and had also served in the federal prison system before going to the state of Washington as superintendent of public institutions. McGee is a quiet, dapper, efficient man who, in the years since 1944, has earned a reputation as one of the best administrators in the state.

The first policies announced by McGee were neither radical nor startling, but required some changes at San Quentin as well as in the other prisons. McGee called for the abolition of anything resembling the con-boss system, prohibited fraternizing between employees and prisoners, encouraged religious activities, gave his blessing to advisory councils of prisoners, restated the importance of the principle of individual treatment of prisoners, prohibited corporal punishment, and called for the segregation of homosexuals. Duffy had anticipated many of these measures; where he had not, he quickly complied. The greatest innovation that the new administration brought about at San Quentin was the conversions of the West Block into a separate institution known as the Reception and Guidance Center, where all new fish were required to spend their first weeks in prison being examined by doctors and phycologists and being indoctrinated to prison life.

All the new policies did not, however, go down easily with the inmates. In March, 1945, McGee decreed the ending of racial segregation in the mess halls. The order was understood to have come from Governor Warren himself and to have the strong backing of Walter Gordon, a prominent Negro lawyer from Berkeley, who had been a football star at the University of California, who had played a leading part in the legislative fight for the Department of Corrections, and who had been the first man appointed to the new Adult Authority. (Gordon was later made governor of the Virgin Islands.) The integration order resulted in a race riot at San Quentin which was not broken up until guards used their rifles. The next day there was a quiet, nonviolent demonstration by men who refused to enter the mess hall until the prison's 447 Negroes had finished their meal and departed. On March 27 nine hundred men were locked in their cells as hunger strikers. McGee and Gordon joined Duffy in appeals over the prison radio system. The disturbance was finally settled, but at the expense of a compromise that made nobody happy. The two segregated mess sections for whites and Negroes were retained, but a third section was set aside for "voluntary integration." Few men elected to sit in the integrated section, and before long the usual color line was again being enforced. Racial segregation in San Quentin has remained a sensitive subject to this day, with the so-called "Black Muslims" most recently exploiting the issue for their own peculiar purposes.

Although since 1944 there have been occasional reports of friction in matters of policy between the warden's office in San Quentin and the director's office in Sacramento, relations between Duffy and McGee seem to have been generally cordial. In any case, whatever differences may have come up were successfully smoothed over before they became public, and, in matters of broad prison philosophy, the two men were clearly headed in the same direction. Although Duffy was not immune to the sort of mass demonstrations that have afflicted other wardens, these troubles were probably due more to the occasional restiveness that is part of prison life than to the policies either of Duffy or of the Department of Corrections. Furthermore, San Quentin's troubles were mild compared with the orgies of violence and destruction that have scarred other prisons in recent years.

Whenever prisoners escaped, as they did in 1942 and again in 1943, there had been suggestions from one quarter or another that Duffy's "coddling" was to blame. This was unfair, for, as we have seen, prisoners have managed to escape under the harshest wardens. Duffy had understandably become sensitive to charges of being too soft, and when, in 1947, the jute-mill gang struck, he reacted with a show of force that not even the toughest warden could have improved on.

As is usual in prison troubles, there were a number of apparent causes for the strike. Hard on the heels of new department rules tightening up mail and visiting privileges, Duffy had announced that forty minutes would be added to the working day and the supper hour moved from three-forty-five to five-fifteen. The changing of the supper hour seemed reasonable enough, as it spread the men's meals over a longer day, and Duffy characteristically wrote in his column in the *San Quentin News*, "I believe you are going to like this procedure...." The jute-mill workers emphatically did not like the longer work day, and went on strike, adding to their list of grievances the complaints that not enough bread was served with meals and that the current task of eighty yards of jute was too much. Duffy called up the entire guard force of four hundred men and reinforced them with contingents from local police forces and the state highway patrol. Under the guns of the guards and police, who one observer thought comprised the largest army seen around San Francisco since the waterfront strike of 1934, the strikers were locked up in their cells while their leaders were herded into a corner of the yard, from which they were taken outside and immediately driven under heavy police escort to Folsom. The troubles lasted for three days.

In spite of the high esteem in which he was held by the general public, Duffy was not immune to raiding expeditions sent out from Sacramento. The most serious criticism from this source came in January, 1950, when an assembly committee charged that San Quentin's inmates were "being systematically broken down and ruined beyond repair." The committee's case was that there were only five psychiatrists (and not all of these served full time) to care for the 2,400 inmates supposed to get psychiatric care. This worked out to a fantastic theoretical case load of 580 patients per doctor. The committee also attacked claims that sex criminals were receiving the psychiatric care ordered for them by the courts. Duffy protested quite properly that the budget which provided for such a small number of psychiatrists was the legislature's responsibility, not his. But it is hard to escape from the impression that Duffy shared responsibility for the general belief that the psychiatric situation was better than it really was. (In his book, *The San Quentin Story*, published a few months later, Duffy called the prison "a huge modern laboratory for the study of criminals and crime." This falls far short of being a candid description of San Quentin, then, now, or at any other time.)

In August, 1950, just after a series of autograph parties for *The San Quentin Story*, Duffy had to hurry back from Carmel, where he was spending a weekend by the sea with Mrs. Duffy. He had been called back by the duty officer, Dr. Stanley, who reported that the men were rioting in the mess hall for no discernible reason. Duffy again went on the radio and threatened the loss of such cherished privileges as baseball, the movies, and the canteen. "I'm accused of being lenient," he told them. "I want to give you all a break, but I'll tighten this place up more than you ever thought possible if there's another outbreak. Think it over, fellows." They thought it over, and the prison went back to normal.

In terms of money the greatest catastrophe that ever occurred at San Quentin was the total destruction of the jute mill by fire in April, 1951. The loss was estimated at $3,000,000, but in humanitarian terms the mill should have been burned down long before. As recently as 1942 the authoritative Osborne Association had called it the worst industry in any prison in the United States. But however undesirable the mill was, its loss created an employment problem calculated to turn a warden's hair gray. As it had been since 1882, the mill was the prison's largest industry, and at the time of its destruction it had been turning out sandbags for the Korean war. Overnight, almost a thousand men were thrown out of work and into the Big Yard, where, if left to themselves, they could not help but grow bored and disaffected. Duffy assigned as many men as possible to other jobs, enlarging the crews who were building the new cotton mill, sending more men to camp, and frankly making work with a cleanup program around the prison.

The jute-mill fire was the last major problem Duffy had to face as warden. In September Governor Warren announced his appointment to the Adult Authority, and at the end of the year Duffy left San Quentin to take up the peripatetic duties of a member of the Authority, a body which meets in turn at the various state prisons, setting terms under the indeterminate sentence law and hearing applications for parole. Duffy's departure from San Quentin was national news, hailed throughout the editorial pages. He left to the accompaniment of warm eulogies both from the convict body and from his free associates.

There were, however, rumors that Warren had promoted Duffy not only to put his experience and talents at the service of the parole board but also as a convenient stratagem to put a new warden in San Quentin. This theory was expressed most succinctly by Jackson Doyle, the *Chronicle*'s able Sacramento correspondent, who, in connection with Duffy's later political activities, wrote:

It is no secret that Duffy, while at San Quentin, had basic differences in matters of prison administration with his boss, Richard A. McGee of the Department of Corrections. Warren sided with McGee, and when the opportunity permitted, elevated Duffy out of the San Quentin wardenship.

Duffy strongly denies that he left San Quentin unwillingly, pointing out that he had been considered for the Adult Authority when it was created, and had applied for appointment as early as 1948. But the point at issue is Earl Warren's motives in appointing Duffy, and this is a matter which may not be cleared up until the chief justice dictates his memoirs.

Two years after his appointment to the Adult Authority Duffy astonished political observers by announcing his candidacy for a seat on the Board of Equalization, a curious hybrid agency that at that time combined taxing functions and the administration of the state liquor laws. Among those caught off base by the announcement was the incumbent, Paul Leake, who had discussed his policies with Duffy at a peace officer's meeting at San Quentin just a day or two before. To an inquiring newspaperman Duffy explained, "I'm an administrator, I've always been one, and I believe election to the Board of Equalization would be an advancement."

Duffy now candidly admits that the Board of Equalization campaign was a mistake, and it would serve no purpose to dwell on its details. To put it briefly, there was a suggestion that, whether he wanted it or not, the liquor industry regarded Duffy as a friendlier candidate than Leake. (In 1947 and 1948, while warden, Duffy had been a silent partner in a motel, restaurant, and bar on the San Francisco peninsula.) Duffy denied the charge, and won the Republican nomination in the June primary, but Goodwin Knight, who had become governor when Warren was appointed to the Supreme Court, declined to endorse him. Duffy lost the election almost two to one.

Since this unfortunate excursion into elective politics Duffy continued to serve on the Adult Authority until September, 1961, which marked the end of his active prison career at the age of sixty-three. He had for some time been vice-chairman of the board, continued to do a great deal of public speaking, and handled a large part of the board's public relations. In recent years he has been speaking out strongly for the abolition of capital punishment and will soon publish a book describing the ninety executions at which he reluctantly officiated.

Clinton Duffy has never suffered from a lack of attention in the press. As we have seen, he succeeded to the wardenship under dramatic conditions, and the years in San Quentin were abundantly filled with the materials for a success story in the classical mold. The prisoners' wartime activities were faithfully reported in the newspapers and magazines and on the radio, often as a stimulus to free citizens to go and do likewise, and by 1946 there was hardly a literate American who could not recognize the name of Clinton Duffy, while radio comedians could refer slyly to Duffy's tavern with the sure knowledge that their audience would get the joke. If there were any citizens who were still ignorant of Duffy's achievements, their ignorance could hardly survive the attention that the warden received in the mass media during the next four years.

In September, 1946, *Reader's Digest* published an article on Duffy and the San Quentin hobby association written by Dean Jennings, a newspaper reporter who was to become the warden's literary collaborator and political manager. In November the movie-going public was treated to a generously fictitious account of the career of a "Warden Kelly" in a movie called *San Quentin*. In October, 1947, *Life* magazine devoted ten lyrical pages to

Duffy and his prison, informing their readers that the inmates "regard him more as a friend than a keeper." In 1949 Duffy's policies received the public endorsement of that unique molder of public opinion, the late Dr. Alfred Kinsey. Duffy's apotheosis came a year later, with the appearance as an eight-part serial in the *Saturday Evening Post* of Duffy's own story, written in collaboration with Jennings. The magazine series was an abbreviated version of the book, *The San Quentin Story,* which appeared in July, 1950. The book went into three printings, appeared later as a paperback reprint, and then in several foreign languages, most recently in Arabic. A movie with the same title was released sometime later.

The picture of Duffy that emerges from this spate of printers' ink and celluloid is of a dedicated man who, possessing a unique insight into convict psychology, transformed San Quentin overnight from a place of medieval horror into the best of the new prisons. There is a measure of truth here, but, like all popular pictures of public figures, it is oversimplified and lacks the dimensions of a picture drawn in perspective. Our concern, of course, is not so much with Duffy as a friendly and personable private individual as with Duffy as the best-known modern prison reformer in the world.

Against the background of the history of San Quentin the main difficulty with the accepted picture of Warden Duffy is that it presents him as the first of San Quentin's modern wardens rather than as the last, and possibly greatest, of the humanitarians who governed the prison through decency, good sense, and the impact of their personalities on the prisoners. Duffy is clearly a direct descendant of Governor John Weller, who in 1858 advocated segregation of different kinds of prisoners, rehabilitation, shorter sentences, intelligent guards, and a fair deal for the discharged convict.

As readers of this book will recognize, Duffy's program of rehabilitation was not so much an original construction as it was an extension of the ideas of other twentieth-century reform wardens, including John Hoyle, James A. Johnston, and Frank Smith. The prison educational system, for example, had flourished since Hoyle's day, and under Johnston had grown until half the prisoners were enrolled, a figure that has remained remarkably consistent until the present day. Early in the 1920's the academic program had included not only compulsory classes in reading and writing, but also more advanced classroom work both in day and night classes, of which the courses offered by the extension department of the University of California were academically the most strenuous.

From 1925 on the roll of prison officers included a professional educator as director of education, and by 1934 the prison faculty consisted of 85 inmates assigned full time to teaching duties. In September, 1930, the school graduated 657 men; in December 1931, 900. In 1931 the workday was shortened by an hour to allow employed convicts to attend school. The educational system continued to expand even in Court Smith's time, with the director of education, Dr. H. A. Shuder, reporting a curriculum of 189 courses in 65 subjects. For at least ten years before Duffy's appointment the wardens of San Quentin had been claiming, with some justice, that their prison school was the best of its kind in the United States.

The segregation of prisoners according to their crimes and their chances of rehabilitation had long been a dream of the reform wardens, going back almost a hundred years. The first practical effort at segregation came when Johnston initiated legislation sending repeaters to Folsom and attempting to turn San Quentin into a prison for the younger and presumably more reformable first-termers. Within San Quentin itself, when the West Block was opened in 1927, almost nine hundred of the younger prisoners were assigned to it, to be housed separately from the older men. In the mid-1930's, under Holohan, there was an ambitious plan to construct a dormitory for a thousand first offenders who could be completely isolated from the rest of the prisoners. The plan died, and it is only recently that something of the sort has been done at Soledad prison.

A staff psychiatrist was appointed as early as 1932, when a "psychiatrical" department was established under Dr. David G. Schmidt, who has remained as chief psychiatrist ever since. From the beginning, Dr. Schmidt and his assistants subjected every newly-received prisoner to a psychiatric interview and engaged in a necessarily limited program of clinical work.

The privilege system of discipline goes back at least to Hoyle, flourished under Johnston and Frank Smith, and survived even under Holohan and Court Smith. The dungeon and the spot were reserved for men regarded as hard cases, but our indignation at the cruelties practiced on these men should not be allowed to obscure the fact that the great majority of entries in the punishment book were "LPFN" or "lost privileges until further notice."

The point of all this is simply that Duffy's reforms did not spring full-blown out of the prison soil on June 15, 1940, but were the fruit of a reform movement which had been changing San Quentin for more than thirty-five years. In spite of the crimes that were certainly committed against the convicts during these years, San Quentin did not stand up badly by comparison with other American prisons. We have, for example, the testimony of a touring member of the British Prison Commission, who told San Francisco interviewers in 1931 that he thought San Quentin was the best prison he had visited in the United States. The Englishman was no doubt being diplomatic, but his statement was accepted at its face value by newspapermen who knew the prison.

Duffy's main accomplishments were two. First, he carried through a broader program of humanitarian measures than had been tried before. Second, with his flair for publicity, he was able to arouse the support of a public that, having survived the kidnapings and gang warfare of the 1930's, had become generally indifferent to the welfare of convicts. Readers of this book will recognize that in these respects there is more than one parallel between Duffy and his predecessor of thirty years before, John Hoyle. Yet it comes as a surprise to read the following words:

"When you contrast some prison officials with some prisoners, there is no reason to lack faith in the prisoners. I have known a minister at the prison who sold pardons. I have known a superintendent of construction who robbed the state. I have known a lieutenant of the yard, a man who held steadfastly to the theory that no convict could be reformed and who took an unholy joy in the discovery of a recidivist. I have known such a man to rob prisoners. When keepers are crooked, why not give convicts a chance?" The speaker was not Clinton Duffy, but the forgotten man of the same surname, Colonel Dennis Duffy, president of the board during Hoyle's wardenship.

It is hard to escape from the conclusion that Warden Duffy's campaign on behalf of prison reform was, if such a thing is possible, too successful. The general public has been left with the impression that the San Quentin formula of education, psychiatry, religion, and sports is an effective solution to the twin problems of running an orderly prison and of inducing criminals to lead lives within the law. So far as the second, and more important, problem goes, this is far from the truth. A humanely run San Quentin is more palatable to our modern sensibilities than a San Quentin built around the dungeon and the jacket, but nobody has ever presented any convincing proof that the modern prison has rehabilitated a larger proportion of its inmates than the tough prison of the last century. (Dr. Stanley has recently published an article arguing that the reverse is true, basing his main argument on the increasing rate of parole violation. In the early 1900's about 10 per cent of men on parole were returned to prison; in the last decade the figure has been about 50 per cent. There have, however, been so many changes in the administration of the parole law that this apparently shocking comparison is close to meaningless.)

The comparatively decent prisons run by such wardens as Clinton Duffy are by far to be preferred to the Alcatraz-like institutions advocated by such such critics as J. Edgar Hoover, who regularly announces that criminals are "mad dogs" and who has called prison reformers "moo-cow sentimentalists," among other names. Nevertheless, decency and common sense, a little psychiatry and a little religion, have proved to be not enough. This, really, is the central dilemma faced by all present-day prison officials and by everybody else who is concerned with the criminal and his law-abiding brother.

Chapter XVII

AFTER DUFFY

SINCE DUFFY the prison has been in the hands of professional careerists in the prison service whose personalities have been subordinated to their job. The odds are that if an inquiring reporter were to walk down San Francisco's Market Street, offering passers-by a ten-dollar bill for the name of San Quentin's present warden or his immediate predecessor, he would go a long way before having to part with any money.

Harley O. Teets, who succeeded Duffy in December, 1951, had entered prison work in the federal service. After ten years at federal institutions, during which he rose to the rank of guard lieutenant, he came to California as captain at Folsom. For five years he was associate warden under Duffy. A mild-looking man, he was known as a better administrator and tighter disciplinarian than Duffy, and during his six years in office he ran the prison pretty much by the book. Teets made few changes, and successfully rode out an investigation into alleged brutality in the psychiatric department. (The investigation, incidentally, was inspired by a series of articles by *Chronicle* reporter Pierre Salinger, who was later to become press secretary to John F. Kennedy.)

When Teets died of a heart attack in 1957 he was still largely unknown outside the prison, except for his unsuccessful attempts to keep Chessman from writing any more books. He was generally respected inside. A prisoner who had served under both Duffy and Teets spoke a fitting epitaph when he told the writer of this book, "When Duffy said *yes,* you weren't sure but maybe he meant *no,* but when Teets said *yes* he meant *yes,* and when he said *no* he meant *no.*" Perhaps Teets' greatest accomplishment was in maintaining order without undue harshness even though the prison population continued to rise. Until the new cotton mill absorbed many of the unemployed in 1955, between five hundred and a thousand men had to spend their days in their cells or milling about in the yard.

If Duffy looks like a professor of economics and if Teets looked like a successful small-town dentist, the present warden, Fred R. Dickson, looks every inch the part. A large, beefy man, he talks like an old-line police captain, but he has done graduate work at Chicago and at Berkeley, and his conversation is larded with terms out of the vocabulary of the social sciences. He was one of Richard McGee's early appointments, coming in 1944 from Nebraska, where he had been superintendent of a juvenile institution. His first appointment was as Duffy's associate warden; later he was on the staff of the minimum-security institution at Chino. He left Chino to set up a modern department of institutions in the state of Washington, returned as superintendent of Chino, and came back to San Quentin on Teets' death. To the newspaper-reading public he is best known as the warden who was obliged to execute Chessman.

When Dickson's personality has shown through, it has been in the form of organizing events such as art shows and jazz concerts at which selected prisoners can mingle with the general public and even with their own families. On a weekend in the summer of 1960, when the public was invited to the prisoners' annual arts-and-crafts show, an estimated ten thousand citizens roamed through the prison's outer grounds and spent $8,000 for paintings, sculpture, and handicrafts. Of these activities Dickson says,

"They help break down the walls and let the people outside know what kind of people we have in here. This is a community like any other community, except that the men are locked up." He has also abolished the tug of war and the grotesque races of the old field day, which he has turned into the championship playoffs for the intramural teams.

There have been no phenomenal changes at San Quentin during Dickson's administration. The prison's population is now limited to 5,000, with the result that the daily count usually reaches as close as possible to 4,999. Prisoners' letters home are no longer postmarked "San Quentin" but "Tamal." The innovation which has attracted most attention in prison circles has been an experiment in a technique called "group counseling," which is part of the statewide program of the Department of Corrections. Unlike "group therapy," in which a group of inmates discuss their troubles with a psychiatrist, psychologist, or psychiatric social worker, group counseling is carried on by the guards and foremen, who in turn have to be trained by professional counselors. The group-counseling sessions take place both on and off the job, but are generally in off-duty hours. Dickson thinks group counseling has been generally successful. On the whole, the warden takes a healthily pragmatic view of his work. "We think we're doing a pretty good job," he said recently, "but sure as hell someday somebody else is going to come along and do a better one."

There have been several major physical changes in the past few years. The Stones at last fell under the wreckers' machines in the winter of 1959, and in the place where it stood there is now a severely functional building called the Adjustment Center, which is in effect a prison-within-a-prison. Here one hundred men who haven't been able to get along with their fellows can be completely isolated from the rest of San Quentin. They need never leave the Adjustment Center. Besides their cells, it contains a small mess hall and even a schoolroom, where the agitators and troublemakers can attend classes which will hopefully bring about improvements in their human relations.

The Garden Beautiful is gone, and so is the Porch, and with it the last physical reminder of the old women's department and such fabled captains of the yard as "Rough-house" New, "Sammy" Randolph, John Edgar, and A. C. McAlister. Although a modernistic Catholic chapel stands in its place, the Porch is not completely gone, for the title "Porch Officer" appears in gold leaf on an office window a few steps from where the old Porch stood.

The site of the old jute mill has been absorbed into the lower yard, which is used for sports and recreation, but its place in the prison economy has been taken by the new cotton mill, a sprawling building with a sawtooth roof. Here several hundred men weave cloth to be used in prisons and hospitals throughout the state. Unfortunately, there are as few cotton mills in California as there were jute mills, with the result that the skills learned there are largely useless.

In spite of these changes, a strong atmosphere of San Quentin's past history can still be sensed by even the casual visitor. Now that the Stones is gone, the oldest buildings remaining are the "Old" (1859) and "New" (1885) hospitals, with the dungeon underneath the former still serving as a storeroom. The dental laboratory is located in the "Old" hospital, while, as it has for years, the Protestant chapel occupies the shabby quarters next door. The "New" hospital serves a variety of purposes, none of them medical.

The ancient horseshoe, which from time immemorial has been wired above the outer count gate, is still in place, but the old-timers, both convict and free, have been departing one by one, and soon there will be no one left who remembers at firsthand the daily procession to the Rose Bowl, the wild day of the Big Break, or the Jockers' Ball.

Clinton Duffy lives in a spacious hilltop house which enjoys a spectacular view of San Quentin and of the bay beyond. James

A. Johnston, "Big Jim" Holohan, and the two Smiths, Frank and Court, are dead. Dr. Stanley has settled down to an active retirement in his estate in the foothills of Mount Tam, from which he occasionally issues a characteristically crusty article about the prison he knew. It is almost fifty years since he first went to San Quentin, and one can detect in his memoirs an active sense of regret for the heroic days of the past.

The ending of this book must necessarily be an anticlimax. It would be more satisfying to conclude either with a mighty denunciation of the stupidity, futility, and cruelty of even the modern San Quentin, or, alternatively, with a confident and clear-eyed view of the wonders that are going to be accomplished by the brave and enlightened men who are now in charge. It is to be regretted that neither of these approaches squares with the facts. The central fact about San Quentin (and, for that matter, about every other prison and reformatory in the country), is that we have run out of any really useful ideas bearing on the treatment of criminals. If we can ever summon up the courage to admit the bankruptcy that hides behind the fine, self-deceiving words, perhaps things will be better sometime in the future.

Harley Teets once said that San Quentin was a blindfolded elephant lumbering along the edge of a precipice. Unhappily, this will probably continue to be the best description of any American prison that has ever been made.

NOTES

I FIRST became interested in the history of San Quentin in 1952, when I took a job at the prison, teaching high-school courses in the day school. Although many of the stories told by the old-timers in my classes turned out to be pure mythology, I was steered into the course of the prison's true history by the chief librarian, Herman K. Spector, who had assembled and published in mimeographed form a bibliography called *San Quentiniana*.

Many of the books in this list are of interest only because they were written by San Quentin officials or by convicts and former convicts. Others, such as Clinton Duffy and Dean Jennings' *The San Quentin Story* (Doubleday, 1950), Dr. Leo L. Stanley and Evelyn Wells' *Men at Their Worst* (Appleton-Century, 1940), and, more recently, Mrs. Gladys Duffy and Blaise Whitehead Lane's *Warden's Wife* (Appleton-Century-Crofts, 1959) are readable accounts of personal experiences, but are not of much value as history.

The same criticism applies to James A. Johnston's *Prison Life Is Different* (Houghton Mifflin, 1937), to Caryl Chessman's generally overrated books, and to the most recent San Quentin book, *The Desperate and the Damned* (Crowell, 1961), a book of reporters' reminiscences written by Bernice Freeman Davis and Al Hirshberg.

To my taste, the best of *San Quentiniana* are Robert Joyce Tasker's *Grimhaven* (Knopf, 1928) and Donald Lowrie's *My Life in Prison* (Mitchell Kennerley, New York, 1912), the first of which has considerable literary merit and both of which are valuable accounts of convict life at the periods when their authors were incarcerated. David Lamson's *We Who Are About to Die* (Scribner's, 1936) which attracted a good deal of attention when it was published, is dreadfully sentimental but sometimes useful. For the chapter about Ed Morrell, I found extremely illuminating his curious autobiography, *The Twenty-Fifth Man* (New Era Publishing Company, Montclair, New Jersey, 1924, and Vantage, 1955). The details of Morrell's experiences, however, are drawn from Lowrie's book mentioned above and his *My Life Out of Prison* (Kennerley, 1915), and Jack London's *The Star Rover* (Macmillan, 1915).

One other item on this list should be mentioned. James H. Wilkins, a former prison director, wrote a history of the years of the lease which was published in the San Francisco *Bulletin,* from June 13 to July 10, 1918, and which was later reproduced in mimeographed form by Clinton Duffy at San Quentin. Mr. Wilkins was a former newspaperman, and his history is lively and always interesting, but, alas, full of grave errors of fact. I have drawn on this history wherever Wilkins was writing from personal experience; otherwise I have treated it with caution. The book by the Lombrosian chaplain, August Drähms, is *The Criminal* (Macmillan, 1900).

Magazine articles about San Quentin are many in number but rather thin in substance, most of them being puff pieces for the warden in charge. The following articles, however, were for one reason or another of more than routine interest:

"The California Penal System" by C. H. Shinn (*Popular Science Monthly,* March, 1899, p. 644) is a useful summary of the enlightened penal thought of the time, with many friendly references to Warden Hale's administration of San Quentin.

Dr. Stanley has written many articles both for professional medical journals and for the general reader. Of the medical articles the most interesting are "Testicle Transplantation" (*Journal of the American Medical Association,* May 29, 1920, p. 1501) and "Tuberculosis in San Quentin" (*California and Western*

Medicine, December, 1938, and January, 1939). In addition, a series of pieces in which Dr. Stanley recalls the old days has appeared at various dates in the "Marin Magazine," a Saturday supplement to the daily *Independent-Journal* of San Rafael.

Two articles by E. B. Block describing Frank Smith's wardenship appeared in *Sunset,* July, 1926, and August, 1927. Block's solemn and straight-faced description of the Jockers' Ball in the first of these is a masterpiece of unconscious humor. Jim Tully's "A California Holiday" (*American Mercury,* January, 1928, p. 22) is a sharp and interesting description of Holohan's San Quentin.

Of the periodical literature on Duffy, the principal articles referred to in this book are Gerald Breckenridge's "Biggest Big House" (*Saturday Evening Post,* November 8, 1941, p. 20), a ten-page picture story in *Life* (October 27, 1947, p. 116), and Duffy and Dean Jennings' "San Quentin Is My Home" (*Saturday Evening Post,* eight installments from March 25, 1950, to May 13, 1950).

Frontier, a California magazine, has recently published two interesting articles: "Prison Reform" (January, 1960, p. 27), which reviews the career of Richard McGee and "Death in the Gas Chamber, Revelations of a Former San Quentin Physician" (May, 1960, p. 13) by William F. Graves, M.D.

When my wife began to do the research for this book in earnest, she found that the most reliable sources were the journals and reports of the state legislature, the periodic reports of the prison directors, and the San Francisco, Marin County, and Sacramento newspapers from the earliest days until the present. Our thanks go to the research librarians of the San Francisco Public Library (particularly Mrs. Mary Moses), the Bancroft Library of the University of California at Berkeley, and the California room of the state library in Sacramento. The information file maintained in the state library was an invaluable source of references to the newspapers.

We are especially grateful to Virginia Keating, head of the

Marin County Free Public Library, Ida Goodrich of her staff, and Betty McKegney and Artelle Farley of the Belvedere-Tiburon branch, for obtaining countless volumes of state records for us, and for their exceeding patience in demanding their return.

Although the officials at San Quentin are in constant danger of being buried under the unending blizzard of paper that is one of the occupational hazards of their work, they were generous with their time and knowledge in digging out the surviving records of the past. Thanks to the long memory of Records Officer Peter J. Murry (now chief records officer of the Department of Corrections), I was able to consult the original handwritten logs for seventeen years between 1856 and 1890, as well as old punishment books, letter files, and many other original documents. C. V. (Jack) Brennan of the records office, who came to San Quentin as a guard in the early 1930's, contributed cheerfully from his memories of older days and made many photographs available to me. Dr. Stanley was both helpful and hospitable at Crest Farm. Even though he knew I was not an uncritical admirer of his administration, Clinton Duffy went out of his way to assist me with the story of his years in the warden's office. My thanks are also due to Director of Corrections Richard A. McGee and Warden Fred R. Dickson for giving me access to the prison records.

The list of people who contributed to this book would not be complete without the name of Roy D. Graves. I first met Mr. Graves in the museum maintained by the Marin County Historical Society, where he is curator. Mr. Graves produced the prison diary kept by the writing master K. H. Keeny and invited me to visit him at his house in San Francisco, where, he said, he had a box of San Quentin material. The box had a curious history. It had been shipped from Philadelphia to a San Francisco hobby shop, where Mr. Graves, who is an energetic and knowledgeable historian, bought it for a few dollars. On inspection, the contents of the box turned out to be a miscellaneous and fascinating assortment of prison records, personal papers, and photographs of the period of Warden John E. Hoyle. Mr. Graves and I share the opinion that the box contains the papers kept in a desk or cabinet in the warden's office and packed up helter-skelter at the time of Hoyle's departure in 1913. How it found its way to Philadelphia remains a moot question as I have not been able to discover if Hoyle ended his life in that city.

Besides the books already mentioned, the following volumes were of more than ordinary value to us:

For the early political history of California, Theodore H. Hittell's four-volume *History of California* (N. J. Stone, San Francisco, 1897) seemed to us far superior both in style and substance to the many, and rather doughy, works of Hubert Howe Bancroft. John Walton Caughey's *California* (Prentice-Hall, 1946) is a useful and well-balanced one-volume work.

Herbert Asbury's *The Barbary Coast* (Knopf, 1933) remains the best account of the criminal history of San Francisco and a model for all other nonacademic social historians. I have also drawn freely from Major Horace Bell's *Reminiscences of a Ranger* (W. Hebberd, Santa Barbara, 1927, and Primavera Press, Los Angeles, 1933), which deserves to be better known than it is.

Of the various works on criminology we consulted, we turned most frequently to Harry Elmer Barnes and Negley K. Teeters standard textbook, *New Horizons in Criminology* (Prentice-Hall, revised edition, 1945). Although Barnes and Teeters' references to San Quentin are sometimes mistaken, their account of the development of American prison systems is based on firmer ground. Mention should also be made of John Bartlow Martin's *Break Down the Walls* (Ballantine, 1954), which has little to say about San Quentin, but which treats American prisons in general with a great deal of extraordinary good sense.

Wherever archaic punctuation and spelling seemed awkward, I have modernized the quoted passages. Prison slang is defined where it first occurs; the page number of the definition is given in the general index that follows.

INDEX